VBA For Dummies,
4th Edition

Interesting VBA Shortcut Keys

Press	To Do This
Alt+F11	Open the VBA editor
Alt+F8	Display a list of macros
Ctrl+Break	Perform an emergency stop of the program
Ctrl+G	Display the Immediate window
Ctrl+I	List the quick information for the selected element
Ctrl+J	List the properties and methods for an object
Ctrl+R	Display Project Explorer
Ctrl+Shift+I	List the parameter information for the selected element
Ctrl+Shift+J	List the constants associated with an enumeration
Ctrl+Tab	Move to the next Code or UserForm window
F1	Get help on any selected item
F2	Display the Object Browser window
F4	Display the Properties window
F5	Start the program
F7	Display the Code window after selecting a form or control
F9	Add a breakpoint
Shift+F7	Display the form that corresponds to the active Code window
Shift+F9	Add a quick watch for the highlighted text

Common VBA Functions

Use This Function	To Do This
Asc, AscB, or AscW	Convert a character into its ASCII, DBCS, or Unicode numeric value
Chr, ChrB, or ChrW	Convert a number into its ASCII, DBCS, or Unicode character
CStr	Convert any expression, including any supported data type, into a string
CVErr	Create a user-defined error number for your program
Format	Change an enumeration or other expression into formatted text
InputBox	Get a single input from the program user
MsgBox	Display a short message box onscreen
Str, Format, or CStr	Convert a number into a string
Val, CByte, CCur, CDbl, CDec, CInt, CLng, or CSng	Convert a string into a number

For Dummies: Bestselling Book Series for Beginners

VBA For Dummies, 4th Edition

Cheat Sheet

Standard VBA Data Types

Type	Size in Bytes	Description
Boolean	2	Stores a value of True (0) or False (–1).
Byte	1	Contains a number in the range of 0–255.
Currency	8	Defines monetary values in the range of –922,337,203,685,477.5808 to 922,337,203,685,477.5807.
Date	8	Defines combination value that includes both date and time; although you certainly don't have to include both. Valid dates range from January 1, 100 to December 31, 9999.
Decimal	14	Defines a precise 28-digit number. You must use the Variant data type for this value. The number is in the range of ±79,228,162,514,264,337,593,543,950,335 with no decimal point and ±7.9228162514264337593543950335 with 28 places to the right of the decimal.
Double	8	Contains a real number in the range of –1.79769313486231 E308 to – 4.94065645841247 E-324 for negative values and 4.94065645841247 E-324 to 1.79769313486232 E308 for positive values.
Integer	2	Contains a number in the range of –32,768 to 32,767.
Long	4	Contains a number in the range of –2,147,483,648 to 2,147,483,647.
Object	4	Any object reference.
Single	4	Contains a real number in the range of –3.402823 E38 to –1.401298 E-45 for negative values and 1.401298 E-45 to 3.402823 E38 for positive values.
String (fixed length)	String length	Contains a set of characters from 1 to approximately 65,400 characters long.
String (variable length)	10 + string length	Contains a set of characters from 0 to approximately 2 billion characters long.
Variant (with characters)	22 + string length	Stores any valid non-numeric data type or data types larger than a Double.
Variant (with numbers)	16	Stores any valid numeric data type up to the size of a Double.

For Dummies: Bestselling Book Series for Beginners

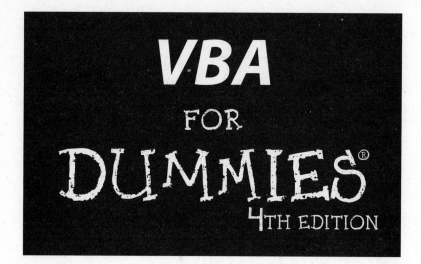

VBA

FOR

DUMMIES®
4TH EDITION

VBA
FOR
DUMMIES®
4TH EDITION

by John Paul Mueller

WILEY

Wiley Publishing, Inc.

VBA For Dummies®, 4th Edition

Published by
Wiley Publishing, Inc.
111 River Street
Hoboken, NJ 07030-5774

www.wiley.com

For general information on our other products and services or to obtain technical support, please contact
our Customer Care Department within the U.S. at 800-762-2974, outside the U.S. at 317-572-3993, or fax
317-572-4002.

Wiley also publishes its books in a variety of electronic formats. Some content that appears in print may
not be available in electronic books.

Library of Congress Control Number: 2003105671

ISBN: 0-7645-3989-2

Manufactured in the United States of America

10 9 8 7 6 5 4 3 2

4B/RZ/QZ/QT/IN

WILEY   is a trademark of Wiley Publishing, Inc.

About the Author

John Mueller is a freelance author and technical editor. He has writing in his blood, having produced 59 books and over 200 articles to date. The topics range from networking to artificial intelligence and from database management to heads-down programming. Some of his current books include several C# developer guides, an accessible programming guide, a book on Web Matrix, and several Windows XP user guides. His technical editing skills have helped over 32 authors refine the content of their manuscripts. John has provided technical editing services to both *Data Based Advisor* and *Coast Compute* magazines. He has also contributed articles to magazines like *SQL Server Professional, Visual C++ Developer,* and *Visual Basic Developer.* He is currently the editor of the *.NET* electronic newsletter for Pinnacle Publishing (`http://www.freeenewsletters.com/`).

When John isn't working at the computer, you can find him in his workshop. He's an avid woodworker and candle maker. On any given afternoon, you can find him working at a lathe or putting the finishing touches on a bookcase. One of his newest craft projects is glycerin soap making, which comes in pretty handy for gift baskets. You can reach John on the Internet at `JMueller@mwt.net`. John is also setting up a Web site at `http://www.mwt.net/~jmueller/`; feel free to take a look and make suggestions on how he can improve it. One of his current projects is creating book FAQ sheets that should help you find the book information you need much faster.

Dedication

This book is dedicated to Ervin and Linda Borleske. Thank you for your friendship and encouragement.

Acknowledgments

Thanks to my wife, Rebecca, for working with me to get this book completed. I really don't know what I would have done without her help in researching and compiling some of the information that appears in this book. She also did a fine job of proofreading my rough draft.

Russ Mullen deserves thanks for his technical edit of this book. He greatly added to the accuracy and depth of the material that you see here. I really appreciated the time that he devoted to checking my code for accuracy.

Matt Wagner, my agent, deserves credit for helping me get the contract in the first place and taking care of all the details that most authors don't really consider. I always appreciate his help. It's good to know that someone wants to help.

Finally, I would like to thank Terri Varveris, Nicole Sholly, Teresa Artman, and the production staff at Wiley for their assistance in bringing this book to print. It's always nice to work with such a great group of professionals.

Publisher's Acknowledgments

We're proud of this book; please send us your comments through our online registration form located at www.dummies.com/register/.

Some of the people who helped bring this book to market include the following:

Acquisitions, Editorial, and Media Development

Associate Project Editor: Nicole Sholly

Acquisitions Editor: Terri Varveris

Senior Copy Editor: Teresa Artman

Technical Editor: Russ Mullen

Editorial Manager: Kevin Kirschner

Media Development Specialist: Greg Stafford

Media Development Manager:
Laura VanWinkle

Media Development Supervisor:
Richard Graves

Editorial Assistant: Amanda Foxworth

Cartoons: Rich Tennant
(www.the5thwave.com)

Production

Project Coordinator: Erin Smith

Layout and Graphics: Amanda Carter, Seth Conley, Lauren Goddard, Michael Kruzil, Lynsey Osborn, Shae Wilson

Proofreaders: John Greenough, Angel Perez, Rob Springer, Brian Walls, TECHBOOKS Production Services

Indexer: TECHBOOKS Production Services

Publishing and Editorial for Technology Dummies

    Richard Swadley, Vice President and Executive Group Publisher

    Andy Cummings, Vice President and Publisher

    Mary C. Corder, Editorial Director

Publishing for Consumer Dummies

    Diane Graves Steele, Vice President and Publisher

    Joyce Pepple, Acquisitions Director

Composition Services

    Gerry Fahey, Vice President of Production Services

    Debbie Stailey, Director of Composition Services

Contents at a Glance

Table of Contents

Introduction

●●

*W*elcome to your first look at Visual Basic for Applications (VBA)! You might think that VBA is a secret code used by advanced computer users to intimidate the rest of us. Nothing could be farther from the truth. VBA is all about doing things your way. When you want an application to perform a task in a certain way, use VBA to extend it. VBA makes *you* the boss.

You might also think that VBA is only for Microsoft Office users. Microsoft has licensed VBA to a number of companies, many of which use VBA (or a VBA derivative) in their programs. After you discover the wonders of VBA, you can customize a number of applications to make them work the way that you want them to work.

VBA is a tool that empowers you to perform tasks that you never thought possible in a fraction of the time that it takes to perform the task by hand. For example, you can add new toolbars, create custom reports, and perform special kinds of data analysis. When you write a VBA program, you become the master of your environment — someone who gets the job done quickly.

When you look at VBA as a tool that helps you work fast, with fewer errors, and with greater freedom, you begin to understand how powerful this tool is. VBA is an exciting application feature to explore. You can experience the VBA advantage, too!

About This Book

VBA For Dummies, 4th Edition is a reference book. You don't have to read it in any particular order, and you can skip anything that you don't find interesting. Readers that have VBA programming experience can skip to the advanced examples at the end of the book or explore new language elements as needed. That said, I did put the book into a logical order. When you begin at Chapter 1 and progress through the book chapter by chapter, you acquire a complete view of VBA, even if you've never used it before.

This book contains many examples from my own library. I write VBA programs for all my applications that support it because I know that using VBA can save me time and effort. In addition, I write VBA programs for some of my consulting clients. This real-world approach to using VBA will help you get started quickly.

Conventions Used in This Book

I always try to show you the fastest way to accomplish any task. In many cases, this means using a menu command such as Tools⇨Macro⇨Visual Basic Editor.

I'm assuming that you've worked with Windows long enough to know how the keyboard and mouse work. You should also know how to use menus and other basic Windows features.

Whenever possible, I use shortcut keys to help you access a command faster. For example, you can also start the VBA Integrated Development Environment (IDE) by pressing Alt+F11.

This book also uses special type to emphasize some information. For example, entries that you need to type appear in **bold**. All code, Web site URLs, and onscreen messages appear in `monofont type`. Whenever I define a new word, you'll see that word in *italics*.

Because you use two applications when working with VBA, I always tell you to move from one application to the next. When a chapter begins, I assume that you're in the VBA IDE unless I tell you otherwise. All the commands in that chapter are for the VBA IDE until I specifically tell you to move to the host application. I also specifically tell you when it's time to move back to the VBA IDE.

What You Should Read

What you read depends on your level of experience — you need to know how to use at least one Microsoft Office application. It also helps to know something about VBA before you tackle the programs at the end of the book. With this in mind, you probably want to read Chapters 1 through 7 in order before you begin discovering other parts of the book.

You might have used VBA before and only want to know what you can add to your knowledge. The programs become progressively more complex and application specific as the book progresses. When you want to find out how to work with Word only, feel free to select Chapter 13. You might find Chapter 18 a good place to start because in it, I tell you about interesting VBA resources that you might not know about. Of course, all the content in this book is great, and I hope that you eventually read it all.

What You Don't Have to Read

Most of the chapters contain some advanced material that only interests some readers. When you see one of these specialized topics, such as writing information to the Windows Registry, feel free to skip it.

You can also skip any material marked with a Technical Stuff icon. This material is helpful, but you don't have to know it to use VBA. I include this material because I find it helpful in my programming efforts and hope that you will, too.

Foolish Assumptions

You might find it difficult to believe that I have assumed anything about you — after all, I haven't even met you yet! — but I have. Although most assumptions are indeed foolish, I made these assumptions to provide a starting point for the book.

I'm assuming you've worked with Windows long enough to know how the keyboard and mouse work. You should also know how to use menus and other basic Windows features. It's also essential to know how to use at least one Office application. Some portions of the book work with Web pages, and others use eXtensible Markup Language (XML); you need to know at least a little about these technologies to use those sections. You don't have to be an expert in any of these areas, but more knowledge is better.

How This Book Is Organized

This book contains several parts. Each part demonstrates a particular VBA feature and helps you build your VBA knowledge. In each chapter, I discuss a particular topic and include example programs that you can use to discover more about VBA on your own. You can find the source code for this book, along with a bonus chapter, on the Dummies.com Web site at `http://www.dummies.com/go/mueller`.

Part I: An Overview of VBA

The main purpose of this part of the book is to help you use the VBA IDE to write programs. In Chapter 1, I tell you about the various windows and other physical features of the VBA IDE. Unbelievably, you write your first VBA program in this chapter! In Chapter 2, I tell you about the parts of a VBA program and show you various methods for running any VBA program that you create. You also gain some experience with the Microsoft help files in this chapter.

Part II: Learning the Ropes

No matter who you are, you have to discover the essentials of any task before you can perform it. The main purpose of this part of the book is to help you understand the VBA language. VBA uses *statements* (commands) to perform work. Just like any language, there are parts to these statements that are very much like human language. In Chapter 3, I show you how to create various kinds of VBA program containers. In Chapter 4, you see how to store and manage data. Controlling a program is important (you don't want it to run amok), so in Chapter 5, you see examples of how to perform this task. We all know the results of buggy programs, so in Chapter 6, I show you how to avoid this problem. Finally, in Chapter 7, I demonstrate methods of interacting with the user.

Part III: Expanding Your VBA Horizons

The main purpose of this part of the book is to help you build your VBA knowledge. In Chapter 8, you see how to work with objects — an essential skill when you discover the benefits of writing programs to create documents automatically. In Chapter 9, I demonstrate how to use *arrays* and *collections,* which are special kinds of data storage containers that VBA uses. Storing information on disk is very important, so read Chapter 10 to discover how to access the disk drive. Microsoft is touting XML as the next best thing for Office users; see Chapter 11 for how to use XML files to your benefit.

Part IV: Programming for Applications

All the chapters to this point are generic. The information could apply to any application that supports VBA. However, you quickly discover that every application that supports VBA implements some features in a slightly different way. The main purpose of this part of the book is to help you become productive by using VBA with a particular application. However, before you begin reading about a specific Office application, in Chapter 12, I show you how to make some Office specific changes by using VBA code. In this part, I discuss the three main Office applications: Word (Chapter 13), Excel (Chapter 14), and Access (Chapter 15). Most of you don't use just one application, so in Chapter 16, I extend the idea of individual application programming into working with multiple applications by using a single program. This advanced technique helps you create one program that could create a chart in Excel that relies on data stored in Access, add text to explain the data by using Word, and finally, create a presentation by using PowerPoint. You can perform all this by clicking one button — Office programs don't get more productive than that.

Part V: The Part of Tens

We all accumulate cool tips and techniques that other people find helpful. In Chapter 17, you discover ten cool things that you can do with VBA. You can do a lot more than that, but these are ten things that I thought you would enjoy knowing. Chapter 18 tells about ten kinds of resources that you can use to make VBA better, easier to use, or simply more productive.

The accompanying Web site

This book contains a lot of code, and you might not want to type it. Fortunately, you can find the source code for this book on the Dummies.com Web site at http://www.dummies.com/go/mueller. The source code is organized by chapter, and I'll always tell you about the example files in the text. The best way to work with a chapter is to download all the source code for it at one time.

The Web site also has a bonus chapter on FrontPage. This chapter describes how you can use VBA to make FrontPage easier to use. In fact, you'll find an application that lets you create the initial part of a Web page automatically. Other programs show how to discover more about FrontPage features and demonstrate how to customize those features to meet specific needs, such as exchanging data between applications.

Icons Used in This Book

Tips are nice because they help you save time or perform some task without a lot of extra work. The tips in this book are timesaving techniques or pointers to resources that you should try to get the maximum benefit from VBA.

I don't want to sound like an angry parent or some kind of maniac, but you should avoid doing anything marked with a Warning icon. Otherwise, you could find that your program melts down and takes your data with it.

Whenever you see this icon, think advanced tip or technique. You might find these tidbits of useful information just too boring for words, or they could contain the solution that you need to get a program running. Skip these bits of information whenever you like.

If you don't get anything else out of a particular chapter or section, remember the material marked by this icon. This material usually contains an essential process or bit of material that you must know to write VBA programs successfully.

Where to Go from Here

It's time to start your VBA adventure! I recommend that anyone who has only a passing knowledge of VBA go right to Chapter 1. This chapter contains essential, get-started information that you need to write your first program.

Those who already know VBA might want to skip to Part IV to sink their teeth into some complex examples. You might want to check out the resources in Part V if you find your current VBA experience lacking. The VBA refresher course begins in Part II and ends in Part III. Start with the part that best suits your needs.

Part I

An Overview of VBA

The 5th Wave · By Rich Tennant

AT THE REAL PROGRAMMERS DATING BAR

WHOA! LOOK AT THE POCKET PROTECTORS ON THIS ONE!

In this part . . .

You might wonder whether you need to visit this part of the book. This section of the book contains essential information that you need to use VBA effectively. In Chapter 1, I introduce all the windows and other graphic elements of the VBA Integrated Development Environment (IDE). In addition, you create your first program in this chapter. In Chapter 2, I describe the steps for creating a program and show you four methods to run it. This chapter contains the first permanent program for the book. The most important idea to take away from these initial chapters is that you can write programs by using VBA — it's not something that just advanced computer users can do.

Chapter 1

Getting to Know VBA

*H*ave you ever talked with someone about an application that you're using and said that you thought that the vendor that created an application was clueless? The application is just too hard or too time-consuming to use because the features are difficult to access. In a few cases, I'll bet you saw a feature that *almost* does what you want it to do . . . but not quite. Something that almost works is frustrating to use, and many of us have wished for a solution to the problem.

At some point, one of the propeller heads at Microsoft came out of his caffeine-induced coma and made something that fixes all these problems and more — Visual Basic for Applications (VBA). VBA is a simple programming language. By using VBA, you can have things your way — you can customize your applications to meet your needs and expectations. No longer are you a slave to what the vendors want. If you use an application that supports VBA, you can add new features — such as automated letter writing and special equation handling — to change things around to the way that you want. In short, it becomes your custom application and not something that the vendor thinks that you want.

VBA works with many applications, including the Microsoft Office applications. You use VBA to write programs to accomplish tasks automatically or change the application environment. Many people think they can't write even simple programs. This book helps you understand that anyone can write a program. In fact, you'll write your first program in this chapter. Of course, first you find out the secret handshake for starting the VBA editor. Using the VBA editor is just a little different from the word processors that you've used in the past. Along the way, you see some interesting uses for VBA and just how many applications that you can modify by using it.

VBA: It's Not Just for Programmers

One of the things that you should think about is why you want to use VBA. I know that some of you are probably just interested in using VBA, but most of you need a good reason for taking time out of your busy schedule. It's important to think about what tasks you can use VBA to do. It won't take out the garbage or fold your laundry, but you can use it to write some types of letters automatically. With this in mind, the following sections tell you about a few things that I've done with VBA. Knowing you, I'm sure you'll come up with more.

Automating documents

I hate writing letters, especially if the letter contains most of the same information that I wrote for the last letter. Sometimes you can automate letters by using mail merge, but that generally doesn't work too well for individualized letters. In those situations, I set up a form that contains the common information that I include in some letters but not others. I check off the items that I need for the current letter, and VBA writes it for me automatically. You can see my automated letter secrets in Chapter 13.

Document automation isn't limited to word processing. You can also automate a spreadsheet. I have several programs that I've created for Excel. For example, whenever I get a new client for my business, I click a button, and VBA creates all the required client entries in Excel for me. Because Excel performs the task the same way every time, I can't forget anything and every client receives the same level of high-quality service. You can see techniques for creating automated Excel worksheets in Chapter 14.

And if you have to move the data that you create in your word processor or spreadsheet to the Internet, VBA can help make the process nearly automatic. Chapter 16 contains everything that you need to know to move information from one Microsoft Office product to another without the usual modification and reformatting. And in the Bonus Chapter on the Web site, you see how to create automated documents in FrontPage.

Customizing an application's interface

Sometimes an application feature just bugs you. I guess that you could turn it off if it bugs you that much, but that might not be an option if you need that function in your work. Use VBA to create a new version of the feature with everything that you need and nothing that bugs you. For example, I never liked how Word performs a word count, so I created my own program to perform the task. Chapter 12 shows you some of my secrets for taming unruly interfaces.

Changing an application interface to your liking is easy. You can create a customized menu system or toolbars. You can move some interface elements out to a form or get rid of them completely. And any interface change that you want to make is probably doable by using VBA. In addition, you don't necessarily have to use just one interface. You can create programs to change the interface as needed for the task that you're performing. For example, I have a program to switch between book, article, and client document writing modes. Chapter 7 shows a number of interesting ways to use forms.

Performing calculations

One of the most common uses of special applications is to perform complex calculations. You can create many types of equations by using any of the Microsoft Office products. However, sometimes you need to change the data before you can use it or perform the calculation differently depending on the value of one or more inputs. Whenever a calculation becomes too complicated for a simple equation, use VBA to simplify things by solving the calculation problem using small steps, rather than one big step. Chapters 4 and 14 show a number of ways to work with calculations.

Sometimes the number that you create using a calculation doesn't mean much — it's just a number until someone makes a decision. Some decisions are easy yet repetitive. Chapter 5 shows the methods that your application can use to make decisions automatically with VBA. Smart applications save you more time for that game of Solitaire.

Getting stuff from a database

I use Access to store a variety of information — everything from my movie collection to a list of clients that I work with regularly. You use databases to store information, although that doesn't help much if you can't get it out. Use VBA to get the information from your database in the form that you need it. For example, you can display that information on a form so that you can review it or use that same data to create a report.

I love databases because they provide the most flexible method for storing repetitive information such as a client list or any other kind of list that you can imagine. Don't assume that databases are so complicated that you'll never understand how they work. Most productivity databases are actually quite simple to use. All you need is a little easily understood VBA code to gain access to them. Chapter 15 shows you everything you need to know to work with productivity databases.

VBA even includes ways of creating temporary databases for those lists that you need only today. This can save you a lot of time and still force the computer to do the work for you. You can see these alternatives in Chapter 9.

Adding new application features

With all the features that vendors have stuffed into applications, you'd think that every possible need would be satisfied. However, I'm convinced that vendors never actually use the applications that they build. (A nifty new screen saver for Windows is not my idea of a necessary feature.) However, the window-sizing program that I really needed came from a third-party vendor.

Most of this book covers adding new application features. Discover how to add specific features by reading specific chapters. (See the preceding sections to find where.) If you read the book from cover to cover, you'll be able to use VBA to add just about any feature to any product that supports VBA. Your friends will be impressed and think that you're a genius. Maybe your boss will become convinced that you're the most valuable employee in the world and give you a large bonus. Reading this book could make you famous, but more importantly, it will make you less frustrated.

Making special tools

If you have to send information to other people who might not have Microsoft Office and they need the information formatted, you might have to work a long time to find a solution. Chapters 10 and 11 contain two methods for storing information in alternative formats. Chapter 10 uses the trusty text file, and Chapter 11 relies on the latest rage — eXtensible Markup Language (XML) files.

Having things your way

Sometimes I'd just like to scream. Microsoft seems to think that it knows precisely what I want — based on what people tell it. Who these other people are remains a mystery, but I wouldn't trust the guy in the dark suit sitting next to you.

Fortunately, you can use VBA to help customize Microsoft's well-intentioned application features. If Word decides that it absolutely must display the information you don't want upon startup, store your settings to disk and restore them every time that you launch Word. The use of automatically executing programs (see Chapter 2) can help you have things your own way. Chapter 10 shows you how to store your settings in text format, and Chapter 11 shows you how to store them in XML format.

Other Products Use VBA, Too

Don't assume that VBA is only good if you're using Microsoft Office or a few other Microsoft products. With VBA at your command, you can control a lot of different applications. Go to the Microsoft site http://msdn.microsoft. com/vba/companies/company.asp to see a list of companies that have licensed VBA. You'll be amazed at the number of applications that you can work with using VBA. Here are a few of my favorites:

- **Corel products** (http://www.corel.com/): Corel makes WordPerfect and Draw. *WordPerfect* is a word processing program, which many legal offices still use. One of my first professional writing jobs required use of WordPerfect. *CorelDRAW,* a drawing program that many professionals enjoy using, supports a wealth of features. All the line art in this book was originally drawn using CorelDRAW, and all my drawing setups are performed automatically by using VBA programs.

- **Micrografx iGrafx series** (http://www.micrografx.com/): This product can help you create flowcharts or organizational charts. Unlike a lot of drawing tasks, both flowcharts and organizational charts are extremely repetitive, making them a perfect place to use VBA.

- **IMSI TurboCad** (http://www.turbocad.com/): I love to work with wood, which means that I have to draw plans for new projects from time to time. TurboCad is the drawing program that I prefer to use. It's relatively inexpensive, and the VBA programs I've created for it automate many of the drawing tasks such as creating ¾" boards.

VBA hasn't been around forever. If you drag out that old dusty copy of WordPerfect for DOS, you'll be disappointed because it doesn't support VBA. The Microsoft vendor participant list doesn't tell you which version of a product supports VBA for the most part, so you either have to check the product packaging or ask the vendor.

A Room with a View

Many people approach VBA with the same enthusiasm and clarity of thought with which the condemned faces the gallows. When you work with an application, you see what the developer wants you to see and not much more. You're in the user room — the one without a view. Approach using VBA like entering a new room: You now have a room *with* a view — you're the one who sees what will happen and when.

Looking at the Integrated Development Environment (IDE)

VBA is a visual programming environment. That is, you see how your program will look before you run it. Its editor is very visual, using various windows to make your programming experience easy and manageable. Figure 1-1 shows what this Integrated Development Environment (IDE) looks like.

An *IDE* is an editor, just like your word processor, spreadsheet, or database form. Just like how application editors have special features that make them especially useful for working with data, an IDE is a programming editor with special features that make it useful for writing instructions that the application should follow. These instructions are *procedural code* — a set of steps.

Project window

Standard toolbar

Code window

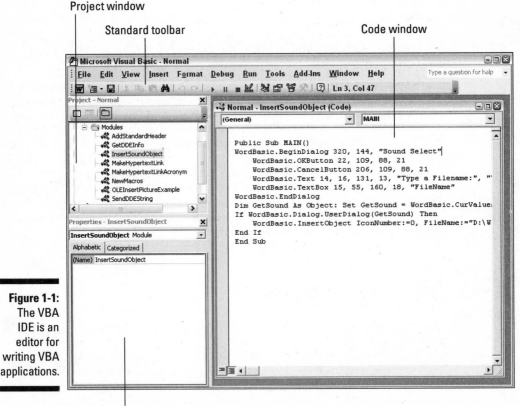

Figure 1-1:
The VBA
IDE is an
editor for
writing VBA
applications.

Properties window

As you can see from Figure 1-1, the VBA IDE consists of a menu system, tool-bars, a Project window, a Properties window, and a Code window to start with. The IDE can show other windows when it needs to, but these are the three windows that you see when you start VBA. Here's a brief summary of what each of the windows do. (The upcoming "Starting the Visual Basic Editor" section shows how to use them.)

✔ **Project:** This window contains a list of the items in your project, which contains all the document elements in a single file. Your application exists within a file that appears in the Project window.

✔ **Properties:** Whenever you select an object, the Properties window tells you about it. For example, this window tells you whether the object is blue or whether it has words on it.

✔ **Code:** Eventually, you have to write some code to make your application work. This window contains the special words that tell your application what to do. Think of it as a place to write a specialized to-do list.

Looking at the VBA Toolbox

You won't have to write code for every task in VBA. The IDE also supports forms, just like the forms that you use to perform other tasks. In this case, you decide what appears on the form and how the form acts when the user works with it. To make it easier to create forms, VBA provides the Toolbox, like the one shown in Figure 1-2, which contains controls used to create forms.

Each Toolbox button performs a unique task. For example, clicking one button displays a text box, but clicking another displays a command button. The form features that these buttons create are *controls*. Chapter 7 shows you how to use all these controls as well as how to add other controls when the controls that the Toolbox provides don't meet a particular need.

Figure 1-2:
The VBA
Toolbox.

Looking at objects

You're going to hear the term *object* quite a bit while you read this book and use VBA to create your own applications. An object used in a program is very much like an object in real life. Programmers came up with this term to make programs easier to understand. Read on while I use the real world example of an apple to explain what an object is in VBA — and to understand why objects are such an important part of VBA and how they make things easier.

Property values are up

When you look at an apple, you can see some of its properties: The apple is red, green, or yellow. VBA objects also have properties — for example, a button can have a *caption* (the text that users see when they look at the button). And some of the apple properties are hidden. You don't know what the apple will taste like until you bite into it. Likewise, some VBA objects have hidden properties.

There's a method to my madness

You can do a number of things with an apple. For example, picking an apple from a tree is a method of interacting with the apple. Likewise, VBA objects have methods. You can move a button from one place to another with the Move method. *Methods* let the developer do something to the object.

And now, for a special event!

An apple usually changes color when it ripens. No one did anything to the apple; it turned ripe because it reached maturity. This is an *event*. Likewise, VBA objects can experience events. A user clicks a command button, and the command button generates a Click event. As a developer, you didn't do anything to the command button. The command button decides when to generate the event. In short, *events* let the developer react to changing object conditions.

Starting the Visual Basic Editor

How you start the Visual Basic Editor depends on the application that you're using. If you're using the Microsoft Office products featured in this book, start the Visual Basic Editor by choosing Tools➪Macro➪Visual Basic Editor. When you execute this command, you see a display similar to the one shown in Figure 1-1.

Depending on which version of Microsoft Office you use and how you set it up at the beginning, the macro security feature might be set too high to allow you to use the examples in this book. To change the macro security level, use the following procedure.

1. **Choose the Tools⇨Options command.**

   The Microsoft Office application displays the Options dialog box.

2. **Select the Security tab.**

3. **Click Macro Security.**

   The Microsoft Office application displays the Security dialog box.

4. **Select the Security Level tab and choose the Low option.**

5. **Click OK twice to close the Security and Options dialog boxes.**

Using Project Explorer

Project Explorer appears in the Project window. You use it to interact with the objects that make up a project. A project is an individual file used to hold your program, or at least pieces of it. The project resides within the Office document that you're using, so when you open the Office document, you also open the project. See Chapter 3 for a description of how projects and programs interact. Project Explorer works much like how the left pane of Windows Explorer does. Normally, you see just the top-level objects like the Excel objects shown in Figure 1-3.

Figure 1-3:
Use Project Explorer to work with project objects.

The objects listed in Project Explorer depend on the kind of application that you're working with. For example, if you're working with Word, you see documents and document templates. Likewise, if you're working with Excel, you see worksheets and workbooks. However, no matter what kind of application you work with, the way that you use Project Explorer is the same.

Figure 1-3 also shows some special objects. A project can contain forms, modules, and class modules. Here's a description of these special objects:

- **Forms:** Contain user interface elements and help you interact with the user. Chapter 7 shows how to work with forms.

- **Modules:** Contain the nonvisual code for your application. For example, you can use a module to store a special calculation. Most of this book contains modules.

- **Class modules:** Contain new objects that you want to build. You could use a class module to create a new data type. Chapter 8 shows how to work with objects.

To select an object so that you can see and change its properties, highlight it in Project Explorer. To open the object so that you can modify it, double-click the object.

Right-clicking everything

Project Explorer has a number of hidden talents, which you can find by right-clicking objects to see what you can do with them. For example, right-click the VBAProject (Book1) entry at the top of Figure 1-3 to see the context menu shown in Figure 1-4.

Figure 1-4:
Right-click
VBA objects
to display
context
menus.

It's amazing to see what's hidden on this menu. Don't worry about using all of the menu entries now. Each of the menu entries appears at least once and probably more often in the book. For example, Chapter 3 shows how to use the VBAProject Properties entry. The important thing to remember now is that most objects have a context menu that you can access by right-clicking or using the Context Menu button on your keyboard.

Working with special entries

Sometimes you see a special entry in Project Explorer. For example, when you work with a Word document, you might see a References folder, which contains any references that the Word document makes. Normally, it contains a list of templates that the document relies upon for formatting.

In many cases, you can't modify the objects in the special folders. This is the case with the References folder used by Word document objects. The References folder is there for information only. To modify the referenced template, you need to find its object in Project Explorer. In this book, I don't discuss special objects because you normally don't need to work with them.

Using the Properties window

Most of the objects that you click in the VBA IDE have properties that describe the object in some way. The earlier "Property values are up" section of the chapter tells about properties if you haven't worked with them before. The following sections provide details about the Properties window (refer to Figure 1-1).

Understanding property types

A property needs to describe the object. When you look at an object, you naturally assume something about the information provided by a particular property. For example, when describing the color of an apple, you expect to use *red, yellow,* or *green.* Likewise, VBA object properties have specific types.

One of the most common property types is text. The Caption property of a form is text. The text appears at the top of the form when the user opens it.

Another common property type is a logic or Boolean value. For example, if a control has a Visible property and this property is set to True, the control appears onscreen. Set this property to False, and the control won't appear onscreen even though it still exists as part of the application.

Object properties can also have numeric values. For example, to describe where to place a control onscreen, set the Top and Left properties to specific numeric values. These values tell how many pixels are between the top and left corner of the screen and the top-left corner of the control.

In some cases, a property can display a drop-down list box from which you can choose the correct value. Other properties display a dialog box like the one for color shown in Figure 1-5.

Figure 1-5:
Some
properties
display a
dialog box
to select the
correct
value.

Getting help with properties

Don't expect to memorize every property for every object that VBA applications can create. Not even the gurus can do that. To tell what a particular property will do for your application, just highlight the property, press F1, and VBA displays a Help window similar to the one shown in Figure 1-6 (in most cases).

Such help screens tell you about the property and how it's used as well as provide you with links for additional information. The additional information is especially important when you start changing the property values in your application code. For example, click the Example link, and the help system shows how to write code that uses that property.

Microsoft Visual Basic Help

BackColor Property

See Also   Example   Applies To   Specifics

Specifies the background color of the object.

Syntax

object.**BackColor** [= *Long*]

The **BackColor** property syntax has these parts:

Part	Description
object	Required. A valid object.
Long	Optional. A value or constant that determines the background color of an object.

Settings

You can use any integer that represents a valid color. You can also specify a color by using the RGB function with red, green, and blue color components. The value of each color component is an integer that ranges from zero to 255. For example, you can specify teal blue as the integer value 4966415 or as red, green, and blue color components 15, 200, 75.

Remarks

You can only see the background color of an object if the **BackStyle** property is set to **fmBackStyleOpaque**.

Figure 1-6:
Help
documents
the
properties
that VBA
supports.

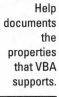

TIP

Click the See Also link in help screens for more information about a topic, such as info about objects, properties, methods, and events associated with the topic. In some cases, you also get recommended ways to work with an object, property, method, or event.

Using the Code window

The Code window is where you write your application code. It works like any other editor that you've used, except that you type in a special language: VBA. Figure 1-7 shows a typical example of a code window with some code loaded.

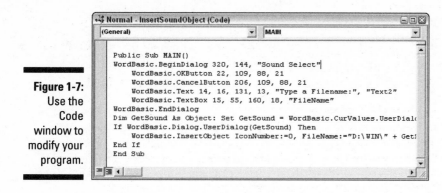

Figure 1-7:
Use the
Code
window to
modify your
program.

```
Public Sub MAIN()
WordBasic.BeginDialog 320, 144, "Sound Select"
    WordBasic.OKButton 22, 109, 88, 21
    WordBasic.CancelButton 206, 109, 88, 21
    WordBasic.Text 14, 16, 131, 13, "Type a Filename:", "Text2"
    WordBasic.TextBox 15, 55, 160, 18, "FileName"
WordBasic.EndDialog
Dim GetSound As Object: Set GetSound = WordBasic.CurValues.UserDial
If WordBasic.Dialog.UserDialog(GetSound) Then
    WordBasic.InsertObject IconNumber:=0, FileName:="D:\WIN\" + Get
End If
End Sub
```

Normal - InsertSoundObject (Code)
(General) *MAIN*

Opening an existing Code window

Sometimes you won't be able to complete an application and need to work on
it later. To open an existing code window, find the module that you want to
open in Project Explorer. Double-click the module entry, and the IDE displays
the code within with your code loaded.

The Code window also appears when you perform other tasks. For example,
if you double-click one of the controls on a form, the Code window appears
so that you can add code to the default event handler. VBA calls the event
handler (special code that responds to the event) every time that the specified event occurs.

Creating a new Code window

When you start a new module within an existing document or template, open
a new Code window by using either the Insert⇨Module or the Insert⇨Class
Module command. After you save this module or class module, it appears in
Project Explorer with the other modules and class modules in your project.

Typing text in the Code window

When you type code, VBA checks what you type. If you make a major error,
such as typing a word that VBA doesn't understand, you see an error message explaining what you did wrong (see Figure 1-8). If you don't understand
the error, click the Help button for additional information.

Figure 1-8:
VBA
displays an
error when
you make a
mistake.

Microsoft Visual Basic

Compile error:

Expected: end of statement

| OK | Help |

While you type the code for your application, VBA also formats it. For example, if you type a keyword in lowercase letters, VBA changes it so it appears as shown in the help file. *Hint:* Keywords also appear in a different color so that you can easily identify them. This book contains examples of the common VBA keywords.

Finding more Code window features

The Code window has a context menu, just like other objects in VBA. When you right-click the Code window, you see a list of optional actions that you can perform. For example, you can obtain a list of properties and methods that apply to the object that you're currently using in the window. Chapter 3 shows how to use many of the special Code window features.

Getting help with code

Because it's hard to remember precisely how to use every function and method that VBA supports, use the VBA help feature. For any keyword that you type in the Code window, highlight the keyword, press F1, and VBA will look for help on the word that you selected.

Make sure that you select the entire keyword, or VBA might not find the information that you need. Double-click the keyword to ensure that you highlight the entire word.

Using the Intermediate window

Although you can use the Intermediate window for debugging applications, this window can actually help you learn about VBA without writing reams of code. You can execute statements one at a time. Use the View⇨Intermediate Window command to display the Intermediate window. This window normally appears at the bottom of the IDE, and it won't contain any information until you type something in it.

Creating a variable in the Intermediate window

Most developers spend their days using the Intermediate window checking their applications for errors. You can use the Intermediate window to ask VBA about the value of a variable, for example. (A variable acts as a storage container for a value such as Hello World.) This feature is always available in the VBA IDE, even if you aren't using VBA for anything at the moment. To try this feature out, type **MyVal = "Hello World"** (don't forget the double quotes) in the Intermediate window and then press Enter. Now type **? MyVal** and then press Enter. Figure 1-9 shows the output of this little experiment.

Figure 1-9:
Use the
Intermediate
window to
check the
value of a
variable.

```
Immediate                                    ☒
MyVal = "Hello World"                         ▲
? MyVal
Hello World
|
                                             ▼
◄ ◄                                    ►
```

Figure 1-9:
Use the
Intermediate
window to
check the
value of a
variable.

You asked VBA to create a variable named MyVal and assign it a value of Hello World. The next step is to ask VBA what MyVal contains by using the ? operator. Figure 1-9 shows that MyVal actually does contain Hello World.

Creating a one-line program

Experimenting with the Intermediate window is one of the fastest ways to learn how to use VBA because you get instant results. You can also copy successful experiments from the Intermediate window and paste them into the Code window. Using this method ensures that your code contains fewer errors than if you type it directly into the Code window.

If you've read the earlier section "Creating a variable in the Intermediate window," you created a variable named MyVal. The variable still exists in memory unless you closed VBA. You can use this variable for a little experiment — your first program. Type **MsgBox MyVal** into the Intermediate window and then press Enter. You see a message box like the one shown in Figure 1-10.

Congratulations! You just completed your first VBA application! The code that you typed asked VBA to use the MsgBox function to display the text in the MyVal variable. Click OK to clear the message box.

Figure 1-10:
The
MsgBox
function
produces a
message
box like this.

```
┌────────────────────────┐
│ Microsoft Excel      ☒  │
├────────────────────────┤
│  Hello World            │
│   ┌──────────────┐      │
│   │      OK      │      │
│   └──────────────┘      │
└────────────────────────┘
```

Using Object Browser

VBA provides access to a lot of objects, more than you'll use for any one program. With all the objects that you have at your disposal, you might forget the name of one or more of them at some time. Object Browser helps you find the objects that you need. In fact, you can use it to find new objects that could be useful for your next project. Use the View➪Object Browser command to display Object Browser, as shown in Figure 1-11. Normally, you need to filter the information in some way.

Figure 1-11:
View the objects that VBA makes available via Object Browser.

Browsing objects

Object Browser contains a list of the contents of all projects and libraries loaded for the VBA IDE. You can view the list of projects and libraries by using the Project/Library drop-down list box. When you start Object Browser, this list box reads `<All Libraries>`, which means that you're viewing everything that VBA has to offer — usually too much for someone to make sense of it all.

Projects and libraries are different, but you won't normally need to worry about them to use the objects that they contain. A *project* is the VBA code contained in one of the files that you load into the application. In most cases, you use a project to store the code that you create. A *library* is external code contained in a Dynamic Link Library (DLL) file. The DLL contains support routines used by the application or VBA. This code is normally written by a developer using a language such as Visual Basic or Visual C++. You can't easily edit the code in a DLL.

The projects and libraries list might look complicated at first, but you can narrow the list down to a few types of entries. Of course, you always see your project templates. In addition to project templates, you find these libraries in the list:

- ✔ **Application:** This library has the name of the application, such as Excel or Word, and also includes the features that the application provides for VBA users. For example, the Excel library has a `Chart` object that contains a list of chart-related methods, properties, and events that Excel supports.

- ✔ **Office:** This library contains a list of objects that Microsoft Office supports. For example, this is where you find the objects used to support Office Assistant. Of course, if you're using an application other than Microsoft Office, you won't see this library. Your application might provide another alternative.

- ✔ **StdOLE:** This library contains some of the Object Linking and Embedding (OLE) features that you use in the application. For example, when you embed a picture into a Word document, this library provides the required support. You can use this library in your VBA applications, too, but the Office or application-related library usually provides access to objects that are easier and faster to use.

- ✔ **VBA:** This library contains special utility objects that VBA developers need. For example, it contains the `MsgBox` function that I demonstrate in the earlier "Using the Intermediate window" section of the chapter.

Whenever you want to browse the libraries for a specific object, limit the amount of material that you have to search by using the options in the Project/Library drop-down list box (*filtering* the content). This is a helpful technique when you perform searches as well.

Looking for names and features in Object Browser

When you remember . . . almost, but not quite . . . the name of a method or other programming feature that you want to use, using the search feature of Object Browser can make your life easier. Simply type the text that you want to look for in the Search Text field (the empty box beneath All Libraries) and then click the Search button (the one with a symbol that looks like binoculars) in Object Browser. The Search Results field shown in Figure 1-12 shows what happens when you look for `MsgBox`.

Whenever you choose (highlight) one of the entries in the Search Results field, the bottom two panes change to show that entry. This feature helps you locate specific information about the search result and see it in context with other methods, properties, and events. Notice that the bottom pane tells you more about the selection item. In this case, it tells you how to use the `MsgBox` function.

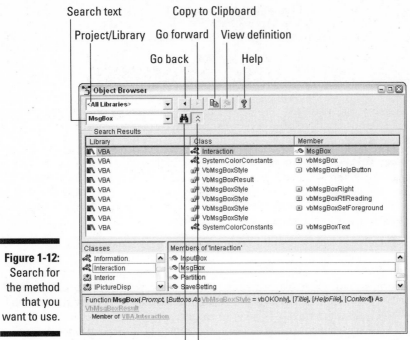

Search text

Copy to Clipboard

Project/Library   Go forward   View definition

Go back   Help

Search   Hide search results

Figure 1-12:
Search for
the method
that you
want to use.

Cutting and pasting in Object Bowser

Whenever you find a method, property, or event that you want to use in Object Browser, you can copy the information to the Clipboard by clicking the Copy to Clipboard button (the one with a symbol that looks like two documents) and then pasting that directly into your application code. Using this feature not only means that you type less code, but you have fewer errors to consider.

Getting help in Object Browser

Sometimes the information at the bottom of Object Browser display isn't enough to tell you about the element that you're viewing. When this happens, highlight the element that you want to know more about, press F1, and VBA displays the help screen for that element.

Chapter 2

Your First VBA Program

In This Chapter

▶ Creating an application plan

▶ Defining the steps to create an application

▶ Using different methods to run your application

▶ Getting and using code found in the help files

*I*n Chapter 1, I show you how to work with the VBA Integrated Development Environment (IDE). In that chapter, I also show you how to use the Intermediate window to create one-line test programs. However, the programs that you create by using the Intermediate window aren't the same as permanent programs (because Intermediate window programs aren't permanent), and you'd find it difficult to perform useful work with them.

This chapter shows you how to move from the Intermediate window into the Code window. The *Code window* is where you create programs of a lasting nature — the kind that you can use to perform the same task more than once. Because of the time required to write the code, it only pays to create an application that you can use more than once. The benefit of writing a program is that you can perform a repetitive task quickly.

One of the tricks that the propeller heads use is to get hold of pre-made code whenever they can. I end this chapter by showing you one of the techniques that they use most — stealing the code directly from Microsoft. The help files that come with VBA contain a lot of code that you can use in a number of ways. Microsoft knows some developers want to use the code, so it tries to make the samples as flexible as possible.

Deciding What to Do

Whenever you decide to create a program, start with a plan. Just like a builder needs a plan to construct a house, you need a plan to construct your program. You could easily tell whether a builder decided to build a house without using a plan, and it's just as easy to determine when someone writes a program without using a plan. Application users can see that the application isn't well designed because it doesn't work as anticipated. The plan that you use doesn't have to be very complicated, but you do need to think about these questions:

- ✔ What will the program do?
- ✔ How will the program accomplish its task?
- ✔ When will the program run?
- ✔ Who will use the program?
- ✔ Why is the program important?

Professional developers use a number of complex and hair-raising methods to answer these questions. You work on much smaller programs, and you can normally answer the questions quite easily. Don't make this more complicated than you need to. You might answer the first question by saying that the program will count the number of words in a document.

The reason that you want to go through this process is to ensure that you've thought about the program that you want to create. It's easier to answer the questions *before* you write any code instead of fixing the code later. Writing your answers down also helps you avoid making the program into something that you didn't intend. This is a common problem for everyone; even developers with a lot of experience write programs that quickly grow beyond the original intent.

Steps to Create a VBA Program

Writing a program usually involves four steps. In this section, I tell you about the four steps while you create your first permanent program — one that you can run as often as you like. The permanent program displays a dialog box, just like the example in Chapter 1.

Step 1: Design the program

In the "Deciding What to Do" section of this chapter, I tell you how to plan your program. I also tell you what questions you should ask in preparation for writing the program. This step is actually part of the design phase, but most developers make it a separate step. Thinking through your application before you commit something to paper is important.

After you plan your application, you can use any of a number of techniques to design the program. Some people use a technique called *flow charting* that uses special symbols to replace programming elements. Other people use specialized engineering software to do the job. You might read about these methods when you get more involved with VBA. However, the best way to design most simple applications is to use a method called *pseudo-coding,* which is a method in which you write down a list of steps in your own words that say what you want VBA to do.

Using pseudo-code is a good way to think about how you want to write the code without getting too concerned about coding issues. This example displays a dialog box. The pseudo-code could be as easy as

```
Display the message box.
See which button the user clicked.
End the program.
```

Don't worry about being too precise about the pseudo-code. The idea is to write a list of steps that you can understand before you begin writing code. If you don't understand what you want to do, it's unlikely that you can tell VBA how to do it. Pseudo-code is a method for putting your words into a form that you can convert to code later.

TIP

You can also add pseudo-code as comments to the VBA code that you write. In Chapter 3, I show you how to use comments in your code. Using your pseudo-code as a basis for comments helps you include the thought process used to design the program in your code. Never write a program that is devoid of comments because you might need to make changes later.

Step 2: Implement the design

The wording for this step is just a fancy way of saying that you need to write some code. You often hear propeller heads use the phrase "implement the design," and it also appears as commonly used jargon in many magazines.

Before you can write some code, you need to open the Visual Basic editor by using the Tools⇨Macro⇨Visual Basic Editor command. I'm using Excel for this example, but the same steps work in Access, Word, FrontPage, PowerPoint, or most other applications that support VBA. The only change is that your screenshots won't look precisely like mine when you use another product.

The first thing to do is create a Code window. To do that, use the Insert⇨ Module command. The Visual Basic editor creates a blank Code window where you can type your program. A blank Code window can be a scary experience, but you don't need to worry because you already have some text (the code snippet in the previous section, "Step 1: Design the program") to put into it. The Code window includes a container in which to store the code called a Sub (for sub-procedure) and the pseudo-code. (Chapter 3 describes the Sub in detail, so you don't need to worry about it for now.) Add a ' (single quote) character in front of each pseudo-code statement to ensure that VBA knows that this is pseudo-code. Figure 2-1 shows how your Code window should look.

Figure 2-1:
The Code window starts blank, but you already have information to add to it.

You could actually run the Sub shown in Figure 2-1, but it wouldn't do anything. To make this example do something, add code to it that VBA understands. This means converting the English statements such as *Display the message box.* into VBA. To display a message box, use the MsgBox function that I describe in Chapter 1.

The MsgBox function is capable of doing more than the Chapter 1 example shows. First, it can return a Result that shows which button the user selected. The Result variable holds the selection information so that you can use it in other ways. You can also tell MsgBox which buttons to display and to provide a title. Here's a more advanced version of the MsgBox function that I use in Chapter 1 — type it directly beneath the ' Display the message box. comment.

```
Result = MsgBox("Click a Button", vbYesNoCancel, "A Message")
```

This code tells VBA to display a message box with "Click a Button" as the text and "A Message" on the title bar. The message box includes the Yes, No, and Cancel buttons. After VBA displays the message box, it waits for the user to make a decision. When the user clicks one of the three buttons, VBA stores the choice in the Result variable. Wow, that's a lot for one piece of text to do!

The pseudo-code says that the code needs to detect which button the user pressed. You can use another message box to display the information like this:

```
MsgBox Result
```

This is the same technique that I use in Chapter 1. The only difference is that the information contained in Result relies on a user selection. You don't know which button the user will select in advance, but this code works no matter which button the user clicks.

The origins of computer bugs

You might wonder why professionals call a programming error a *bug*. There are many versions of this story, but all of them begin in the early annals of computer history. At that time, computers were immense devices that could take up an entire building. Instead of the small chips used in today's computers, these older devices used switches and vacuum tubes. The story holds that one day a programmer of one of these massive machines experienced an error. After a long search, the programmer found an actual bug in one of the switches used to control the computer. The term stuck — all programming errors are now blamed on insects.

The final piece of pseudo-code says that VBA should end the program. You do this with the End Sub statement shown in Figure 2-1. Whenever VBA runs out of instructions to process, it ends the program. Figure 2-2 shows what your code should look like now. Make sure that you save the code at this point by using the File⇨Save command.

Figure 2-2: Writing code is easy when you use pseudo-code to describe it first.

```
Sample Programs.xls - Module1 (Code)
(General)                          SayHello
Sub SayHello()
' Display the message box.
Result = MsgBox("Click a Button", vbYesNoCancel, "A Message")
' See which button the user clicked.
MsgBox Result
' End the program.
End Sub
```

Step 3: Test, test, test

It's time to run the application for the first time. The easiest way to run an application is to click the Run Sub/User Form button on the toolbar. (It's the one that looks like the Play button on a VCR.) Click the button to see the first message box. It should look like the one shown in Figure 2-3. If the program won't run, use the Tools⇨Options command to display the Options dialog box. Select the Security tab and click the Macro Security button. Set the security level to Medium or Low and click OK twice.

The message box contains the title, message, and buttons that you asked VBA to display in the code. Checking the contents of the message box to verify that it contains everything that you thought it would contain is *testing*. If you want to ensure that your program always works the way you originally designed it, you need to test as many features as possible.

Figure 2-3:
The first message box asks the user to click a button.

A Message

Click a Button

| Yes | No | Cancel |

Click Yes to see another message box like the one shown in Figure 2-4. Look at the code again. Notice that this message box contains the result (the return value) of the MsgBox function. The number 6 isn't very useful to humans, but it's quite usable for the computer. An actual program converts this number to something that humans can understand. For now, you know that clicking Yes produces a number 6.

Figure 2-4:
The MsgBox function return value.

Microsoft Excel

6

OK

When you click OK, the program ends, and you don't see any other message boxes. This condition verifies that the last step of the pseudo-code is complete.

Don't assume the testing process is over; there are two other buttons on the initial message box. Unless you test the buttons, you won't know that they work. Run the program again, but try the No button the second time and the Cancel button the third time.

The return value displayed in the second message box (refer to Figure 2-4) should change for each button. Clicking No should produce a value of 7, and clicking Cancel should produce a value of 2. If you don't see these values, your program has an error. Professionals call a programming error a *bug*.

Step 4: Swat the bugs

Bugs can appear when you test your program. Planning and writing your code carefully reduces the number of bugs, but everyone makes mistakes. It's often a matter of not understanding how a function works. Testing your programs helps you find the bugs. After you find the bugs, you have to look at your code and discover the coding errors that create the bugs.

Not every bug is even your fault — it could be an error in the documentation for the function. Microsoft is well known for committing mistakes of this sort and then telling everyone that it really meant to do that. (Microsoft is fond of calling this an *undocumented feature*.) You might find that a bug isn't actually in your program but somewhere in VBA itself. Microsoft might tell you about these errors, but it often leaves them as a surprise for you to discover.

Microsoft won't knock on your door to tell you that it made a mistake. You have to search for these errors on your own at a central Web site that Microsoft has set up. The Microsoft *Knowledge Base* is a special kind of search engine that helps you find information about problems with VBA and the associated fix. You can find the Microsoft Knowledge Base at `http://search.support.microsoft.com/search/default.aspx`.

It's important to get rid of as many bugs as possible in your program. This task is so important that I devote an entire chapter to it: In Chapter 6, I provide details on how to locate and fix bugs in your program. This chapter also tells you how to keep the user from making mistakes by detecting the error before the program does. The important idea for this chapter is that you need to fix bugs in your application; don't worry too much about the precise details for this task right now.

Four Ways to Run Your Program

Running your program from within the Visual Basic editor is fine when you want to test it. However, the goal is to run it from the application and not have to open the Visual Basic editor first. You have a lot of choices for running any VBA program — more than most people want to remember. VBA provides four common methods for running applications, but most VBA users never need to think beyond the first method, which is using the Macro dialog box.

Using the Macro dialog box

The Macro dialog box is the most common way to run a VBA program. Every time that you create a new Sub, it appears in the list of macros that you can run. You don't have to do anything special. This feature means that you can always access every program that you create by using this method, which is why it's the most popular method.

Use the Tools⇨Macro⇨Macros command to display the Macro dialog box as shown in Figure 2-5. You can also display this dialog box by pressing Alt+F8 in Office applications. (Other applications use different key combinations.) Notice that Figure 2-5 shows the macro, SayHello, that appears in the earlier "Step 2: Implement the design" section of this chapter.

Figure 2-5:
Use the
Macro
dialog box
to access
the
programs
that you
create.

When you want to run the program, highlight it and then click the Run button. Try it now. You should see the same, two dialog box sequences that you saw when you tested the program earlier in the chapter.

You can also use this dialog box to perform other tasks. Highlight the macro name and then click the Edit button; the application opens the Visual Basic editor. The Code window displays the code associated with the program that you highlighted. You can also remove old programs by clicking the Delete button.

Notice the Macro Name field near the top of the Macro dialog box in Figure 2-5. This field normally contains the name of the macro that you've highlighted in the list. However, you can also use the Macro dialog box to create new programs. Type **SayGoodbye** in the Macro Name field, and the Macro dialog box enables the Create button and disables everything else, as shown in Figure 2-6. You can use this dialog box to create any new programs that you need.

Figure 2-6:
Typing a
non-existent
macro name
in the
Macro
Name field
enables the
Create
button.

Using the quick launch methods

It isn't always convenient or efficient to open the Macro dialog box to run the programs that you design. If you use the same program several times a day, opening the Macro dialog box can become a time-wasting event. What you need is a *quick launch method* — a way to start the program that doesn't require you to open the Macro dialog box.

Defining a shortcut key

The Macro dialog box shown in Figure 2-5 has one other use that helps you create quick launch programs. Open the Macro dialog box by using the Tools⇨Macro⇨Macros command. Highlight the program that you want to launch quickly (SayHello for this example). Click the Options button. Excel opens the Macro Options dialog box. Type **h** in the Shortcut Key field and **This is a simple program.** in the Description field. Your dialog box should look like the one in Figure 2-7.

Figure 2-7:
Make a
program
quick
launch by
using the
Macro
Options
dialog box.

> **Macro Options**
>
> Macro name:
> SayHello
>
> Shortcut key:
>   Ctrl+ h
>
> Description:
> This is a simple program.
>
> [OK]   [Cancel]

Click OK to close the Macro Options dialog box and then click Cancel to close the Macro dialog box. When you press Ctrl+H, the program that you created earlier should run and display the same two dialog box sequence as before.

Defining a toolbar button

Using shortcut keys is fine when you don't have a lot of them to remember and you don't mind performing finger gymnastics. However, you don't have to limit yourself to keyboard shortcuts. You can place a button on a toolbar that starts your program. Using this method means that all you have to remember is to look at the toolbar.

Many people place custom buttons on the same toolbars that the application uses for other purposes. This is fine if you don't mind seeing the toolbar grow longer and longer, right off the right side of the screen. It's better to create a custom toolbar so that you can show or hide the buttons associated with your programs when you need them.

To add a VBA program to a toolbar, you can begin by creating a custom toolbar for the task or you can select an existing toolbar. The SayHello example uses an existing toolbar, Standard, to speed things up. The Standard toolbar is provided with just about every Windows application that uses VBA, but you might need to use another toolbar. The following steps show how to add a program to your toolbar:

1. **Right-click in the toolbar area and then choose Customize from the context menu that appears.**

   The Customize dialog box appears.

2. **Select the Commands tab and scroll through the Categories list until you find Macros.**

   Figure 2-8 shows that you have two options for adding macros to your toolbar — as a menu item or as a button.

Figure 2-8:
Add your program to the toolbar by using either a button or a menu item.

Use a button when you need to save space on a toolbar. However, make sure that you add a name to the button that explains what the button is used for, or you might forget its purpose. Use a menu item to make it easier to remember the button's purpose. Choosing the menu item option displays a new toolbar button bearing the name that you assign on the toolbar, making it easier to see what the button does.

3. **To add a custom button, drag a Custom Menu Item object from the Customize dialog box to the Standard toolbar.**

   The application should add a new (blank) button to the toolbar.

4. **Right-click the new button on the toolbar and then select the Name option. (This entry has a text box next to it.)**

5. **In the Name field, type** &Say Hello.

This action assigns a name to the button. The & (ampersand) places an underline beneath the S in Say. A user can press Alt+S to access the button quickly when the toolbar is selected.

6. **Right-click the new button on the toolbar and then select Assign Macro.**

   An Assign Macro dialog box appears, like the one shown in Figure 2-9.

Figure 2-9:
Use the
Assign
Macro
dialog box
to add a
macro to the
toolbar
button.

7. **Highlight the SayHello entry and then click OK.**

8. **Click Close to close the Customize dialog box.**

   That's it! The Say Hello toolbar button is now functional. Click it to see the same, two dialog box sequence that you see in the previous examples.

Defining a menu entry

You might use a program often enough to attach it to a regular program element but not often enough to take up space on a toolbar. In this case, you can use a menu to hold the quick launch option. You use the same set of steps shown in the preceding "Defining a toolbar button" section to perform this task. The only difference is that you drag the custom button or custom menu item to the menu that you want to use instead of to a toolbar (Step 3).

Accessing the program from other VBA code

Never write a piece of code twice when you can write it once and use it everywhere. Saving time is one of the reasons to use VBA, so saving time by writing VBA code is a good way to increase the benefits that you receive. In Chapter 3, I discuss many of the methods that you can use to reuse code.

However, the first idea that you have to understand is that you can *call* (tell VBA to execute) any VBA program that you create from another program. Here's a simple example that you can add to the Code window.

```
Sub SayHello2()
' Show that we're using the SayHello2 program.
MsgBox "We're in SayHello2!"

' Call SayHello
SayHello
End Sub
```

Notice how this sample uses pseudo-code to describe what happens when you run the program. Remember that *pseudo-code* is a list of steps that the program must perform written in a form that you can understand. The first task is to prove that you executed the SayHello2 program by displaying a message box that contains a message that doesn't appear in SayHello. The second task is to call SayHello. Make sure that you save your program at this point.

When you run this program, it displays three message boxes. The first one reads We're in SayHello2! The second and third message boxes look just like the ones you've seen for the SayHello program used throughout this chapter.

Executing the VBA program automatically

In rare cases, you need to write a VBA program that does something when you start the associated application or perform some other task such as opening a document. You should use this method of executing your programs automatically only if it serves a very special purpose. Using this technique to perform a setup that you only use once in a while doesn't make sense. If there's something that you set up every day, it usually pays to make it a permanent part of the application configuration rather than run a program to make the changes.

The smartest VBA users avoid using this technique for several reasons. First, many users have disabled automatic macro execution on their machines, which means that this technique won't work at all. The reason why people disable automatic macro execution is that some *crackers* (nefarious fiends who write viruses) have used automatic macro execution as a weapon in the past. (You can read more about macro viruses at http://www.esafedesktop.com/ Macro%20Viruses.htm — this is just one of over 400 sites that I've found that discuss this problem.) Second, the precise method for creating an automatically executing program varies by application. The technique used in Word might not work in Excel and vice versa.

The program used most often in this chapter is SayHello. The name that you give your program is important because it can have special effects on the application. When you name your program AutoExec, the application (Word, Excel, Access, and so on) automatically executes the macro whenever it's started. Table 2-1 contains a list of special program names that you can use to perform tasks automatically in some applications.

Table 2-1	Special Program Names That Automatically Execute
Name	**When It Runs**
AutoClose	When the user closes a document
AutoExec	When the application starts
AutoExit	When the application ends
AutoNew	When the user creates a new document
AutoOpen	When the user opens an existing document

Using Help to Your Advantage — Stealing Microsoft's Code

This book contains a lot of code — most of it very practical code that you can use today to improve your Microsoft Office experience. Even with as much as this book has to offer, you still won't find examples of every function that VBA has to offer. Fortunately, Microsoft does provide you with lots of sample code in the help files. In fact, you can even copy this code right out of the help file and use it for your next program.

To see the sample code associated with a function, open the help page to that function. You might want to highlight one of the MsgBox entries in the sample code for this chapter and then press F1. In Chapter 1, I describe some of the information on this page. However, notice the links at the top of the page. Three of the most common links are See Also, Example, and Specifics. Click Example to see a new window open like the one shown in Figure 2-10.

This code is a little complex for right now, but in this book, I show you how to read and understand it. More importantly, you can highlight the code, right-click it, and then select Copy from the context menu that appears. Paste the code into the Code window for your VBA program to use it.

Figure 2-10:
Copy any of the code that you need from the help file to reduce program-ming time and effort.

The image shows a Microsoft Visual Basic Help window containing:

MsgBox Function Example

This example uses the **MsgBox** function to display a critical-error message in a dialog box with Yes and No buttons. The No button is specified as the default response. The value returned by the **MsgBox** function depends on the button chosen by the user. This example assumes that DEMO.HLP is a Help file that contains a topic with a Help context number equal to 1000.

```
Dim Msg, Style, Title, Help, Ctxt, Response, MyString
Msg = "Do you want to continue ?"     ' Define message.
Style = vbYesNo + vbCritical + vbDefaultButton2     ' Define buttons.
Title = "MsgBox Demonstration"    ' Define title.
Help = "DEMO.HLP"     ' Define Help file.
Ctxt = 1000     ' Define topic
        ' context.
        ' Display message.
Response = MsgBox(Msg, Style, Title, Help, Ctxt)
If Response = vbYes Then     ' User chose Yes.
    MyString = "Yes"     ' Perform some action.
Else     ' User chose No.
    MyString = "No"     ' Perform some action.
End If
```

Part II
Learning the
Ropes

The 5th Wave   By Rich Tennant

They're moving on to the Array Programming section. That should daze and confuse them enough for us to finish changing the tire and get the heck out of here.

ANSI
Document
Publishers

In this part . . .

Every adventure begins with a discovery phase. This part of the book is all about discovery. You consider all the elements that define VBA as a language. Good structure is the basis of most projects in life. When you build a house, you create the basic structure first and then add onto it. Chapter 3 is all about VBA program structure. You discover how to create a framework for the programs that you build later.

In Chapter 4, I help you understand how to manage data by using VBA. Data management is the single most important skill that a programmer can learn. In Chapter 5, I tell you how to control program flow by using several techniques. Controlling program flow lets you do things like make decisions. In Chapter 6, I show you some techniques that you can use to make the task easier. In this chapter, I also demonstrate how you can use some of these techniques in other ways to make programming faster and easier. In Chapter 7, I help you discover the joys of creating a user interface.

Chapter 3

Writing Structured VBA Programs

• •

In This Chapter

▶ Discovering the structure used by most programs

▶ Using structure to your advantage

▶ Creating a program by using a `Sub`

▶ Creating a program by using a `Function`

▶ Hiding some program elements by using scope

▶ Adding white space to programs

▶ Adding comments to your code

• •

*I*n Chapters 1 and 2, I concentrate on the basics of VBA programming without discussing an important element that most VBA programs need — structure. Adding structure makes code easier to read and use. It's also a mandatory part of the development process.

There are a number of ways to look at structure in a program. Just like you use an outline to structure a presentation, you need to add structure to your program to make it work properly. Using structure in a program is like using a checklist with a large customer order — it helps you ensure that all the program elements are in place. The structure that you add to a program is like presenting numeric information with a graph — it makes the content of the program easier to see and understand.

In this chapter, I present various forms of structure. The obvious structuring element is physical. By using physical structure, you can divide your program into small pieces that are easy to write and understand.

Another form of structure includes the concept of privacy. You need to consider who can see your program and how they can use it. *Scope*, which is the act of determining the range of program access, is important because you want to make some parts completely private and other parts completely public.

Finally, there are visual elements of structure. How you use white space when you write your program can make the difference between reading it and scratching your head. In Chapter 2, I discuss some use of comments in the form of pseudo-code, but you might find that you need additional comments to help someone truly understand your program (and to jog your memory when you need to make alterations).

Parts of a Program

The examples in Chapters 1 and 2 use some physical structure. You can't write a program, not even a simple one, without at least a little structure because VBA needs that structure to understand what you want it to do. A VBA user can ignore the structure, but VBA can't. This chapter formalizes the meaning for each structural element.

Defining the parts of a program

Programs are the highest level of physical structure. A *program* contains everything needed to perform a given task. It can cross module, class module, and form boundaries. (*Modules, class modules,* and *forms* are special containers for holding program code — you can save them as individual files, but they're normally embedded within an application document.) The concept of a program comes from the very earliest use of computers. A program acts as a container for the code used to implement a set of features required by the operating system or the user.

Some people have a hard time understanding what a program is because modern software packages often define the term incorrectly. When you open a copy of Word, you're using a *program.* Conversely, Microsoft Office is a set of programs, or an *application suite.* Microsoft Office isn't a single program; it's a set of programs that includes Word, Access, Excel, and other individual programs. Likewise, when you open a copy of Notepad — that's a program. Notepad and Word each contain a set of features required by the user to perform a given task.

Programs also extend into other areas of computing. A single device driver, say the driver that you installed for your mouse, is a program. The user interface that helps you configure the mouse is often a separate program. It's not part of the device driver even though it controls the device driver's actions.

Don't assume that a program equates to a project. (A *project* is the container used to hold the embedded modules, class modules, and forms associated with a given document.) You're not creating a new program when you create a new project. A *VBA project* can actually contain a number of VBA programs. Every public Sub that a user can access by using the Macro dialog box (as I describe in Chapter 2) is a separate program. The SayHello program that I use in Chapter 2 is an example of a simple program that relies on a single Sub, but you can create programs of any complexity.

In Chapter 17, I demonstrate that a single program can cross project boundaries. All the examples in that chapter rely on the services of at least two Microsoft Office products to perform a single task. Even though the program is calling on the services of more than one Microsoft Office product, and it resides in more than one location, it's still a single program. Each example contains a set of features required by the user to perform a given task. The physical location and the use of external modules don't affect this definition.

Understanding the VBA programming blocks

A VBA program consists of building blocks. In fact, because programming is abstract, people tend to use physical examples to explain how things work. You still need to know about the abstract elements of VBA programming, or you can't write a program. This section explains the basic constructs of VBA programming. In the upcoming "Taking the Lego Approach" section of this chapter, I use a physical example as a means of describing these abstract elements in detail. You need to consider only the four elements that I describe here:

- **Project:** The project acts as a container for the modules, class modules, and forms for a particular file. In Word, you normally see a minimum of three projects loaded into the Visual Basic editor: the normal template, the document template, and the document. Excel users normally see just one project for the file that they currently have open.

- **Module, class module, and form:** These three elements act as containers for main programming elements such as class descriptions and procedures. A single project can have multiple modules, class modules, and forms in it. However, each of these elements requires a unique name.

- Function **and** Sub: The Function and Sub elements hold individual lines of code (also called *statements*). A Function returns a value to the caller, but a Sub does not.

✔ **Statement:** Many people call an individual line of code a *statement.* The pseudo-code in Chapter 2 shows why. Each line of pseudo-code is a statement of what the application should do. The example in the "Step 2: Implement the design" section of Chapter 2 shows how these lines of pseudo-code are translated into code that VBA can understand. You're still making a statement when you use VBA code to perform a task — you're just doing it in VBA's language.

Using Subs

I use a sub-procedure, or Sub, in Chapter 2. A Sub is the easiest method of packaging code, and it's the only packaging method that appears in the Macro dialog box. In fact, the example in the "Writing Your First Function" section (later in this chapter) demonstrates this feature. Consequently, the one place where you always use a Sub is the main entry point for a program unless the program is a utility that you use only for programming purposes.

A second way to use a Sub is to perform a task and not receive a direct return value. You could use a Sub to display an informational message such as the ones in Chapter 2. A Sub can modify information in a number of ways; it just can't return a value — only a Function can do that. However, you can use arguments as one method for modifying information by using a Sub (see the upcoming "Writing Your First Function" section example). A second method relies on global variables (see the later "Defining the effects of scope" section example).

Many VBA users also use the Sub as a means of breaking up code. Instead of creating code that goes on for miles and miles, using several Subs can break up the code into page-sized pieces. Using this method makes the code a lot easier to read.

Using Functions

You might not see a use for the Function after spending some time working with the Sub. However, not every problem is a screw requiring use of a screwdriver or a nail in search of a hammer. You use a Function for different problems than a Sub can answer. In most cases, there's definitely a correct answer to using a Function or a Sub. For example, you always use a Sub when you want to access program code from within the host application, and you always use a Function when you want to perform a calculation with a return result.

A `Function` always returns a value, which makes it different from a `Sub`. For this reason, you can write functions that contain code that you plan to repeat a lot within a program. To process a list of names, you might create a `Function` to process each name individually and then call that `Function` once for each name. The `Function` can provide the processed information as a return value. In Chapter 5, I describe how to create repeating code.

You can also use a `Function` for public code that you don't want to list in the Macro dialog box. You normally won't see a `Function` listed in the Macro dialog box — this dialog box usually lists only `Subs`.

Modifying the project settings

So far, you've used VBA without configuring many of the options, and the examples have relied on defaults that VBA normally uses. Most of the VBA program levels have some type of configuration, including the project. In this section, I describe the various project setting options.

To open the project settings, right-click the project in the Project window and then choose the project Properties option from the context menu that appears (see Figure 3-1). See the "Looking at the Integrated Development Environment (IDE)" section of Chapter 1 for description of the Project window. (Note that I've already filled out the various options that I describe in the following sections.)

Figure 3-1:
Define basic
information
for your
projects.

Describing your project

Describing your object makes it easier to track when you view it in the VBA IDE windows. Start by giving your project a meaningful name. It shouldn't be long, but calling your project *VBAProject* isn't all that meaningful because it doesn't describe what the project does. The Project Name field shown in Figure 3-1 has a meaningful project name for this chapter because the examples show how to add structure to your programs.

Although the Project Name field value shows up in a number of places, the Project Description field value only shows up in Object Browser. You can write a longer text description of the project so that it's easier to track each entry that Object Browser shows. Otherwise, you might have a hard time finding the project that you want.

Some people don't see help files as a necessary project description, but a *help file* is a detailed description of what your project can do. The Help File Name field tells where to locate the help file and which help file to use. The Project Help Context ID field contains the number of the help topic that relates to the project. This entry normally contains the topic number of an overview page.

Adding conditional compilation

Conditional compilation is an essential feature for creating multiple versions of your program. Normally, VBA goes through your list of statements and performs them one at a time. However, using conditional compilations allows VBA to perform a task in one way while you write and test the program and in another way when you finish it.

The most common use for this feature is to help debug a program. In Chapter 6, I show you how to use conditional compilation for this purpose. However, for now, just to have a little fun, you can create a very simple program that shows how this feature works. First, make sure that you type **myDebug = 0** in the Conditional Compilation Arguments field and then click OK. Then type the following program in a module (see the "Step 2: Implement the design" section of Chapter 2 for instructions on creating a module):

```
Public Sub CheckConditional()
    #If myDebug = 0 Then
        MsgBox "In Standard Mode"
    #Else
        MsgBox "In Debug Mode"
    #End If
End Sub
```

This program says that if myDebug is set to 0, the program should display a message box that reads In Standard Mode. If myDebug is set to any other value, the program should display a message box that reads In Debug Mode. Run the program, and you should see a message box that reads In Standard Mode.

Open the project Properties dialog box again. Change the Conditional Compilation Arguments field so that it reads **myDebug = 1**. Click OK and then run the program again. The program displays a message box that reads In Debug Mode.

Locking your code

At some point, you might decide that you want to lock your code away forever so that no one can modify it. The Protection tab of the project Properties dialog box, as shown in Figure 3-2, helps you accomplish this task. Simply select the Lock Project for Viewing check box and then supply the same password in both the Password and the Confirm Password fields. Click OK to complete the process.

Figure 3-2:
Locking
your code
can keep it
safe from
prying eyes.

Locking your project might seem like a good idea, but you should carefully consider doing so for a number of reasons. The most important reason is that you can't unlock the project without the password. If you forget the password, the project might remain locked forever. The second reason is that locking your project doesn't prevent someone from viewing your code. The only thing that locking the project does is to prevent someone from modifying the code. Consequently, when you need to hide the code for some reason, VBA isn't the best tool for the job. (If hiding your code is essential, you need a native code compiler such as Visual C++.)

Defining compiler options

When you first start VBA, it makes certain assumptions about how you want to write code. These assumptions might not be accurate, so Microsoft provides a way for you to tell VBA to do something else. The compiler options that appear in Table 3-1 help you define how VBA works with your code. (A *compiler* reads your code and translates the words into instructions that Windows can understand.) You can add these options at the very beginning of a module, class module, or form before any other code.

Table 3-1	Compiler Options for VBA
Option	*Description*
Option Base <Number>	Use this option to change how VBA numbers array elements. You can number array elements beginning at 0 or 1. In Chapter 9, I describe how to use arrays.
Option Explicit	Smart VBA programmers always add this compiler option to their code. This option tells VBA that you want to define variables before you use them. Not only does this option make your code easier to read, but it can also help you to find typos in your code. Although the standard setting treats MyVar and MVar as two variables, this option forces VBA to question the misspelled version.
Option Compare <Method>	Use this option to change how VBA compares strings. When using the Binary technique, VBA considers *hello* and *Hello* different because the first form is in lowercase. Using the *Text* method means that VBA considers *hello* and *Hello* as the same word because it won't take the case of the letters into consideration. The Database technique is only available in Access — it uses the database sort order for string comparison purposes.
Option Private Module	Use this option to make a module private so that no other module can see what it contains. The concept of public and private is the object's scope. The upcoming section "Getting the Scoop on Scope" describes what scope means in greater detail.

The `Option Explicit` statement is so important that you should always add it to a program. Listing 3-1 is a short example of how this feature works.

Listing 3-1   Using Option Explicit to Reduce Errors

```
' Tell VBA to ensure we define variables.
Option Explicit

' This Sub will fail because it doesn't
' define the variable.
Public Sub OptionCheck()
    MyVar = "Hello"
    MsgBox MyVar
End Sub

' This Sub will succeed.
Public Sub OptionCheck2()
    ' Define the variable.
    Dim MyVar As String

    ' Add a value to the variable.
    MyVar = "Hello"

    ' Display a message box.
    MsgBox MyVar
End Sub
```

In both cases, the `Sub` defines a value for a variable named `MyVar`. The `OptionCheck` `Sub` fails because it doesn't define the variable before it uses it. VBA doesn't know anything about `MyVar`, so it can't use it. Look at the second `Sub`, `OptionCheck2`. This `Sub` works because it defines `MyVar` first and then assigns a value to it. Although using the `Option Explicit` statement might seem like a lot of work, it really does save a lot of time debugging typos in your program.

Taking the Lego Approach

It's easy to make writing a program harder than it needs to be by getting caught up in the abstract nature of code. The biggest mistake that you can make is to write one long program that goes on for pages and pages that no one can understand — not even you. Code that looks more like a copy of *War and Peace* rather than a simple set of instructions is usually called *spaghetti code*.

Understanding the Lego approach

I call the method that I describe in this chapter *the Lego approach* because most people are familiar with this toy and it's an easy way to explain good programming technique. Some people use other names for this kind of programming. You might hear it called *modular programming* because it relies on modules to hold individual pieces of code. Don't confuse all these terms with object-oriented programming, which I describe in Chapter 8.

The Lego approach to writing code is one in which the programmer breaks the program up into easily understood modules and writes just one module at a time. Using this approach helps you write code that is easy to modify later and that most people can understand with ease. The Lego approach also makes it easy for you to move pieces of code when writing another program.

Creating an application plan

In Chapter 2, I describe how to use pseudo-code to write a program. The program in that chapter only uses one module because it's quite simple. Not every program that you create is that simple. Sometimes a program performs complex tasks, and you need to create an *overview,* or *application plan,* first. Think of the Lego approach again: Each block is separate, but you don't get the whole picture until you put the blocks together. The application plan shows how to put the blocks together to get a particular result. You have three sizes of blocks that you can use:

- ✔ Projects
- ✔ Modules, forms, and class modules
- ✔ Sub-procedures and functions

Think about the writing a VBA program this way. You have a pile of blocks, and you have a picture of what you want to create in your mind. To make the creation a reality, you need to choose and add blocks that look like they fit. You can choose standard blocks from this book, the VBA help file, or online sites such as the FreeVBCode.com at http://www.freevbcode.com/.

You can use a number of techniques to create your application plan. I usually start with a list of major tasks such as printing a report or finding a word. This isn't pseudo-code. You're not writing a procedure for VBA to follow. All that you're thinking about is the major tasks that VBA has to perform. Maybe your program only performs one major task. In that case, you might be able to get by with a single project, module, and sub-procedure like the example in Chapter 2.

Defining the project

You might never need to define more than one project for a program. This is especially true of Access and Excel projects in which everything needed to hold the data appears in one file. You can also place everything that you need into a single Word template if this is the only template that you need and the program is appropriate for use with more than one document.

However, think about Word for a moment, and you discover something about projects. Figure 3-3 shows a typical Project window setup. Notice that this window contains three projects: Normal, Project (Document2), and TemplateProject (LETTER).

Figure 3-3: A single program can span more than one project.

Word always loads the `Normal.dot` template. You might also use a custom template. Finally, you also have the document, which also counts as a project. In this case, I wrote a program for the individual document that uses template specific sub-procedures and functions in the Letter template as well as generic utility sub-procedures and functions in the Normal template. You can see this example in Chapter 13. You might run into some situations like this when you create your Word programs, too.

Another situation in which you use multiple projects is when you create programs in which multiple applications have to work together. I have a program for Word that asks CorelDRAW to import a drawing and convert it into a form that Word can use. Word receives the converted drawing and places it in the current document. Word then asks Access to look up the drawing in a database. Access performs this task and returns a description of the drawing to Word, which then formats the description and places it under the drawing in the current document. If I had to perform this whole loop every time that I needed a drawing, it would take 20 minutes per drawing. My Word VBA program can perform the task in less than a minute, and the results are perfect every time.

Defining the program means figuring out how many building blocks that you need to accomplish a task. You can take the simple approach and use just one project for many programs. However, don't make life difficult. If you need to use multiple projects, VBA makes it easy to use them.

Adding a module

Most of your beginning programs use a single module. However, good design begins with module definitions. You could create a huge module called *utility* that contains every utility program you've ever written, but it would be a mess. It's like the overstressed dresser drawer that hides the tie tack or other jewelry that you want to wear tonight. After you throw all the contents of the drawer out into the room, you finally find the one item that you were looking for. Instead of creating a single utility module, try creating a module for disk utilities and another for data manipulation. Be unique! Try arranging your modules to see what works best.

When your programming skills improve, you might want to interact with the user in some way. You might want to ask the user questions. This task requires that you add a form to your program. Every form that you want to create requires a separate form addition to the program. Make sure that you create forms that ask for one kind of information — don't confuse the user by asking for all kinds of unrelated information on one form. (See Chapter 7 for a description of forms and how to use them.)

Working with objects means using classes. To create a special object, add a class module to your application. Like when adding forms, you should add one class module for every new object that you want to create. Make sure that any object that you create performs only one task. (Chapter 8 demonstrates methods for working with objects.)

Designing procedures

Most of the example programs in this book rely on a single project and a single module. You might find that most (if not all) of your programs rely on just one of each of these blocks, too. When using this strategy, think about how to break your program into sub-procedures and functions. Use the information found in the earlier "Using Subs" and "Using Functions" sections to determine which kind of module to use.

The important thing when working at the sub-procedure and function level is to write code in convenient chunks. Use your sub-procedures and functions as containers to hold a certain kind of task. Think again about Legos. Every Lego is an individual unit. You need to write sub-procedures and functions so you can break them apart easily — making each element an individual unit. The examples in this book show you various methods for breaking your code apart because this is one of the most important programming skills.

It's easy to figure out how to break apart simple code. The `MsgBox` function that you've used so often is a good example. Look at how this function works: You send some information to it, and the function takes care of all the details for displaying the message box onscreen. You don't have to worry about how `MsgBox` accomplishes this task, and there aren't any weird conditions for using `MsgBox`.

Writing statements

After all the other organization is complete, you're left with one or more projects that contain one or more modules that contain at least a sub-procedure. All your Legos are put together, but they're empty. The statements that you write ultimately create the program. All the organization makes the task of writing the statements easier because you only need to concentrate on one task as a time.

In Chapter 2, I emphasize the importance of using an organized approach to writing statements. You begin by creating a pseudo-code procedure, and then you change that pseudo-code into statements that VBA can understand. This process provides two levels of organization for your program: code and documentation. However, there are two other forms of organization. In the upcoming "Creating Readable Code" section, I describe the importance of using white space to make your code readable. In the upcoming "Telling Others about Your Code" section, I show how to use comments to describe how your code works.

Writing Your First Sub

Most of the Microsoft Office products provide a Properties page for documents that contains a Summary tab similar to the one shown in Figure 3-4. You can also find a variation of this Properties page for most third-party products. The Summary tab can provide a lot of valuable information for your programs. You can find out basic statistics such as the author's name and the company that created the document. The document information also includes statistics, such as the number of words that the document contains. See the BuiltinDocumentProperties help topic in the VBA help file for additional information.

Figure 3-4:
Many
applications
include a
Summary
tab like
this one.

Structure.xls Properties

General | Summary | Statistics | Contents | Custom

Title:
Subject:
Author: John Paul Mueller
Manager:
Company: DataCon Services
Category:
Keywords:
Comments:
Hyperlink base:
Template:
☐ Save preview picture

OK   Cancel

This is the first example where you work directly with an object. The property that you want to use is BuiltinDocumentProperties. This property is available for most of the Microsoft Office products, but it's attached to a different object in each one. When using Word, you find this property attached to both the Word.Document and the Word.Template objects. Excel users find the property attached to the Excel.Worksheet object. Use the Object

Browser (press F2 to display the Object Browser if necessary) that I discuss in Chapter 1 to find this property for your product. Type **BuiltinDocumentProperties** in the Search Text field and then click Search. Figure 3-5 shows typical results for Excel.

Figure 3-5: The documentation often tells you about an interesting property but not where to find it.

Notice the text at the bottom of Figure 3-5. The information includes the full object name for the property, which comes in handy when you write the code shown in Listing 3-2. Here's the code that you need to create this example in Excel. Change the `ActiveWorkbook` object to the object that your application supports, such as `Document` or `Template` in Word, when using another application.

Listing 3-2   Getting Author Information from a Document

```
Public Sub GetSummary()
    ' Declare a DocumentProperty object to hold the
    ' information.
    Dim MyProperty As DocumentProperty

    ' Set the DocumentProperty object equal to the author
    ' information.
    Set MyProperty = _
        ActiveWorkbook.BuiltinDocumentProperties("Author")

    ' Display a message box containing the property value.
    MsgBox MyProperty.Value, vbOKOnly, "Author Name"
End Sub
```

This example begins by declaring a variable named `MyProperty`. However, `MyProperty` is different from other variables because it's actually an object. This is a `DocumentProperty` object that can hold any document property, including the author or company name.

The next line of code sets `MyProperty` equal to the author information provided by the `BuiltinDocumentProperties("Author")` object. You can set one object equal to another if they're the same kind of an object. It's like looking at two apples: You can say that one apple is like another, but you can't say that an apple is like an orange. In this case, you're storing the author information located in the `BuiltinDocumentProperties("Author")` object into `MyProperty`.

If a line of code is too long, you can continue it on the next line in VBA by adding an underscore, _, like the one shown in the example code. The underscore is called a *continuation character*. You should add a continuation character when the text onscreen requires scrolling. It's easier to read the code if you don't have to scroll from side to side.

The last line of code displays the `Value` of the `MyProperty` object. VBA already knows how to work with other variables that you have seen. An object usually requires special handling. In this case, you ask `MyProperty` what its value is and display it in a message box.

Run this program to see a dialog box containing the name of the document creator. In most cases, the creator is you. Try changing the Author field entry shown in Figure 3-4 to something else. The output of the program changes to match whatever you type in this field.

Writing Your First Function

The example in the preceding "Writing Your First Sub" section (Listing 3-2) is nice, but you might want more than one piece of information. VBA users commonly rely on functions to perform repetitive tasks (see the earlier "Using Functions" section). That's what the example in this section shows.

Listing 3-3 uses a `Sub` named `GetSummary2` to call the `GetDocProperty` function multiple times. In every case, a special variable stores the result. At the end of the program, `GetSummary2` displays all the information that the program has accumulated.

Listing 3-3   Using a Function to Retrieve Document Information

```
Public Sub GetSummary2()
    ' Declare a string to hold the output information.
    Dim DocumentData As String

    ' Store the name of the information.
    DocumentData = "Author Name: "

    ' Get the author name.
    DocumentData = DocumentData + GetDocProperty("Author")

    ' Add an extra line.
    DocumentData = DocumentData + vbCrLf

    ' Store the name of the information.
    DocumentData = DocumentData + "Company: "

    ' Get the company name.
    DocumentData = DocumentData + GetDocProperty("Company")

    ' Display a message box containing the property value.
    MsgBox DocumentData, vbOKOnly, "Summary"
End Sub

Private Function GetDocProperty(Name As String) As String
    ' Declare a DocumentProperty object to hold the
    ' information.
    Dim MyProperty As DocumentProperty

    ' Set the DocumentProperty object equal to the author
    ' information.
    Set MyProperty = _
        ActiveWorkbook.BuiltinDocumentProperties(Name)

    ' Return the information.
    GetDocProperty = MyProperty.Value
End Function
```

Listing 3-3 begins with GetSummary2. Much of what you see looks
similar to previous examples. However, notice how the code works with
DocumentData. The example builds the text output by adding the previous
content of the string to itself. So, first DocumentData contains "Author
Name: ", and then you add the actual author name to it by using
GetDocProperty.

Another new addition is the use of a constant. The `vbCrLf` constant contains special characters that act the same as when you press Enter at the end of a line of text in a word processor.

The `GetDocProperty` function introduces several new ideas. The first idea is a return value. Functions can return a value to the caller. The second idea is the use of an argument. An *argument* is input to a `Sub` or `Function`. In this case, `Name` is the input to the `GetDocProperty` function.

The actual code within the `GetDocProperty` function looks the same as the example in the earlier "Writing Your First Sub" section. However, in this case, the code uses `Name` (a variable) as input to `ActiveWorkbook.BuiltinDocumentProperties` instead of a constant. Also notice that the code makes the function equal to the `MyProperty.Value` property. This is how you return a value to the caller. Figure 3-6 shows the output of this example.

Figure 3-6: Combining everything you know so far shows you can create a nice informational display.

Summary

Author Name: John Paul Mueller
Company: DataCon Services

OK

Getting the Scoop on Scope

You might think the concept of scope is confusing and difficult to understand because you think it's complex. Actually, *scope* is simply the range of what a program can see and how much it lets others know. When you look at the `MsgBox` function, you care about the inputs that you provide and the output that the function produces. These are the public (or visible) elements of the `MsgBox` function. You don't care too much about what happens inside the `MsgBox` function even though this information is important to the `MsgBox` function itself. These inner workings — the ones that you can't see — are the private (or invisible) elements of the `MsgBox` function.

There are two reasons that scope is important to you as a VBA user. First, if every part of a program could see every other part of a program, chaos would result because there would be too much information to track. Second, programs have to protect their data to ensure that it doesn't get damaged in some way. In short, you want to make some parts of your program visible so that people can use them, but other parts have to remain invisible so that they remain protected.

Understanding the purpose of scope

You've seen two keywords used for all the Sub and Function examples so far: Public and Private. These two keywords can affect other elements as well. You can use them to define the scope of variables or of classes. Scope has an affect on just about every kind of programming element that you use in the book, so it's important to understand how it works.

- ✔ Public: Tells VBA that it should allow other program elements to see the affected elements
- ✔ Private: Tells VBA that it should hide the affected element from other programming elements

Defining the effects of scope

The best way to learn about scope is to begin working with it. You can experiment with simple uses of scope to see how a change in scope affects your programs. The most important rule is that scope only affects everything outside the current block. That's right, the Lego example works here, too. (See the earlier section "Taking the Lego Approach.")

Making a module private by adding Option Private Module at the beginning of the module means that everything in that module is invisible to the outside world. Even if the module contains a Public Sub, only the other elements inside the module can see it — the Public Sub is invisible to everything outside the module. Likewise, when declaring a Private Sub, everything within the current module can still see it, but nothing outside the current module can.

Listing 3-4 demonstrates some of the basic elements of scope. Other examples in the book refine this concept, but this is a good starting point.

Listing 3-4   Using Global Variables

```
' Declare a private global variable.
Private MyGlobalVariable As String

Public Sub GlobalTest()
    ' Set the value of the global variable.
    MyGlobalVariable = "Hello"

    ' Display the value.
    MsgBox MyGlobalVariable

    ' Call the GlobalTest2 Sub
    GlobalTest2

    ' Display the value on return from the call.
    MsgBox MyGlobalVariable
End Sub

Private Sub GlobalTest2()
    ' Show that the global variable is truly global.
    MsgBox MyGlobalVariable

    ' Change the value of the global variable.
    MyGlobalVariable = "Goodbye"
End Sub
```

Notice that MyGlobalVariable is private. You can't access this global variable outside the current module. However, both of the sub-procedures in this module can access the global variable.

As another example, GlobalTest is a public Sub, but GlobalTest2 is private. You can verify the use of scope in this case by opening the Macro dialog box by using the Tools⇨Macro⇨Macros command. You see GlobalTest listed, but GlobalTest2 won't appear in the list.

Type and run the example code in Listing 3-4 to see how the two Sub elements affect each other. You should see three dialog boxes. The first dialog box reads Hello because GlobalTest sets the value of MyGlobalVariable. The second dialog box also reads Hello because MyGlobalVariable is truly global. Even though the value of this variable was set in GlobalTest, GlobalTest2 can read it. Finally, the third dialog box reads Goodbye because GlobalTest2 has set MyGlobalVariable to another value.

Creating Readable Code

You might have noticed how the examples in this chapter use white space to make the code more readable. If you type all the statements for your program one right after the other, the code still works. VBA doesn't care about white space. However, you might care because code without white space is nearly unreadable.

Most VBA users rely on two kinds of white space. You've seen the first type in this chapter. Notice that every comment and statement pair in the code is followed by a blank line. This blank line tells anyone reading the code that he has reached the end of this particular statement or step in the procedure.

The second kind of white space is indention. The examples in this chapter indent the code within a Sub or Function to make the body of the Sub or Function clear.

Telling Others about Your Code

The pseudo-code technique that I describe in Chapter 2 is a good way to start documenting your code. However, at some point, you need to add additional information because simply reading the procedure presented by the pseudo-code might not be enough. You might want to add your name, a project title, and other forms of documentation to your code.

Writing basic comments

Comments can take a number of forms. The pseudo-code comment is the first kind of comment that everyone writes because it's the kind of comment that's most natural to use. Developers quickly move on to adding documentation comments, such as who wrote the program, when it was originally written, and a list of updates made to code. Some developers move on to better comments at this point.

One of the more important comments that you can add to your code is why you chose to write the program in a certain way. Simply saying that the code performs a specific task isn't enough because you can usually perform the same task in several different ways. Telling why you made certain choices can reduce mistakes during code updates and serve as reasons for performing updates later when your coding technique improves.

As a good programmer, you should also include mistakes that you make in the code as comments if you think that someone else might make the same mistake. These experiential comments have helped me in many situations because I actually end up using them for notes. When I start a new project, I look back at my notes for things that I should avoid.

Knowing when to use comments

Use comments wherever and whenever you think that you need them. You might think that comments are difficult to type and only include one or two paltry comments for each program that you write. You're correct — writing good comments can be time consuming and could be difficult because writing them makes you think yet again about the code. However, the programs with the fewest comments usually generate the most head scratching during an update. In fact, I've seen a few situations where the lack of comments in code actually caused a company to start writing the code from scratch during an update rather than paying someone to spend the time relearning what the old code means.

Understanding how to create a good comment

A *good* comment is one that you can understand. Don't use fancy terms — write everything in plain terms that you can understand. When you feel that you need to explain something, feel free to do it. Good comments should answer the six essential questions: who, what, where, when, why, and how. Make sure that your comments are complete and that they fully answer any questions that someone reading your code might have.

Chapter 4

Storing and Modifying Information

● ●

● ●

*I*n this chapter, I refine the concept of a variable by describing variable types and how you can modify their content. Understanding how a computer stores information is very important. Computers don't see information in the same way that you do — many methods of representing information that seem obvious to you are invisible to the computer.

As far as the computer is concerned, everything is a series of bits that it has to move around. Data types were invented, sometimes by trial and error, to make the bits easier for humans to understand. For example, when you see the letter *C* on the display, all that the computer sees is a series of 8-bits that form a special number. Interpretation of this number as the letter C is for your benefit. Understanding that everything is a series of bits makes this chapter easier to understand.

When you begin to realize that you're in control — that you decide how to organize and interpret the bits the computer is moving around for you — you've taken a large step in understanding how VBA works. VBA helps you tell the computer how you want the bits moved around. In the following sections, I describe various ways how you can interpret and modify the bits that the computer stores for you.

Understanding Variables and Constants

VBA provides many levels of data interpretation. Some data interpretations help you make your program reliable, others make it run faster, still others provide accuracy, and a few make the data easier to interpret. One of the two big distinctions is between variables and constants. You can modify a *variable* anytime that the program can actually access it. A *constant,* however, retains the same value all the time.

Making the declaration

All data in a VBA program looks like a series of bits to the computer. The computer doesn't understand the difference between a constant and a variable — this distinction is provided for your benefit. You use different methods to mark variables and constants in your program.

Variables have a scope and a data type. See the "Defining the Data Types" section later in this chapter for data type descriptions and how to use them. See the "Getting the Scoop on Scope" section of Chapter 3 for scope issues. Declare variables with both scope and data type so that VBA knows how to work with them. Listing 4-1 shows some examples of variable and constant declarations.

Listing 4-1   Examples of Variable and Constant Declarations with Scope

```
Option Explicit

' This variable is visible to other modules.
Public MyPublicVariable As String
' This variable is visible only to this module.
Private MyPrivateVariable As String
' Using Dim is the same as making the variable private.
Dim MyDimVariable As String

' A constant is only used for conditional compilation.
#Const MyConditionalConstant = "Hello"
' This constant is visible to other modules.
Public Const MyPublicConstant = "Hello"
' This constant is visible only to this module.
Private Const MyPrivateConstant = "Hello"

Public Sub DataDeclarations()
    ' Only this Sub can see this variable.
    Dim MyDimSubVariable As String

    ' Only this Sub can see this constant.
    Const MySubConstant = "Hello"
End Sub
```

The variable declarations rely on `Public` and `Private` for scope as well as a data type keyword following the variable name to define the data type. All the variables are strings (or text). Using the `Dim` keyword makes a variable private. However, actually using the word `Private` is clearer, so that's what you should use in your code.

Notice the first constant declaration is for conditional compilation. You can use this declaration in place of the Conditional Compilation Arguments field entry (see the "Adding conditional compilation" section of Chapter 3 for details). You can't define this type of constant as private or public because the value is hidden from other modules.

The other two kinds of constant declaration do rely on `Public` or `Private` for scope. Notice that you do include the keyword `Const` to mark the value as a constant. The constant has a name and a value assigned to it. However, notice that it doesn't have a data type because you can't assign one to a constant. VBA stores constants as a series of bits by using the type of the information that you provide. Because you can never change the value of a constant, the question of data type isn't important.

Variables or constants defined within a `Sub` or `Function` are private to that `Sub` or `Function`. Consequently, VBA requires that you use the `Dim` keyword in this case. Notice that the constant still includes the `Const` keyword but lacks a `Private` or `Public` keyword for the same reason.

Knowing which storage type to use

At first, it might seem like you should always use variables so that you can always access the data and change it. Variables do provide flexibility that constants don't provide, and you can use them more often than not to store your data. However, constants also have distinct advantages including

- ✔ **Speed:** Using constants can make your application faster. Constants require less memory, and VBA can optimize your program to perform better when you use them.

- ✔ **Reliability:** Constants have a reliable value. If a constant has a specific value when you start the program, that value remains until the program ends.

- ✔ **Ease of reading:** Most VBA users rely on constants to make their programs easier to read. The `vbCrLf` constant shown in the examples in Chapter 3 is the same no matter how many programs you create. Every developer who sees this constant knows that VBA adds what amounts to pressing Enter (adding a carriage return and line feed combination).

There are other reasons to use constants in place of variables. For example, the Object Browser makes it easy to work with constants. Whenever you highlight a constant in the Object Browser, you see the value associated with that constant, as shown in Figure 4-1. Notice that the entry at the bottom of the Object Browser tells you that the highlighted entry is a public constant with a value of `"Hello"`.

Figure 4-1: Use constants to provide quick access to standard values in the Object Browser.

The "Using enumerated constants" section of Chapter 8 demonstrates another use of constants. Enumerated constants help document objects that you create and make them easier to use. Using enumerated constants also reduces the potential for error when someone uses an object that you create.

Defining scope

Listing 4-1 demonstrates that variable and constant scope rules work about the same. Always use `Private` to keep a variable or constant hidden from the outside world. Use `Public` to provide access to the variable or constant outside the current module. Any variable or constant that you define within a `Sub` or `Function` is always private to that `Sub` or `Function`. See the "Getting the Scoop on Scope" section of Chapter 3 for additional information.

Defining the Data Types

A *data type* is a method of defining the data to make it easier to work with in a program. The computer still sees the data as a series of bits, but VBA works with different data types in different ways. The computer can see the binary value, 1000001b, but it doesn't do anything special with that value. VBA can see this binary value as the number 65 or the letter A depending on the data type that you assign to the value. The data type is important in understanding the value and working with it. Using a data type also ensures that the program follows certain rules. Otherwise, the data could become corrupted because the program could mishandle it.

VBA supports a number of standard data types including `Byte`, `Boolean`, `Integer`, `Long`, `Currency`, `Decimal`, `Single`, `Double`, `Date`, `String`, `Object`, and `Variant`. In addition to the defined data types, you can also create user-defined data types so that you can mark the information as needed for your program. A user-defined data type gives you the power to extend the VBA interpretation of data. (The computer still looks at the data as binary information.) Each of the data type descriptions that follows has a different purpose, and you can work with the data type in a variety of ways.

Using strings for text

The first data type that I discuss in this chapter is one that you've already seen in the message box examples: the string. When you create a message box, you use a string as input. The string is the most useful and most-often used data type in VBA.

In this chapter, I discuss only the essential string functions. VBA provides a rich set of string manipulation functions. You can discover more about these functions in the Working with Strings help topic. Always access VBA help topics from within the VBA Integrated Development Environment (IDE) by using the Help⇨Microsoft Visual Basic Help command or by pressing F1.

Understanding strings

Programmers often use fancy terms for things that the average person easily recognizes. *Strings* are simply text, just like the text that you're reading now.

A *string* is a sequence of characters. The characters aren't always printable but can include control characters that determine how the text appears onscreen. A string can also include special characters, such as punctuation, or even special features, such as a circumflex or an umlaut. Although a string can contain all these elements, the main content of a string is always text.

Using character codes

Strings can contain a number of elements. In previous examples, I show you strings that contain control character constants such as `vbCrLf`. This constant actually contains two control characters: a carriage return and a line feed. The carriage return sends the cursor back to the beginning of the line; the line feed places the cursor on the next line. The result of using both control characters together is the same as pressing Enter on the keyboard.

Strings can also use a special function, `Chr`, to create special characters. You can combine this function with the Character Map utility (normally available on the Start➪Programs➪Accessories menu) to produce any character that you need for your program. Figure 4-2 shows a typical Character Map display.

Figure 4-2: Character Map displays all the printable characters available for a particular font.

When you hover the mouse over a character, the balloon help displays the Unicode character number in hexadecimal or base 16 (see the upcoming "Defining hex and octal values" section for details). Selecting the character displays the Unicode number in the lower-left corner of the Character Map dialog box and displays the character in a larger size. Listing 4-2 shows `Chr` function in use.

Listing 4-2   Creating Special Characters

```
Public Sub ShowCharacter()
    ' Declare the string.
    Dim MyChar As String

    ' Tell what type of character the code displays.
    MyChar = "Latin Capital Letter A with Circumflex: "

    ' Add the character.
    MyChar = MyChar + Chr(&HC2)

    'Display the result.
    MsgBox MyChar, vbOKOnly, "Special Character"
End Sub
```

This program displays a capital letter A with a circumflex when you run it. Notice how the code uses the `Chr` function. The hexadecimal value from Character Map appears as `&HC2`. The &H demotes a hexadecimal value, and the `C2` is the number of the character.

You can also get the Unicode number for a special character. A program might use this number to ensure that the string actually contains the requested value. The `Asc` function converts any single character into its numeric equivalent. Listing 4-3 shows an example of the `Asc` function.

Listing 4-3   Getting the Numeric Value of a Character

```
Public Sub GetCharacter()
    ' Declare the output variables.
    Dim MyChar As String
    Dim CharNum As Integer

    ' Add the special character to MyChar.
    MyChar = Chr(&HC2)

    ' Determine the Unicode number for the character.
    CharNum = Asc(MyChar)

    ' Display the result as a decimal value.
    MsgBox "Character " + MyChar + _
        " = Decimal Value " + CStr(CharNum), _
        vbOKOnly, _
        "Special Character Decimal Value"
End Sub
```

The program shows that the capital letter A with circumflex has a decimal value of 194. This value equates to the hexadecimal value of C2h shown in the code. Note that when you see a lowercase *h* follow a number, the number is a hexadecimal value. VGA always writes hexadecimal numbers with a leading &H, such as &HC2. This program also includes the CStr function, which accepts an expression such as a number as input and outputs a string. See the upcoming "Defining hex and octal values" section for more information on the CStr function.

Removing excess space

Some strings come with extra baggage in the form of spaces that you don't need. The spaces can appear at either end of the string or at both ends. VBA provides three essential functions for removing excess space:

- ✔ LTrim: Removes the excess spaces from the left side of the string
- ✔ RTrim: Removes the excess spaces from the right side of the string
- ✔ Trim: Removes excess spaces from both ends of the string

You can combine these three functions with other string functions to produce specific information. Listing 4-4 shows the LTrim, RTrim, and Trim functions in action. It also demonstrates how to combine these three functions with other functions to produce new information.

Listing 4-4   Removing Spaces from a String

```
Public Sub RemoveSpace()
    ' Declare a string with spaces.
    Dim IStr As String

    ' Declare an output string.
    Dim Output As String

    ' Add a string to IStr
    IStr = "     Hello     "

    ' Show the original string length.
    Output = "Original String Length: " + CStr(Len(IStr))

    ' Get rid of the spaces on the left.
    Output = Output + vbCrLf + _
            "LTrim Length: " + CStr(Len(LTrim(IStr))) + _
            " Value: " + Chr(&H22) + LTrim(IStr) + Chr(&H22)

    ' Get rid of the spaces on the right.
    Output = Output + vbCrLf + _
```

```
                "RTrim Length: " + CStr(Len(RTrim(IStr))) + _
                " Value: " + Chr(&H22) + RTrim(IStr) + Chr(&H22)

    ' Get rid of all the extra spaces.
    Output = Output + vbCrLf + _
                "Trim Length: " + CStr(Len(Trim(IStr))) + _
                " Value: " + Chr(&H22) + Trim(IStr) + Chr(&H22)

    ' Display the result.
    MsgBox Output, vbOKOnly, "Trimming Extra Spaces"
End Sub
```

The program begins by creating a string that has extra spaces on both ends. It then performs four steps to create an output string that demonstrates the various string features. The first step determines the current string length by using the Len function. However, the Len function outputs a number, so the code uses the CStr function to convert the number to a string. Notice how the Len function acts as input to the CStr function. You can *nest* functions like this to produce special effects.

The three function strings work the same. The code first computes the output string size and places it in the Output string. It then removes the excess spaces and places this value into the Output string as well.

Notice that the code uses Chr(&H22) in several places. This function and value produce a double quote. Because VBA uses the double quote to show the beginning and ending of string values, this is one of the few ways that you can add a double quote to your string. In this case, the double quote shows the beginning and end of the string so that you can better see the space removal feature.

Getting the data you need

Strings can contain more information than you actually need or contain it in a form that you can't use. You might use a string to provide storage for several pieces of information that you need to send to another location. When the string arrives at its destination, the receiving program unpacks the individual data elements from the string.

All these actions rely on some form of *parsing*, which is the act of removing and interpreting sub-elements from a storage element such as a string. You can create a single string that contains Hello World and separate it into two pieces, Hello and World, by using parsing. A program could store these separate elements and use this for various purposes.

The three functions that you use to extract information from a string are Left, Right, and Mid. As their names suggest, you use the first to extract the left side of the string, the second to extract the right side, and the third to extract the middle. These three functions require location information and input on where to start and stop extracting information. You use the `InStr` and `InStrRev` functions to find this information. Listing 4-5 shows some of the techniques that you can use to parse a string.

Listing 4-5   Finding Information in Strings by Using Parsing

```
Public Sub ParseString()
    ' Create a string with elements the program can parse.
    Dim MyStr As String

    ' Create an output string.
    Dim Output As String

    ' Fill the input string with data.
    MyStr = "A String To Parse"

    ' Display the whole string.
    Output = "The whole string is: " + MyStr

    ' Obtain the first word.
    Output = Output + vbCrLf + "The First Word: " + _
            Left(MyStr, InStr(1, MyStr, " "))

    ' Obtain the last word.
    Output = Output + vbCrLf + "The Last Word: " + _
            Right(MyStr, Len(MyStr) - InStrRev(MyStr, " "))

    ' Obtain the word String.
    Output = Output + vbCrLf + "The Word String: " + _
            Trim(Mid(MyStr, _
                InStr(1, MyStr, "String"), _
                Len(MyStr) - InStr(1, MyStr, "To")))

    ' Output the result.
    MsgBox Output, vbOKOnly, "Parsing a String"
End Sub
```

The code begins by creating two variables: one to hold the input data and a second to hold the output data. The input string has a simple phrase that code can parse. The first parsing task is easy — locate the first word in the phrase. To perform this task, the `Left` function retrieves text starting at the first character and continuing until the first space. The `InStr` function returns the position of the first space as a number.

The second parsing task is more complicated. The `Right` function returns the right end of the string. The `InStrRev` function returns the number of characters from the beginning of the string to the last space. The `Len` function returns a value of 17 (the length of the string), and `InStrRev` returns 12 (the number of characters from the beginning of the string to the last space). The result is 5. Count the number of letters in *Parse* (the last word in the string) — it contains five characters. The `Right` function returns `Parse` in this case.

The third parsing task is to look for the word *String* in `MyStr`. The example code shows that you can perform nesting as needed. The nesting begins with the `Trim` function, which removes any extra characters. The `Mid` function requires three arguments for this example. The first is the string that you want to work with. The second is the starting position. Notice the code uses the `InStr` function, but it searches for *String* and not a space this time. The third is the length of the string. The length of the string is still 17, and the position of *To* within the string is 10, for a total of 7 characters. The seven characters include the word *String* and the space that follows, which is the reason for using the `Trim` function.

Using numbers for calculations

Numbers form the basis for a lot of the information computers store. You use numbers to perform tasks in a spreadsheet, to express quantities in a database, and to show the current page in a document. Programs also use numbers to count things such as loops, to determine the position of items such as characters in a string, and to check the truth value of a statement. Finally, VBA uses numbers in a myriad of ways, such as determining which character to display onscreen or how to interact with your code.

Understanding the numeric types

You look at numbers as a single entity — a number is simply a number. The computer views numbers in several different ways. The reason for this diversity of viewpoints is that the processor actually works with different kinds of numbers in different places. At one time, the math coprocessor used to work with money and numbers with decimal points was a separate chip within the computer. The four basic number types include

- **Integer:** This is a number without a decimal. An *integer* can hold any whole number, such as 5, but not a number with a decimal, such as 5.0. Although these two numbers are the same, the first is an integer, and the second isn't.

- **Real:** A *real* number is one that contains a decimal point. The decimal portion doesn't have to contain a value. The number 5.0 is a perfectly acceptable real number. A real number is stored in a completely different format than an integer. (The storage technique only matters to the processor — you don't need to know it to use VBA.)

✔ **Currency:** Financial calculations usually require special accuracy. Even a small error can cause problems. The currency numeric type stores numbers with extreme precision but at an equally large cost in both processing time and memory use.

✔ **Decimal:** Computers normally store information by using a base 2 or binary format. You use a base 10 or decimal format for working with numbers. Small errors can occur when converting from one numbering system to the other and accumulate to create huge errors. The decimal numeric system stores numbers in a simulated base 10 format, which eliminates many computing errors. However, this system requires more memory and processing time than any other numeric type.

Computers also determine a numeric type based on the amount of memory that the data requires. VBA supports three integer types including Byte (1 byte of storage), Integer (2 bytes of storage), and Long (4 bytes of storage). The extra memory stores larger numbers: 0 to 255 for Byte; –32,768 to 32,767 for Integer; and –2,147,483,648 to 2,147,483,647 for Long. See the Data Type Summary help topic for additional details. Listing 4-6 is an example that demonstrates various data types.

Listing 4-6   **Demonstrating the Differences in Data Type Ranges**

```
Public Sub DataRange()
    ' Declare the numeric variables.
    Dim MyInt As Integer
    Dim MySgl As Single
    Dim MyDbl As Double
    Dim MyCur As Currency
    Dim MyDec As Variant

    ' Define values for each variable.
    MyInt = 30 + 0.00010001000111
    MySgl = 30 + 0.00010001000111
    MyDbl = 30 + 0.00010001000111
    MyCur = 30 + 0.00010001000111
    MyDec = CDec(30 + 0.00010001000111)

    ' Display the actual content.
    MsgBox "Integer:" + TwoTab + CStr(MyInt) + _
           vbCrLf + "Single:" + TwoTab + CStr(MySgl) + _
           vbCrLf + "Double:" + TwoTab + CStr(MyDbl) + _
           vbCrLf + "Currency:" + vbTab + CStr(MyCur) + _
           vbCrLf + "Decimal:" + TwoTab + CStr(MyDec), _
           vbOKOnly, _
           "VBA Data Types"
End Sub
```

The first few variable types use standard declarations. However, notice that you can't declare the decimal data type directly — you must declare it as a Variant in VBA. See the upcoming "Working with variant data" section for more information about the Variant type. The code assigns each variable the same value. Notice that the code must use the CDec function to insert a decimal value into the Variant.

The output shown in Figure 4-3 demonstrates something interesting about the numeric data types. Each type silently dropped any decimal data that it couldn't hold. This is just one of many reasons why you have to carefully consider the numeric data type that you use.

Figure 4-3:
Seeing the
actual
content of
the numeric
types dem-
onstrates
their range.

```
VBA Data Types                        ⊠

   Integer:      30
   Single:       30.0001
   Double:       30.0001000100011
   Currency:     30.0001
   Decimal:      30.0001000100011

              [    OK    ]
```

Defining hex and octal values

Using base 10 numbers is natural. You usually don't worry about anything other than base 10 numbers. However, computers use base 2 or binary numbers. The switch in the circuitry is either on or off – 1 or 0.

Working in binary is quite difficult because even small numbers require many digits. Using either octal (base 8) or hexadecimal (base 16) numbers is easier. Both octal (also abbreviated as *oct*) and hexadecimal (also called *hex*) convert directly to base 2. The binary bit positions convert easily to these other two bases, so VBA doesn't even support binary numbers directly.

Generally, the need to work with other bases is obvious. The VBA documentation might provide values in hex for you to use in your program. You might have to convert a number from one base to another because a program supports only a specific base. Your program might also rely on *flags,* which are essentially on or off indicators based on the value of a specific bit within a number.

Most people don't work well with other bases of numbers. We just don't use them often enough. To keep yourself from going crazy, you can use the

Calculator that comes with Windows. Switch to scientific mode by using the View⇨Scientific command. Figure 4-4 shows what the Calculator looks like. To convert a number by using this program, click the initial base of the number (Hex, Dec, Oct, or Bin), type any number that you need to convert to another base into the input area, and then click the base that you want to see as an output. The result shows in the input area where you typed the original number.

Figure 4-4: The Calculator provides a fast and easy method for converting between numeric bases.

VBA also provides a number of helpful functions and formatting features that you can use to work with other bases. Listing 4-7 is an example of all these features in action.

Listing 4-7   Converting between Numeric Bases

```
Public Sub ShowBase()
    ' Define the three number bases.
    Dim OctNum As Integer
    Dim DecNum As Integer
    Dim HexNum As Integer

    ' Define an output string.
    Dim Output As String

    ' Assign an octal number.
    OctNum = &O110

    ' Assign a decimal number.
    DecNum = 110

    ' Assign a hexidecimal number.
```

```
    HexNum = &H110

' Create a heading.
    Output = vbTab + vbTab + vbTab + "Oct" + _
            vbTab + "Dec" + _
            vbTab + "Hex" + vbCrLf

    ' Create an output string.
    Output = Output + "Octal Number:" + _
            vbTab + vbTab + Oct$(OctNum) + _
            vbTab + CStr(OctNum) + _
            vbTab + Hex$(OctNum) + _
            vbCrLf + "Decimal Number:" + _
            vbTab + vbTab + Oct$(DecNum) + _
            vbTab + CStr(DecNum) + _
            vbTab + Hex$(DecNum) + _
            vbCrLf + "Hexidecimal Number:" + _
            vbTab + Oct$(HexNum) + _
            vbTab + CStr(HexNum) + _
            vbTab + Hex$(HexNum)

    ' Display the actual numbers.
    MsgBox Output, _
            vbInformation Or vbOKOnly, _
            "Data Type Output"
End Sub
```

The code begins with three integers. It then assigns values to each of these integers. Notice that the octal number is set by using the &O prefix (that's the letter *O* and not a zero), and the hex number is set by using the &H prefix.

This example also adds a new constant to your list. The vbTab constant adds a tab character to the output string. (See the Visual Basic Constants help topic for a complete list of VBA constants.) Notice that this example provides both a header and data in the dialog box, which shows how to display data in a tabular format.

Whenever you want to convert a number to a string, you need to use a conversion function. This example shows the three common conversion functions for octal (Oct$), decimal (CStr), and hex (Hex$) numbers. Run this program to see how the functions interact. Notice that you can see the header and each of the numbers in different bases.

Performing conversions between numbers and strings

Most display features, such as the MsgBox function and forms, require strings, even for numbers. When you work with numeric data, you convert the data to a string. The preceding "Defining hex and octal values" section shows some techniques for converting numbers to strings (and vice versa), but this example is only the beginning. Listing 4-8 demonstrates some of the essential string-to-number and number-to-string conversion functions.

Listing 4-8   Converting between Numbers and Strings

```
Public Sub NumberConvert()
    ' Create some variables for use in conversion.
    Dim MyInt As Integer
    Dim MySgl As Single
    Dim MyStr As String

    ' Conversion between Integer and Single is direct
    ' with no data loss.
    MyInt = 30
    MySgl = MyInt
    MsgBox "MyInt = " + CStr(MyInt) + _
            vbCrLf + "MySgl = " + CStr(MySgl), _
            vbOKOnly, _
            "Current Data Values"

    ' Conversion between Single and Integer is also direct
    ' but incurs data loss.
    MySgl = 35.01
    MyInt = MySgl
    MsgBox "MyInt = " + CStr(MyInt) + _
            vbCrLf + "MySgl = " + CStr(MySgl), _
            vbOKOnly, _
            "Current Data Values"

    ' Conversion between a String and a Single or an
    ' Integer can rely on use of a special function. The
    ' conversion can also incur data loss.
    MyStr = "40.05"
    MyInt = CInt(MyStr)
    MySgl = CSng(MyStr)
    MsgBox "MyInt = " + CStr(MyInt) + _
            vbCrLf + "MySgl = " + CStr(MySgl), _
            vbOKOnly, _
            "Current Data Values"

    ' Conversion between a Single or Integer and a String
    ' can rely on use of a special function when making a
    ' direct conversion. The conversion doesn't incur any
    ' data loss.
    MyInt = 45
    MySgl = 45.05
    MyStr = MyInt
    MsgBox MyStr, _
            vbOKOnly, _
            "Current Data Values"

    ' You must use a special function in mixed data
    ' situations.
```

```
        MyStr = "MyInt = " + CStr(MyInt) + _
                vbCrLf + "MySgl = " + CStr(MySgl)
        MsgBox MyStr, _
                vbOKOnly, _
                "Current Data Values"
End Sub
```

The code begins by declaring an Integer, a Single (a real number), and a String. Although the code relies on these three data types, the principles shown apply to any of the data types. Notice that you can perform direct conversion between numeric types without relying on a function. An integer value can always convert to a real number without data loss. Be careful about going the other way though because you can run into problems with data loss. The conversion process drops the decimal value but does use proper rounding, as do the CInt and CLng functions.

Conversion from a string to a numeric value might not require the special functions shown in the code. Use the conversion functions as shown (CInt for Integer conversion and CSng for Single conversion) to ensure that VBA converts the data correctly. Try changing the source code so that it reads MyInt = MyStr — it works as normal in this case, but this behavior isn't guaranteed.

The code also shows that you can assign a numeric value directly to a string as long as that's the only assignment that you make. Always use the correct conversion function when you work with mixed data types. Read the Type Conversion Functions help topic to see other data conversion functions.

Using Boolean values to make decisions

The Boolean type is the easiest to use and understand. This type is used to indicate yes or no, true or false, and on or off. You can use this type to work with any two-state information. It's commonly used to represent data values that are diametrically opposed. Chapter 5 shows how to use Boolean values to make decisions. Listing 4-9 shows several conversion techniques that you can use with Boolean values.

Listing 4-9   Making Decisions with Boolean Values

```
Public Sub BooleanCheck()
    ' Create a Boolean data type.
    Dim MyBool As Boolean

    ' Set MyBool to True
```

(continued)

Listing 4-9 *(continued)*

```
        MyBool = True

        ' Display the native value.
        MsgBox "MyBool = " + CStr(MyBool), _
               vbOKOnly, _
               "Native Value"

        ' Display the numeric value.
        MsgBox "MyBool = " + CStr(CInt(MyBool)), _
               vbOKOnly, _
               "Numeric Value"

        ' Make MyBool equal to a number. Only the number
        ' 0 is False; everything else is True.
        MyBool = CBool(0)
        MsgBox "MyBool = " + CStr(MyBool), _
               vbOKOnly, _
               "Converted Numeric Value"
End Sub
```

The code begins by declaring a Boolean variable and setting its value. As with numeric variables, you can assign a Boolean variable directly to a string as long as that's the only thing that you do. When working in a mixed data type environment, such as the one shown in the code, you must use the appropriate function (such as CStr) to perform the conversion.

The Boolean type isn't numeric — it's logical . . . simply a decision value. You can convert it to a number as shown in the example code. The value is always -1 for True values and 0 for False values.

VBA also lets you convert a numeric value to a Boolean type by using the CBool function shown in the code. Any value that you store in the Boolean, other than 0, equates to True. Converting the Boolean back to a number still shows -1 for True values and 0 for False.

Using scientific values for math calculations

VBA provides a number of math functions normally used for scientific calculations. You can use the Atn, Cos, Sin, and Tan functions for trigonometric calculations. The Abs and Sgn functions help you work with the sign of a number. Listing 4-10 shows some of the math functions in action.

Listing 4-10   Performing Scientific Calculations

```
Public Sub ScientificCalcs()
    ' Define an input value
    Dim MyInt As Integer
    MyInt = 45

    ' Create an output string.
    Dim Output As String

    ' Display the trigonometric values for a 45 degree
    ' angle.
    MsgBox "The original angle is: " + CStr(MyInt) + _
            vbCrLf + "Arctangent is: " + CStr(Atn(MyInt)) + _
            vbCrLf + "Cosine is: " + CStr(Cos(MyInt)) + _
            vbCrLf + "Sine is: " + CStr(Sin(MyInt)) + _
            vbCrLf + "Tangent is: " + CStr(Tan(MyInt)), _
            vbOKOnly, _
            "Trigonometric Values"

    ' Change the sign of the number using Sgn and Int.
    ' Add the value to Output each time.
    Output = "The sign of 0 is: " + CStr(Sgn(0))
    MyInt = -45
    Output = Output + vbCrLf + _
            "The sign of " + CStr(MyInt) + " is: " + _
            CStr(Sgn(MyInt))
    MyInt = Abs(MyInt)
    Output = Output + vbCrLf + _
            "The sign of " + CStr(MyInt) + " is: " + _
            CStr(Sgn(MyInt))
    MsgBox Output, vbOKOnly, "Using Sgn and Abs"
End Sub
```

The code begins by defining an input value. The VBA documentation leads you to believe that you can only use a Double as input to the trigonometric functions. This example shows that you can use any numeric type as long as the value that it contains is correct. The code builds an output string for the first message box by using the various trigonometric functions.

The second portion of the example begins by showing the output of the Sgn function when you supply a value of 0. The output is 0 to show that the number is neither positive nor negative. The input value is set to a negative value for the next part of the Output string construction, so the Sgn function returns -1. Finally, the code uses the Abs function to remove the sign from MyInt and calls on Sgn once again to show that the value is indeed positive.

The Math Functions help topic contains more information on the math functions that VBA supports. The Derived Math Functions help topic contains additional examples of how to combine the math functions to produce specific results.

Using currency values for money calculations

Money usually requires special handling on a computer because you don't want to introduce rounding or other errors. Even small incremental errors can result in large errors if they accumulate over time. The Currency data type provides special handling for money calculations but at a slight performance hit because the Currency data type requires additional memory and processing cycles.

Along with the Currency data type, VBA provides a number of special functions for calculating common monetary values. These are the same special functions available to you in your Excel spreadsheet. For example, you still have access to the Pmt function. The main concern when working with monetary values in a VBA program is to ensure that you use the Currency data type as needed. Listing 4-11 shows how the Currency data type and the Pmt function work together.

Listing 4-11   Working with Monetary Values

```
Public Sub ShowPayment()
    ' Create the required variables. All non-monetary
    ' values use the Double type to ensure accuracy. The
    ' monetary values use the Currency data type.
    Dim Rate As Double
    Dim Periods As Double
    Dim PresentValue As Currency
    Dim FutureValue As Currency

    'Calculate the monthly payment on a mortgage.
    Rate = 0.005            ' 6 Percent divided by 12 Months
    Periods = 60            ' 5 years
    PresentValue = 120000   ' $120,000.00 loan
    MsgBox CStr(Pmt(Rate, Periods, PresentValue)), _
        vbOKOnly, _
        "Mortgage Output"

    ' Calculate the monthly payments required to build
    ' a savings account to 120000
```

```
        Rate = 0.0025          ' 3 Percent divided by 12 Months
        Periods = 240          ' 20 years
        PresentValue = -5000   ' $5,000 current savings.
        FutureValue = 120000   ' $120,000.00 savings in 20 years
        MsgBox CStr(Pmt(Rate, Periods, PresentValue, _
                    FutureValue)), _
            vbOKOnly, _
            "Savings Output"
End Sub
```

The code shows two examples. The first determines the minimum that you
would need to pay each month on a 5-year loan of $120,000.00 compounded
at a 6 percent interest rate. The second shows how much you would need to
pay into a savings account each month to have $120,000.00 saved at 20 years
when starting with $5,000 in the account, and the bank gives you a 3 percent
interest rate. Running the example shows that the mortgage payment is
$2,319.94 per month and that the savings rate is $337.79 per month.

Using date and time values

Tracking time and date in your program can be important. Client contact
entries in Access usually require the date that the client was last contacted. A
spreadsheet might require dates for each entry in a ledger. It's helpful to
include dates in Word documents so that you know the last time that someone accessed or changed it. You might need to know how long a task takes or
have an indicator of when time has elapsed.

Both date and time variables rely on the Date data type. This data type contains both date and time information. However, you can separate the information as needed. You can also assign date and time independently to the
variable by using the Date and Time functions or assign both date and time
by using the Now function. These are the same functions that you use to perform this task within a spreadsheet.

Like a spreadsheet, you can work with time values individually. Listing 4-12
demonstrates various time functions. Notice that you can control individual
elements, making it easy to change just what you need.

Listing 4-12   Keeping Track of the Time

```
Public Sub ShowTime()
    ' Create a time variable.
    Dim MyTime As Date

    ' Obtain the current time.
```

(continued)

Listing 4-12 *(continued)*

```
    MyTime = Time

    ' Display the hours, minutes, and seconds.
    MsgBox "The current time is: " + _
           vbCrLf + "Hours: " + CStr(Hour(MyTime)) + _
           vbCrLf + "Minutes: " + CStr(Minute(MyTime)) + _
           vbCrLf + "Seconds: " + CStr(Second(MyTime)), _
           vbOKOnly, _
           "Current Time"
End Sub
```

VBA provides access to the whole time value by using the Time function. You can also use the Hour, Minute, and Second functions for specific information. Not shown in the example is how you can set the current time by using Time on a line by itself and supplying a time value such as Time = #1:0:0# (for 1 a.m.). In this case, Time acts as a property, rather than a statement, and accepts input in any valid format, such as #1 PM# for 1 p.m. (or 1300 military time). Notice that time and date values always appear within the # symbol rather than the double quotes used for strings.

Using dates is similar to using time in a program. Listing 4-13 demonstrates that you can use the Date function directly instead of placing the information in a variable. It also shows how to set the date (provided that you have sufficient security rights on the workstation that you use).

Listing 4-13   Displaying Date Values

```
Public Sub ShowDate()
    ' Create a date variable.
    Dim MyDate As Date

    ' Obtain the current date.
    MyDate = Date

    ' Set the date.
    Date = #1/1/1980#

    ' Display the Day, Month, and Year
    MsgBox "The current date is (DD/MM/YYYY): " + _
           CStr(Day(Date)) + "/" + _
           CStr(Month(Date)) + "/" + _
           CStr(Year(Date)), _
           vbOKCancel, _
           "Modified Date"

    ' Reset the date.
```

```
        Date = MyDate
        ' Display the Day, Month, and Year
        MsgBox "The current date is (DD/MM/YYYY): " + _
               CStr(Day(MyDate)) + "/" + _
               CStr(Month(MyDate)) + "/" + _
               CStr(Year(MyDate)), _
               vbOKCancel, _
               "Actual Date"
    End Sub
```

The code begins by creating MyDate and using it to store the current date information. The next step is to change the date by using Date as a property. Like when using Time, you can modify Date by using any valid date format. You must have sufficient security to perform this task. If the program fails, ask your network administrator whether you have time and date setting privileges. The code creates a message box to demonstrate that the date change actually occurred. You can verify this change by looking at the clock area of the Taskbar Notification area.

After you click OK, the code continues by resetting the date to its original value. Again, the code displays a message box to show that the change has actually occurred. Notice how the code relies on the Day, Month, and Year functions to display both message boxes.

Working with variant data

The earlier "Understanding the numeric types" section demonstrates one use of the Variant data type: A Variant can hold any data type, including objects. A program can use a Variant when VBA doesn't provide direct support for a data type (such as the Decimal type) or when the type of information that the program user will provide is unknown when you write the program. In short, a Variant is the universal data type for VBA.

VBA does track the data type of the Variant variables that you create. In Chapter 6, I demonstrate how you can see this information while debugging the program. The data type names begin with Variant and end with the native data type. Thus, a Date stored in a Variant would appear as a VariantDate data type.

You can also use the Variant type as a means for data conversion. Place a date within a Variant, such as 1/1/80, and you can convert it to a String or an Integer. The Integer value for this date normally appears as 29221 when using the default Windows settings. You can use the Integer value as input to the Date function to convert the number back into a Date and place the result back into the Variant.

Presenting data in a pleasing format

Most programs can use the default formatting that VBA provides for output. However, you might need some way to present the data in another way, such as a short or long date (04/24/03 or 24 April 2003). It's important to know how to format data so that you can create astounding reports and concise analysis.

Using the Format function

The Format function is the most common way to change the appearance of data. It accepts any valid expression as input. You can also supply an expression that defines how to format the data. The Named Date/Time Formats help topic describes predefined formats for date and time, and the Named Numeric Formats help topic describes numeric formats. Listing 4-14 demonstrates some of the common, named formats for time and date.

Listing 4-14   Changing the Format of a Date

```
Public Sub FormatDemo()
    ' Create the date variable
    Dim MyDate As Date

    ' Fill MyDate with the current date and time.
    MyDate = Now

    ' Display the date using standard formats.
    MsgBox "Standard Format =" + vbTab + CStr(MyDate) + _
        vbCrLf + "Long Date =" + vbTab + _
        Format(MyDate, "Long Date") + _
        vbCrLf + "Short Time =" + vbTab + _
        Format(MyDate, "Short Time"), _
        vbOKOnly, _
        "VBA Named Formats"
End Sub
```

The program displays the standard date/time format, the long date format, and the short time format. You get the raw format by using the CStr function. The Format function requires the MyDate variable and a string containing the named format as input.

Creating custom formatting

Named formats don't always provide the output that you need. In these cases, you can create your own formatting by using custom strings. The elements of these strings are described in three help topics: User-Defined Date/Time Formats, User-Defined Numeric Formats, and User-Defined String

Formats. (Press F1 in the VBA IDE to access help.) Listing 4-15 shows how you can create a custom date and time string.

Listing 4-15   Defining a Custom Date Format

```
Public Sub CustomFormatDemo()
    ' Create the date variable.
    Dim MyDate As Date

    ' Fill MyDate with the current date and time.
    MyDate = Now

    ' Display the date using standard formats.
    MsgBox "Custom Date/Time = " + _
           Format(MyDate, "dd mmmm yyyy Hh:Nn:Ss"), _
           vbOKOnly, _
           "VBA Custom Formats"
End Sub
```

The essential difference in this example is the string input for the Format function. This example tells VBA that you want a date/time display that uses a day with a leading 0, the full month name, and a four-digit year. The time appears as hours, minutes, and seconds — all of which have a leading 0 when needed.

Working with other formatting functions

VBA provides four custom formatting functions: FormatNumber, FormatDateTime, FormatCurrency, and FormatPercent. These functions don't do anything that you can't do with the Format function. The reason why some VBA users rely on these functions is that their names make the purpose of the formatting clearer, and using them requires less typing.

All four functions return a string, just like the Format function. The only input that you must provide is the expression that you want formatted. The default settings return a formatting string that relies on the regional settings that the user has set for the computer. You can override these settings by specifying the optional arguments provided for each function.

Working with Operators

Operators determine how VBA works with two variables and what result it produces. The examples in this chapter use operators to add numbers and *concatenate* (add) strings. In both cases, your code uses the + operator to perform the task. However, the result differs. When using numbers, the result is a summation, such as `1 + 2 = 3`. When using strings, the result is a concatenation, such as `Hello + World = Hello World`. VBA groups operators into four areas:

- ✔ **Arithmetic:** Operators that perform math operations such as addition (+), subtraction (-), division (/), and multiplication (*)

- ✔ **Comparison:** Operators such as less than (<), greater than (>), and equal (=) that compare two values and produce a Boolean result

- ✔ **Concatenation:** Operators such as & and + used to add two strings together

- ✔ **Logical:** Operators such as `Not`, `And`, `Or`, and `Xor` used to perform Boolean operations on two variables

The Operator Summary help topic explains each of these operator categories and the associated operators in detail. The examples in this book demonstrate how to use the various operators, such as the + (plus) operator shown in Listing 4-15.

VBA also assigns operators a *precedence*, or order of use. When your code contains the equation `MyVal = 1 + 2 * 3`, VBA performs the multiplication first and then the addition to receive a value of 7 because multiplication has a higher precedence than addition. However, the equation `MyVal = (1 + 2) * 3` has a result of 9 because parentheses have a higher precedence than multiplication. The rules that VBA uses for precedence are the same rules that you learned in math class. See the Operator Precedence help topic for more information.

Applying What You Know to Design an Excel Report

All the examples up to this point in the book have worked with abstract (or demonstration) code. *Abstract code* is useful for presenting concepts, but you wouldn't actually add it to a document because it doesn't perform useful work. The reason that you use VBA is to accomplish useful work.

The example in this section relies on code to create an Excel report. You begin by typing the entries shown in Figure 4-5. These entries serve as a basis for the report.

The report contains data entries. It also has a summary when the code executes. Listing 4-16 provides the code to use.

Listing 4-16 Designing an Excel Report

```
Public Sub CreateReport()
    ' Create some output variables.
    Dim DataSum As Integer
    Dim Output As String

    ' Begin by adding data to the report.
    Sheet1.Cells(3, 2) = 1
    Sheet1.Cells(4, 2) = 2
    Sheet1.Cells(5, 2) = 3

    ' Create a sum of the cell content.
    DataSum = Sheet1.Cells(3, 2) + _
              Sheet1.Cells(4, 2) + _
              Sheet1.Cells(5, 2)

    ' Create an output string.
    Output = "The sum of the three numbers is: " + _
             CStr(DataSum)

    Sheet1.Cells(7, 1) = Output
End Sub
```

The code begins by declaring two variables. The first, DataSum, holds the sum of the three data entries that the code creates. The second, Output, contains a string that holds the report summary. The worksheets in an Excel file are objects, just like any other object. You access the worksheet objects by using the name assigned to them — Sheet1 in this case.

Worksheets contain Cells objects. Each Cells object uses two numbers to identify its row and column. You can assign a value to the cell by using the = operator as shown in the code.

It's also possible to retrieve values from the Cells objects. The code shows how to use this feature to create a summation of the three numbers entered on the worksheet as data.

The last two lines of code create a summary statement that includes the summation in DataSum. Figure 4-6 shows the result of running this program.

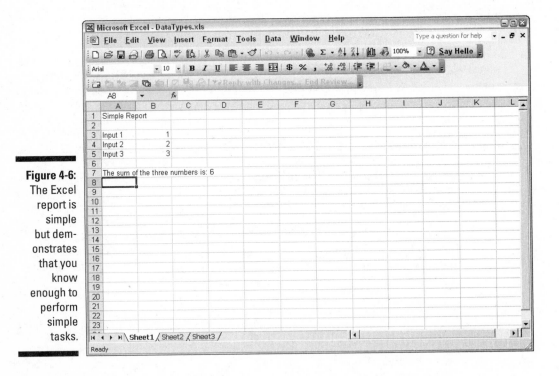

Figure 4-6: The Excel report is simple but demonstrates that you know enough to perform simple tasks.

Chapter 5

Creating Structured Programs

● ●

In This Chapter

▶ Using the If...Then statement

▶ Using the Select Case statement

▶ Using Do loops

▶ Using For Next loops

▶ Using the GoTo statement

● ●

*S*tructures help organize your VBA code so that it can perform more tasks more efficiently. Special *statements* can help organize the code so that it accomplishes tasks based on decisions or performs the same task multiple times. In this chapter, I demonstrate how to use the special statements used to make decisions, perform tasks more than once, or redirect control to another area of the program. The result of using these statements is increased program structure, which makes controlling program execution easier.

These statements also improve program flexibility. A program that uses the right statements can perform a wider variety of tasks and take outside conditions into account, such as the day of the week or the current state of the computer. Statements that control program flow are essential to writing programs that need less input from you and perform more tasks automatically. For example, VBA can help you create Word documents that automatically reflect special days such as a business anniversary or Excel reports where VBA automatically tracks business quarters.

Exercising Control with Structures

Few programs use all the statements in the program file all the time. You might want the program to perform one task when you click Yes and another task when you click No. The statements for both tasks appear in the code, but the program only executes one set of statements.

To control program execution, the developer adds special statements — such as the If...Then statement — that show the beginning and end of each task and also decide which task to execute. You might think that letting the computer decide which task to execute would cause the developer to lose control of the program. However, the developer hasn't lost control of the program because the decision-making process is predefined as part of the program design.

Most developers refer to the beginning and ending statements for a task as a *control structure* because the statement combination adds control to a program. When you see the If...Then statement with its accompanying End If statement in code, the two statements combine to form an If...Then structure.

Because the program contains more than one task, it has more than one path of execution. When you add control structures, the number of execution paths increases exponentially. For example, a program with one control structure has two paths of execution, but a program with two control structures has four paths. As you can imagine, the task of debugging the application becomes harder when you add control structures, so designing your program carefully is important.

You can also *nest* control structures. A program might require multiple decision points to address a specific need. For example, the program might need to decide whether you requested an apple or an orange. When you select an apple, the program then might have to decide between a yellow, green, or red apple. The program can't make the second decision without the first, so the second decision is nested within the first.

Making a Decision with the If...Then Statement

Most programs require decision-making code. When you need to make the same decision every time that you perform a task and the outcome of the decision is always the same, then making the decision something that you can tell VBA to do for you by using the If...Then statement. Decision-making code has several benefits:

- ✓ **Consistency:** The decision is made by using the same criteria and in the same manner every time.

- ✓ **Speed:** A computer can make static decisions faster than humans. However, the decision must be the same every time, and the decision must have the same answer set every time.

✓ **Complexity:** Requesting that the computer make static decisions can reduce program complexity. Fewer decisions translate into ease of use for most people.

All forms of `If...Then` statements can use any expression that equates to a Boolean value, including a variable of the `Boolean` data type. The term *expression* refers to any equation or variable that VBA can interpret as a means of determining when it should perform the tasks within the `If...Then` structure. The expression `2 > 1` is true, so VBA would perform the tasks within the `If...Then` structure. You can also use variables for an expression such as `A = B`. Anything that equates to a Boolean value is useable as an expression for the `If...Then` statement.

Using the If...Then statement

The `If...Then` statement is the simplest form of decision-making code. This statement tells VBA to perform a task if a condition is true. If the condition isn't true, VBA ignores the statements within the `If...Then` structure.

The example in this section checks the highlighted text in a document. To test the `If...Then` statement in VBA, create a Word document. Type **Hello**, press Enter, and then type **Goodbye**. Then double-click the word Hello to select the text. The code in Listing 5-1 shows how a simple `If...Then` statement works. (You can find the source code for this example on the Dummies.com site at `http://www.dummiescom/go/mueller`.)

Listing 5-1   Using an If...Then Statement for Decisions

```
Public Sub IfThenTest()
    ' Create a variable for the selected text.
    Dim TestText As String

    ' Get the current selection.
    TestText = ActiveWindow.Selection.Text

    ' Test the selection for "Hello."
    If TestText = "Hello" Then

        ' Modify the selected text to show it's correct.
        TestText = "Correct!" + vbCrLf + "Hello"
    End If

    ' Test the selection for end of line.
    If TestText = Chr(13) Then

        ' Modify the selected text to show the control
```

(continued)

Listing 5-1 *(continued)*

```
        ' character.
        TestText = "End of line selected!"
    End If

    ' Display the selected text.
    MsgBox TestText
End Sub
```

The code begins by creating a variable to hold the selected text. It then shows how to use a new object, ActiveWindow. The ActiveWindow object is useful for a number of tasks, but in this case, you use it to get hold of the currently selected text, if any.

The first If...Then structure determines whether you select the word Hello. If so, the statement TestText = "Correct!" + vbCrLf + "Hello" executes. Otherwise, VBA ignores the statement and moves on to the next test.

The second If...Then structure determines whether the cursor is at the end of the line. This test tells you two things about selections. First, VBA always sees at least one character selected. If you haven't selected anything, ActiveWindow.Selection.Text returns the next character in line. Second, the vbCrLf constant actually does have two control characters in it. The code tests for Chr(13) or a carriage return because that's always the first character in the vbCrLf sequence. If you set the cursor at the end of the line, VBA modifies TestText as shown in the code.

The final line of code shows whatever TestText contains. Unless you select Hello or the end of the line, the message box contains the selected text. Try out the example code by using various selections or set the cursor at the end of the line, and you can see the usefulness of this feature.

Using the If...Then...Else statement

The If...Then...Else statement makes one of two choices. If the expression controlling the statement is true, VBA executes the first set of statements. On the other hand, if the expression is false, VBA executes the second set of statements.

The example in this section determines whether two numbers are equal or whether one is greater than the other. To test the If...Then...Else statement, create a new Excel worksheet. The code relies on input from the worksheet for test purposes. Figure 5-1 shows the setup and some sample input.

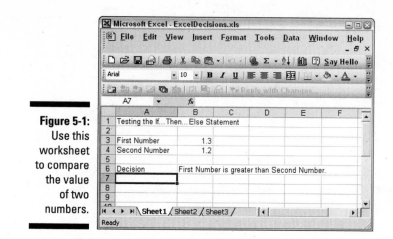

Figure 5-1:
Use this
worksheet
to compare
the value
of two
numbers.

The code used for this example makes three checks: equal to, greater than, or less than. Listing 5-2 shows the code that you need to make these three checks. (You can find the source code for this example on the Dummies.com site at http://www.dummiescom/go/mueller.)

Listing 5-2   Using the If...Then...Else Statement for Comparisions

```
Public Sub CompareNumbers()
    ' Create variables to hold the two numbers.
    Dim Input1 As Double
    Dim Input2 As Double

    ' Create an output string.
    Dim Output As String

    ' Fill the variables with input from the worksheet.
    Input1 = Sheet1.Cells(3, 2)
    Input2 = Sheet1.Cells(4, 2)

    ' Determine if the first number is greater than or equal
    ' to the second number.
    If Input1 >= Input2 Then

        ' Determine if they are equal.
        If Input1 = Input2 Then

            ' Tell the user they are equal.
            Output = "The values are equal."

        Else

            ' The first number must be greater than the
```

(continued)

Listing 5-2 *(continued)*

```
        ' second.
        Output = "First Number is greater than " + _
                    "Second Number."
    End If

Else

    ' The first number is less than the second.
    Output = "First Number is less than Second Number."
End If

' Place the output on the worksheet.
Sheet1.Cells(6, 2) = Output
End Sub
```

The code begins by getting the contents of the two input cells from the worksheet. Always use a `Double` data type when you don't know what kind of number that you might type into a worksheet because this data type is more flexible than an `Integer`. The first number for the `Cells` property is always the row, and the second is the column. Although the worksheet uses letters for the columns, you must use numbers.

You might find it confusing to constantly convert between column letters and numbers when working with large worksheets. To avoid this problem, you can define global constants with the numbers. A `Column_A` constant would equal 1 and so on. Using this technique can make your code easier to read when you use large worksheets.

The first `If...Then` statement checks whether the first number is greater than or equal to the second. You might wonder why the code doesn't simply check for equality. Using this technique reduces the amount of code that you have to write. Notice that the second `If...Then` statement immediately chooses between equality and greater than. It relies on a nested `If...Then...Else` structure to choose between two values for the `Output` string. This is a good example of how to use nesting within your programs.

If the first `If...Then` statement is false, the `Else` statement immediately executes. Notice how the use of nesting saves VBA two checks. When you use individual `If...Then` statements, VBA must make three decisions every time that it compares the two numbers. Using the nested `If...Then...Else` structure shown in the code reduces the number of decisions to one.

The final line of code outputs the comparison results to the worksheet. Try various numbers, and you can see how the nested decision technique works.

Using the If...Then...ElseIf statement

When making multiple comparisons, you can use the `If...Then...ElseIf` statement to make the code easier to read. Using this format can also reduce the number of decisions that VBA must make, which ensures that your code runs as quickly as possible. Listing 5-3 shows an alternative form of the example in the preceding "Using the If...Then...Else statement" section. (You can find the source code for this example on the Dummies.com site at `http://www.dummiescom/go/mueller`.)

Listing 5-3   Using the If...Then...ElseIf Statement for Comparisions

```
Public Sub CompareNumbers2()
    ' Create variables to hold the two numbers.
    Dim Input1 As Double
    Dim Input2 As Double

    ' Create an output string.
    Dim Output As String

    ' Fill the variables with input from the worksheet.
    Input1 = Sheet1.Cells(3, 2)
    Input2 = Sheet1.Cells(4, 2)

    ' Determine if the first number is greater than
    ' the second number.
    If Input1 > Input2 Then

        ' Tell the user the first number is greater.
        Output = "First Number is greater than " + _
                "Second Number."

    ' Determine if they are equal.
    ElseIf Input1 = Input2 Then

        ' Tell the user they are equal.
        Output = "The values are equal."

    Else

        ' The first number is less than the second.
        Output = "First Number is less than Second Number."
    End If

    ' Place the output on the worksheet.
    Sheet1.Cells(6, 2) = Output
End Sub
```

The first thing that you should notice is that this code avoids nesting, which makes it easier to read. VBA will see the first `If...Then` statement and determine whether `Input1` is greater than `Input2`. If the first statement is true, VBA sets the value of `Output` and leaves the structure. However, if the first statement is false, VBA checks the `ElseIf` statement. Finally, if the first two statements are false, VBA executes the statements within the `Else` part of the structure. You can use as many `ElseIf` statements as you need to check every possible condition in your code.

This code is almost as efficient as the first version — it requires just one decision for greater than, two for equality, and three for less than. The ease of reading might become more important to you when the complexity of your programs increases, so this is a perfectly acceptable way to write your code. In short, this example demonstrates that there's usually more than one way to write a program, many of which work fine; the choice of which method to use depends on your personal tastes.

Using the IIf function

You might need to make a decision in a single line of code instead of the three lines (minimum) that other decision-making techniques require. The `IIf` function is a good choice when you need to make simple and concise decisions in your program. It has the advantage of providing decision-making capability in a single line of code. Listing 5-4 shows an example of the `IIf` function in action. (You can find the source code for this example on the Dummies.com site at `http://www.dummies.com/go/mueller`.)

Listing 5-4   Using IIf to Make Inline Decisions

```
Public Sub IIfDemo()
    ' Create variables to hold the two numbers.
    Dim Input1 As Double
    Dim Input2 As Double

    ' Create an output string.
    Dim Output As String

    ' Fill the variables with input from the worksheet.
    Input1 = Sheet1.Cells(3, 2)
    Input2 = Sheet1.Cells(4, 2)

    ' Use nested IIf functions to check all three
    ' conditions.
    Output = IIf(Input1 = Input2, _
                "The values are equal.", _
```

Chapter 5: Creating Structured Programs

```
                    IIf(Input1 > Input2, _
                        "First Number is greater.", _
                        "Second Number is greater."))

    ' Place the output on the worksheet.
    Sheet1.Cells(6, 2) = Output
End Sub
```

This example begins by getting the input from the worksheet. It also creates an Output string.

The IIf function requires three arguments, none of which are optional. The first argument is an expression. The second is a single-line statement of what to do if the expression is true, and the third is a single-line statement of what to do if the expression is false.

The first IIf function determines whether Input1 is equal to Input2. If the expression is true, the first IIf function returns The values are equal. to Output. Otherwise, the first IIf function calls the second IIf function.

The second IIf function determines whether Input1 is greater than Input2. If it is, the second IIf function returns First Number is greater. to the first IIf function, which returns it to Output. Likewise, if the expression is false, the second IIf function returns Second Number is greater.

You can see that this technique could easily become impossible to read and is nearly impossible to comment. However, it only uses one line of code. (Note the continuation characters at the end of each line of code in the book.) The nearest contender appears in the preceding "Using the If...Then...ElseIf statement" section, and it requires seven lines of code.

Making a Choice by Using the Select Case Statement

You can use the If...Then...Else or If...Then...ElseIf statements to meet all decision-making needs. However, using these statements can quickly make your code hard to read when you need to make a lot of decisions in rapid succession. Using these statements is required when you want to perform complex expression checking. VBA provides the Select Case statement as an easier-to-read choice when making a single selection from a list of choices. If you know that a variable contains one of several choices and all you need to check is the choice, using the Select Case statement makes sense.

Using the Select Case statement

The Select Case structure begins with the Select Case statement and ends with an End Case statement. You provide a variable that the Select Case statement can use for selection. Within the Select Case structure are Case *clauses*, or values that the Select Case structure uses for comparison. When the value of a clause matches the value of the input variable, the Select Case structure performs all tasks required by that clause.

In this section, I use examples of the Select Case statement to make a choice of which room to use to store a product. You could easily make this example into a database program, but this section uses a spreadsheet for ease of explanation. Figure 5-2 shows the two input columns used for this example along with typical output in the third column.

Figure 5-2: Make a choice by using this worksheet and associated program.

This decision-making process uses the Bin Number column as input to a Select Case structure. Each clause assigns a number based on a particular number or a range of numbers. Listing 5-5 shows the code that you need to make the choices. (You can find the source code for this example on the Dummies.com site at http://www.dummies.com/go/mueller.)

Listing 5-5 . Using a Select Case Statement for Multiple Decisions

```
Public Sub MakeChoice()
    Dim CursorPosition  As Integer   ' Current row selection.
    Dim BinValue As Integer          ' Bin for selected row.
    Dim Output As Integer            ' Storage room number.

    ' Determine if the user has selected more than one row.
    If ActiveWindow.RangeSelection.Rows.Count = 1 Then

        ' Get the cursor position.
        CursorPosition = ActiveWindow.RangeSelection.Row
    Else

        ' Tell the user to select only one cell.
        MsgBox "Select only one cell!", _
            vbExclamation Or vbOKOnly, _
            "Selection Error"

        ' Exit the Sub without further processing.
        End
    End If

    ' Get the selected bin number.
    BinValue = Sheet2.Cells(CursorPosition, 2)

    ' Select a choice of storage room based in the bin.
    Select Case BinValue
        Case 1
            Output = 1
        Case 2
            Output = 2
        Case 3 To 4
            Output = 1
        Case 5 To 6
            Output = 3
    End Select

    ' Store the number in the worksheet.
    Sheet2.Cells(CursorPosition, 3) = Output
End Sub
```

This example demonstrates some new techniques. The code begins by checking the number of rows that you select. If you only select one row, the code retrieves this value by using the `ActiveWindow.RangeSelection.Row` property. You can also get hold of the column number by using the `Column` property or the row and column by using the `Address` property.

When you select more than one row, it's hard for the program to know which row to work with. The code displays an error message and then exits without performing further processing by using the End statement. This is the first time that you've used *error trapping* in a program, which is figuring out that an error will happen before it can cause problems. See Chapter 6 for more information on debugging and error trapping.

The next step is to retrieve the Bin Number entry by using the row information contained in CursorPosition. The BinValue variable acts as input to the Select Case statement. Notice how this statement uses Case clauses to determine which action to take. You can provide a single value, a range of values, or a list of values separated as commas. The final step is to place the Output value in the worksheet.

Using the Case Else clause

A Select Case statement should normally contain the optional Case Else clause to ensure that you handle all cases, even those that you don't expect when you write the program. Adding this clause requires little time and adds an important error-trapping feature to your program. You could easily change the program from the previous section to include a Select Case statement like the one shown in Listing 5-6. (You can find the source code for this example on the Dummies.com site at http://www.dummies.com/go/mueller.)

Listing 5-6   Handling Unforeseen Decisions with Case Else

```
' Select a choice of storage room based in the bin.
Select Case BinValue
    Case 1
        Output = 1
    Case 2
        Output = 2
    Case 3 To 4
        Output = 1
    Case 5 To 6
        Output = 3
    Case Else
        ' Tell the user to select only one cell.
        MsgBox "Provide a Bin Number between 1 and 6", _
               vbExclamation Or vbOKOnly, _
               "Bin Number Input Error"

        ' Exit the Sub without further processing.
        End
End Select
```

The older version of the code could cause problems when you type a non-existent bin number. This version provides an error message telling you what range of numbers to use. It exits before the code has a chance to create an error condition.

Performing a Task More than Once by Using Loops

Many tasks that you perform require more than one check, change, or data manipulation. You don't change just one entry in a worksheet; you change all the affected entries. Likewise, you don't change just one word in a document; you might change all occurrences based on certain criteria. Databases require multiple changes for almost any task.

Loops provide a method for performing tasks more than one time. You can use loops to save code writing time. Simply write the code to perform the repetitive task once and then tell VBA to perform the task multiple times.

When using loops, you decide how the code determines when to stop. You can tell the loop to execute a specific number of times or to continue executing until the program meets a certain condition.

Using the Do While...Loop statement

A `Do While...Loop` statement keeps performing a task until a certain condition is true. The loop checks the expression first and then executes the code within the structure if the expression is true. You use this loop to perform processing zero or more times. A `Do While...Loop` works especially well if you can't determine the number of times that the loop should execute when you design your program.

One example of a file that could require zero or more changes is a Word document. You might need to format certain words in a specific way for each file, but you have no idea which words you'll use or whether you'll use them at all. The code in Listing 5-7 shows a technique for checking specific words and formatting them. You could easily adapt this program to meet your formatting needs. (You can find the source code for this example on the Dummies.com site at `http://www.dummies.com/go/mueller`.)

Listing 5-7   Modifying Words by Using a Do While...Loop Statement

```
Public Sub ChangeWords()
    Dim CurrentWord As Long ' Current word selection.
    Dim TotalWords As Long  ' Total number of words

    ' Get the total number of words.
    TotalWords = ActiveDocument.Words.Count

    ' Select the first word in the document.
    ActiveDocument.Words(1).Select
    CurrentWord = 1

    ' Keep selecting words until we run out.
    Do While CurrentWord < TotalWords

        ' Make a change based on the word.
        Select Case Trim(ActiveWindow.Selection.Text)
            Case "Hello"
                Selection.Font.Italic = True
            Case "Goodbye"
                Selection.Font.Bold = True
            Case "Yes"
                Selection.Font.Color = wdColorGreen
            Case "No"
                Selection.Font.Color = wdColorRed
        End Select

        ' Move to the next word.
        CurrentWord = CurrentWord + 1
        ActiveDocument.Words(CurrentWord).Select
    Loop
End Sub
```

The code begins by getting the word count for the active document — the one currently selected for editing. The program uses this number to determine when to stop making changes. The `ActiveDocument.Words` document has a number of other interesting uses (such as those shown in the example code), so you should keep it in mind when working with Word.

The next task is to select the first word in the document. You do this by telling `ActiveDocument.Words` which word to select and then using the `Select` method as shown. It's also important to keep track of the current word selection, so the code sets `CurrentWord` to 1. This variable uses the `Long` data type because `ActiveDocument.Words.Count` can return a `Long` value. VBA won't tell you whether you use the wrong data type — you must verify the data type needs by viewing the return data type from method calls and properties.

The `Do While...Loop` structure compares the `CurrentWord` value with the `TotalWords` value. If `CurrentWord` is less than `TotalWords`, it executes the statements contained within the structure.

Notice how the code uses a `Select Case` statement to choose between word choices. This `Select Case` statement also lacks a `Case Else` clause because it doesn't rely on user input. This is one example where the `Case Else` clause can't contribute anything to error trapping or default processing. This example also introduces techniques for modifying the font characteristics of text in a document.

The next two lines of code are especially important. First, the code updates `CurrentWord`. You must do this, or the loop will continue forever because `CurrentWord` is always less than `TotalWords`. Not updating the `CurrentWord` value results in an endless loop — a common source of bugs in programming code. The second statement moves the selection to the next word in the document by using the updated `CurrentWord` value. Note the order of the statements. You must update `CurrentWord` first and then move to the next word in the text. Figure 5-3 shows the document used to test this program with the interesting formatting in place.

Figure 5-3: Create programs that help you perform repetitive tasks such as formatting text.

Using the Do...Loop While statement

The `Do...Loop While` statement works the same as the `Do While...Loop` statement. The difference is that this statement always executes once because the expression used to verify a need to loop appears at the end of the structure. Even if the expression is false, this statement still executes at least one time. You can use this statement when you want to ensure that a task is always completed at least one time.

Using the Do Until...Loop statement

The `Do Until...Loop` statement continues processing information until the expression is false. You can view the `Do While...Loop` statement as a loop that continues while a task is incomplete. The `Do Until...Loop` statement continues until the task is finished. The subtle difference between the two statements points out something interesting — they rely on your perspective of the task to complete. These two statement types are completely interchangeable. The big difference is how you define the expression used to signal the end of the looping sequence.

Using the Do...Loop Until statement

The `Do...Loop Until` statement is the counterpart of the `Do Until...Loop` statement. This statement examines the expression at the end of the loop, so it always executes at least once even if the expression is false.

Using the For...Next statement

The `For...Next` statement is very handy for performing a task a specific number of times. As long as you can determine how many times to do something in advance, this is the best looping option to use because there's less chance of creating an infinite loop. You can create absurdly large loops, but they eventually end.

The `Sub` created in the earlier "Using the Select Case statement" section and augmented in other areas of this chapter works fine for determining the storage room for a single entry. Figure 5-2 shows multiple entries, however, so creating a method for processing all of them would make it easier to assign storage rooms to a new worksheet. The code shown in Listing 5-8 does just that — it makes changing all rows possible with a single program execution. (You can find the source code for this example on the Dummies.com site at `http://www.dummies.com/go/mueller`.)

Listing 5-8   Changing Datasheets With the For...Next Statement

```
Public Sub ChangeAllRooms()
    Dim ActiveRows As Integer    ' Number of active rows.
    Dim Counter As Integer       ' Current row in process.

    ' Select the first data cell in the worksheet.
    Range("A5").Select

    ' Use SendKeys to select all of the cells in the column.
    SendKeys "+^{DOWN}", True

    ' Get the number of rows to process.
    ActiveRows = ActiveWindow.RangeSelection.Rows.Count

    ' Reset the cell pointer.
    Range("C5").Select

    ' Keep processing the cells until complete.
    For Counter = 5 To ActiveRows + 5

        ' Call the Sub created to change a single cell.
        MakeChoice3

        ' Move to the next cell.
        Range("C" + CStr(Counter)).Select
    Next
End Sub
```

This example shows several new functions that you can use. The code begins by selecting the first data row in the worksheet. This selection is important because you want to start at the very beginning of the entries.

The SendKeys function call comes next. This function is interesting because it helps you duplicate keystrokes that you normally make in the worksheet using code. The advantage of this method is that after you get used to the special characters, you can make writing a program very similar to using the program normally. This example sends a Shift (+), Ctrl (^), down arrow sequence (+^{DOWN}) to the worksheet, which selects the entire column. The SendKeys Statement help topic provides full documentation of this function. You can also find other SendKeys examples in other parts of the book.

The SendKeys function is extremely useful. However, don't use it in place of functions that VBA supplies for specific tasks. Using SendKeys can make your code difficult to read and can also slow execution of the program.

By using the ActiveWindow.RangeSelection.Rows.Count property, the code determines how many rows it must process. The code places this value in ActiveRows for later use. Unfortunately, now the worksheet has a range of rows selected rather than a single cell. The code calls upon the Range("C5").Select method to select a single cell again.

The For...Next statement requires three inputs as a minimum. You must provide a counter variable so that the statement knows the current count. The second variable sets the counter to a specific value. This value can be any integer. The code uses 5 in this case because that's the first data row in the worksheet. The third input is the ending count. Counter equals ActiveRows + 5 when the loop completes.

The worksheet is ready to receive the first storage room value, so the code calls MakeChoice3. This is an augmented version of the code in the earlier "Using the Select Case statement" section of this chapter. MakeChoice3 modifies a single cell at a time, so when it returns, only the first data cell has a storage room value in it. The Range("C" + CStr(Counter)).Select method call moves the cell pointer to the next storage room cell. The code continues until all the cells have appropriate storage room numbers.

Using the For Each...Next statement

The For Each...Next statement is similar to the For...Next statement in operation. However, this statement doesn't rely on an external counter. It uses an object index as a counter. The advantage of using this statement is that you don't have to figure out how many times to perform the loop — the object provides this information. The disadvantage of using this statement is that you lose a little control over how the loop executes because the counter is no longer under your control.

You can use this statement for a number of purposes, but generally, it's easier and faster to use the For...Next statement for standard code. You must use the For Each...Next statement with arrays and collections. See Chapter 9 for details on using arrays and collections.

Redirecting the Flow by Using GoTo

You might run into situations where the existing program flow won't work, and you have to disrupt it to move somewhere else in the code. The GoTo statement provides a means of redirecting program flow. Used carefully, the GoTo statement can help you overcome specific programming problems.

Unfortunately, the GoTo statement has caused more problems (such as creating hard-to-understand code and hiding programming errors) than any other programming statement because it has a great potential for misuse. Novice programmers find it easier to use the GoTo statement to overcome programming errors rather than to fix these problems. Always use the GoTo statement with extreme care. Designing your code to flow well before you write it and fixing errors when you find them are both easier than reading code with misused GoTo statements.

Using the GoTo statement correctly

The GoTo statement does provide an essential service of helping you redirect program flow. Before you use the GoTo statement, ask yourself whether there's some other means of performing the redirection, such as using a loop. If there isn't any other way to perform the programming task efficiently, using a GoTo is acceptable. Listing 5-9 shows an example of correct GoTo usage. It's an update of the example shown in the earlier "Using the Select Case statement" section of this chapter. (You can find the source code for this example on the Dummies.com site at http://www.dummies.com/go/mueller.)

Listing 5-9   Using the GoTo Statement

```
' The restart point.
RestartCheck:

' Determine if the user has selected more than one row.
If ActiveWindow.RangeSelection.Rows.Count = 1 Then

    ' Get the cursor position.
    CursorPosition = ActiveWindow.RangeSelection.Row
Else

    ' Tell the user to select only one cell.
    Result = MsgBox("Select only one cell!" + vbCrLf + _
                "Choose the first row in the range?", _
                vbExclamation Or vbYesNo, _
                "Selection Error")

    ' Determine if the user selected Yes.
    If Result = vbYes Then

        ' Modify the selection.
        Range("A" + _
            CStr(ActiveWindow.RangeSelection.Row)).Select

        ' Try the check again.
        GoTo RestartCheck
    End If

    ' Exit the Sub without further processing.
    End
End If
```

This version of the code extends the error trapping found in the earlier "Using the Select Case statement" section of this chapter. The original version correctly identifies an error condition, but then it rudely ends without helping you fix the problem. Rude programs make people mad, so it's best to provide some helpful assistance when you can.

Notice that the message box now displays a message that gives you a chance to fix the error. Result is a VbMsgBoxResult data type and stores the button click information.

When you click Yes, the code changes the current selection by using the Range function. Notice how the code converts the numeric ActiveWindow. RangeSelection.Row property value to a string and combines it with a column letter for the Range function. After the code moves the selection point, it uses the GoTo statement to return to a point before the row selection check in the code. Because there's only one row selected now, the check completes successfully.

Avoiding misuse of the GoTo statement

Many programmers misused the GoTo statement so severely in the past that most books tell you not to use it at all. Misuse of the GoTo statement leads to buggy code that is hard to read. In addition, GoTo statements can hide poor program design. However, the GoTo statement can also accomplish useful work, so the goal is to avoid misuse of the GoTo statement and concentrate on useful tasks. Here are some ways to avoid misusing the GoTo statement.

- ✔ **Loops:** Never use a GoTo statement as a loop replacement. The statements used for loops signal others about your intent. In addition, standard loop statements contain features that keep bugs, such as endless loops, to a minimum.

- ✔ **Exits:** Avoid using a GoTo statement as a means of exiting a program. You can always use the End statement for that task.

- ✔ **Program flow problems:** If you detect problems with the flow of your program, check your pseudo-code and design documents again. Make sure that you implement the design correctly. The design might require change as well. Don't assume that the design is correct, especially if this is a first attempt.

Chapter 6

Trapping Errors and Squashing Bugs

*E*ven the best programmer in the world makes mistakes. It's part of the human condition. Don't be surprised when a bug creeps into your well-designed and well-implemented VBA program. Bugs are the gremlins of the computer industry — they're insidious and evil.

Fortunately, you can hunt down bugs and squash them. You can also prevent bugs from occurring in the first place by coding your VBA program carefully. The goal of this chapter is to help you understand what you can do to prevent bugs in your VBA program and what to do when they get in anyway.

You won't figure out how to write perfect programs because no one does. As a result, you use *error trapping* to detect bugs and do something about them before they can cause problems. In the cases where you can't detect the bug, you use *error handling* to fix the problem that the bug causes and to help your VBA program recover.

Knowing the Enemy

Users look at bugs as non-entities devoid of any characteristics. All a user knows is that a bug causes the program to crash and lose data. You can't afford to have that perspective. Bugs have personalities, in that they vary by

- ✔ Type
- ✔ Cause
- ✔ Effect
- ✔ Severity
- ✔ Other factors that you include in your personal classification system

Locating a bug means knowing about its personality so that you can find it quickly. It helps to classify the bug by type. Each bug type has a different prevention and troubleshooting method. You can classify bugs into the following four types:

- ✔ Syntax
- ✔ Compile
- ✔ Run-time
- ✔ Semantic

The best way to find bugs is to know your coding style. Keeping notes helps you understand patterns in your programming so that you can correct techniques that lead to bugs. More importantly, understanding your personal style helps you develop techniques for finding bugs based on past mistakes. Knowing what you did in the past helps you locate and squash bugs today.

Understanding syntax errors

Syntax errors are the easiest errors to avoid but are also some of the hardest errors to find. A *syntax error* can include a spelling mistake, misuse of punctuation, or a misuse of a language element. When you forget to include an `End If` for an `If...Then` statement, it's a syntax error.

Typos are a common syntax error. They're especially hard to find when you make them in variable names. For example, VBA views `MySpecialVariable` and `MySpecialVaraible` as two different variables, but you might miss the typing error. Adding `Option Explicit` to the beginning of every module, form, and class module that you create eases this problem. (See the upcoming "Understanding compile errors" section for details on using `Option Explicit`.) You can rely on VBA to find most variable typos when you add this simple statement to your code. In fact, this statement should become a standard part of every program that you create.

You can easily miss some of the subtle aids to locating syntax errors if you don't view tasks carefully enough that the Integrated Development Environment (IDE) performs. The balloon help shown in Figure 6-1 for the `MsgBox` function provides a cue that you could miss. VBA displays the balloon help shown in the figure only when it recognizes the function name that you type. When you don't see the balloon help, it's a cue that VBA doesn't recognize the function name, and you need to look at your code. Unfortunately, this feature works only where VBA normally displays balloon help — it doesn't work when you type property names.

Figure 6-1:
Balloon help
helps locate
syntax
errors in
your code.

Balloon help

No matter what you do, a few syntax errors can slip by and cause bugs in your program. You can look at the errors for hours and not actually see them because you've worked with the code for so long. Asking someone else to look at your code often helps because that person isn't familiar with the code. Make sure that you ask someone with the same or better programming skills that you have to ensure that they understand your code.

Syntax errors also include errors in *logic* (the construction of expressions in your program). You can create a loop that processes the loop structure statements once too often or not often enough. An `If...Then` statement can use an expression that works most of the time but isn't quite right, so it doesn't produce the correct result all the time. Code with logic errors runs because VBA doesn't know that the expression is incorrect. The only way to find this kind of syntax error is to debug the program. See the upcoming "Time for a Bug Hunt" section for details.

Understanding compile errors

The VBA *compiler* is actually a syntax checker. Unlike compilers used by other languages, the VBA compiler doesn't produce a free-standing module that you can execute outside the Office environment. VBA uses the compiler to look for errors that prevent the program from running properly. You might create an If...Then statement and not include the corresponding End If statement. The compiler runs constantly, so VBA finds some mistakes almost immediately after you make them.

VBA uses the compiler to find many of the syntax errors that you make and displays an error message similar to the one shown in Figure 6-2. You can try this feature. Open a new project, create a Sub (the name isn't important), and type **MsgBox()**. Then press Enter. VBA displays the message box shown in Figure 6-2. When you use parentheses after MsgBox, VBA expects that you want to include a result variable to hold the result, such as MyResult = MsgBox("My Prompt"). You should also notice that the errant line of code appears in a highlight color, which is normally red.

Figure 6-2:
VBA finds
some syntax
errors.

Missing elements are another syntax error that VBA finds with relative ease. When you fail to include an End If for an If...Then statement, VBA always finds it and displays an error message similar to the one shown in Figure 6-2. However, VBA won't find this error in most cases until you try to run the program. In addition, it doesn't show the errant If...Then statement — VBA normally highlights the End Sub or End Function statement instead, thus making this error a little harder to find.

The compiler also finds many of the punctuation errors that you can make in your code. When a line of code becomes too long and you try to move to the next line without adding a continuation character, the compiler notices the error and tells you about it. (See the "Writing Your First Sub" section of Chapter 3 for a description of the continuation character.) The complier also notes missing periods between elements of a statement or missing parentheses from function calls (when needed).

When you add `Option Explicit` to your code, the compiler checks variables for a number of problems. You could try to assign a string value to an integer. VBA allows you to make this error when you type the code. However, when you try to run the code, the compiler sees the type mismatch and tells you about it. The compiler can detect many variable errors that would go unnoticed otherwise, thus making your code less likely to contain errors.

Understanding run-time errors

Run-time errors happen when something outside your program is incorrect. A disk access request can fail, or you can type the wrong information. Your VBA code is correct, but the program still fails because of this external error. Run-time errors are the reason why many large companies such as Microsoft run beta programs. (A *beta program* is a vendor-sponsored method of getting a program before the developers have finished it for the purpose of testing and evaluation.) A large base of users can help you find run-time errors that depend on a particular machine configuration or a specific kind of user entry technique.

You can trap run-time errors or change the program flow to ensure that they don't happen. In Chapter 5, I show several forms of error trapping. See the upcoming "Prevention Is Better than a Cure" section of this chapter for additional examples. The remainder of the book contains yet more examples of error trapping because this is an important topic. Error trapping helps your program overcome errors that you can't predict when you write a program.

Understanding semantic errors

A particularly difficult error to find and understand is the *semantic error,* which is an error that happens when the VBA code and logic are correct, but the meaning behind the code isn't what you intended. For example, you could use a `Do...Until` loop in place of a `Do...While` loop. Even if the code is correct and you use the correct logic, the code won't produce the result that you expected because the meaning of a `Do...Until` loop is different from a `Do...While` loop.

The meaning that you assign to your code has to match the words that you use to write the code. Just like a good book uses precise terms, a good program relies on precise statements to ensure that VBA understands what you want to do. The best way to avoid semantic errors is to plan your application carefully, use pseudo-code to pre-write the design, and then convert the pseudo-code to VBA code. When you skip steps in the process, you can introduce semantic errors because you won't communicate your ideas well to VBA.

Introducing semantic errors in subtle ways is easy. Writing an equation the wrong way can result in output errors. When you use the wrong equation to determine the next step in a loop, the problem becomes worse because the error looks like a syntax or runtime error. The steps between loops or the expression used to make a decision are very important. The most common error is leaving a parenthesis out of an equation. For example, VBA interprets 1 + 2 * 3 as 7 but (1 + 2) * 3 as 9. A missing parenthesis is easy to miss when you frantically search for an error.

Prevention Is Better than a Cure

Avoiding an error is always easier than trapping or handling it later. However, any form of prevention is better than letting the error occur without any intervention at all. Whenever your program experiences an unhandled error, it stops running (crashes). Here are some reasons why you want to handle errors instead of just letting them happen:

- You can provide specific error information.
- Programs can recover from many errors.
- Programs can reduce or prevent data loss.
- You can include special handling that tracks the error for later debugging.
- The host application (such as Office) can help reduce the effects of the error.
- The operating system can help with some errors and reduce the effect of others.

Avoiding run-time errors

Run-time errors can include many unforeseen events. You can't handle all run-time errors in your program. For example, a storm that removes power from the computer isn't something that you can control. You need an uninterruptible power supply (UPS) attached to the computer to handle that error. Even so, such an error can result in data loss.

However, you can avoid other kinds of run-time errors. Input errors are one of the most common run-time problems that you face when working with VBA. In Chapter 5, I show some techniques for avoiding run-time errors due to improper input. You can also use these techniques:

✔ Check every input for data type, length, value, and meaning.

✔ Provide easy-to-understand prompts for your application.

✔ Make the prompts and error messages as specific as possible.

✔ Offer to fix the problem automatically whenever possible.

✔ Offer to retry the operation after you correct the error whenever possible.

✔ Reduce the chances of error by providing complete context-sensitive help that includes examples and other resource information.

Checking the input is the most important task that your program can perform. If the program needs a word, don't accept a number as input. Ensure that the length of the input matches expectations. This check is especially important to avoid *buffer overrun,* which is a condition where the program receives too much input. Buffer overrun errors often make the news as security breaches. If possible, look for specific values. Even if you don't have specific input values, check for strange characters or values that seem out of place. It's also possible to examine the meaning of the input in some cases. A street address usually requires a street number and name. When you want to ensure that the address information is correct, try looking for this information in the input.

Program resource problems are the second-most common source of run-time errors. You might not have enough space on the hard drive to save a file, or the program might not find a file that it needs. Checking for the resource before you need it helps avoid the associated run-time error. If the resource is something that you can fix, such as a lack of hard drive space, include code that allows you to perform this task and then ask the program to check again.

Recovering from an error

Recovering from an error is important. Adding recovery code means that you can count on your program to help you overcome problems with the system and keep your data safe. You can add two kinds of recovery code to your program:

✔ Code that recovers before the error happens.

✔ Code that recovers after the error happens.

It's always better to detect an error and recover from it before the error actually happens. You can always recover from a resource error, such as lack of hard drive space, before the error happens. Likewise, you can always recover from input errors by making the required checks and asking for the correct input. The only time when you must wait for the error to happen is when you can't predict the error, such as a sudden loss of power.

A common run-time error is lack of hard drive space. To add a drive-checking feature to your program, you need to add a new library to your program. Use the Tools➪References command to display the References dialog box as shown in Figure 6-3. Notice that the Microsoft Scripting Runtime check box is selected. Look for this entry in your dialog box and select it. Click OK. The new library is ready for use.

The Microsoft Scripting Runtime has many powerful features that I explore in detail in other parts of the book. The feature that you use in this section (see Listing 6-1) demonstrates how to check for disk space and recover from an error when the disk drive doesn't have enough space. (You can find the source code for this example on the Dummies.com site at http://www.dummies.com/go/mueller.)

Figure 6-3:
Use this dialog box to add a new library to your program.

Listing 6-1   Determining the Amount of Free Disk Space

```
Public Sub DriveTest()
    ' Create a variable to hold the free space.
    Dim FreeSpace As Long

    ' Create a reference to the file system.
    Dim MyFileSystem As FileSystemObject

    ' Create a reference for the target drive.
    Dim MyDrive As Drive

    ' Create a dialog result variable.
```

```
    Dim Result As VbMsgBoxResult

  'Provide a jump back point.
DoCheckAgain:

  ' Fill these two objects with data so they show the
  ' available space on drive C.
  Set MyFileSystem = New FileSystemObject
  Set MyDrive = MyFileSystem.GetDrive("C")

  ' Determine the amount of free space.
  FreeSpace = MyDrive.AvailableSpace

  ' Make the check.
  If FreeSpace < 1000000000 Then

     ' The drive doesn't have enough space. Ask what to
     ' do.
     Result = MsgBox("The drive doesn't have enough " + _
                  "space to hold the data. Do you" + _
                  " want to correct the error?" + _
                  vbCrLf + _
                  Format(FreeSpace, "###,###") + _
                  " bytes available, " + _
                  "1,000,000,000 bytes needed.", _
                  vbYesNo Or vbExclamation, _
                  "Drive Space Error")

     ' Determine if the user wants to correct the error.
     If Result = vbYes Then

        ' Wait for the user to fix the problem.
        MsgBox "Please click OK when you have freed" + _
               " some disk space.", _
               vbInformation Or vbOKOnly, _
               "Retry Drive Check"

        ' Go to the fallback point.
        GoTo DoCheckAgain
     Else

        ' The user doesn't want to fix the error.
        MsgBox "The program can't save your data " + _
               "until the drive has enough space.", _
               vbInformation Or vbOKOnly, _
               "Insufficient Drive Space"

        ' End the Sub.
        Exit Sub
     End If
  End If
End Sub
```

The code begins by creating some variables. The `FileSystemObject` object contains information about every drive that you can access from your machine. The `Drive` object contains information about a specific drive. The code uses the `Set` keyword with objects. You `Set` a variable equal to an object. See Chapter 8 for details on using objects.

The code places the amount of space available into `FreeSpace` and compares it with the space needed to hold the information. You might have to change the value in the `If...Then` statement to match your drive. Make the number larger than the space that your drive has available.

Because the drive doesn't have enough space, the code displays an error message. The message shown in the code might seem long and complicated, but it provides all the information needed to make a decision. It tells what's wrong, provides you with a choice of actions, and contains specifics about the amount of space needed. Notice the use of the `Format` function for the message. It shows how to use a custom formatting string to display the free space with comma separators but without a decimal point.

If you say that you want to fix the drive space error, the code presents a message box that tells you to click OK when it's okay to make the change again. The code uses the `GoTo` statement to redirect execution to the drive space check again.

On the other hand, if you decide not to fix the error, the program tells you the result of the action. It then exits the `Sub` without doing anything else. This step is important. Otherwise, the program attempts to save the file, and the error occurs.

Understanding error handlers

Error handlers are your option of last resort in dealing with bugs. You use an error handler to work with any errors that you can't trap. The important thing to remember is that the error has happened — you can't prevent it at this point. The best that you can do is to display a message box saying that the error happened and to tell whether your program can recover from the error.

When your program can't recover, it should fail gracefully. However, failing gracefully shouldn't be a standard option — always try to recover from the error. A program that fails gracefully performs the following tasks.

- The program doesn't rely on the standard VBA message. It uses a custom message that contains detailed failure information instead.

- The user is always informed about the consequences of the failure, possible fixes, and whom to contact (when necessary).

✔ The reporting information should also appear in the Windows Event Log when necessary to ensure that the administrator sees the error. VBA doesn't support this feature directly.

✔ If possible, the program includes you as part of the reporting loop so that you can keep track of bugs in your application.

✔ The host application doesn't fail (and cause data loss) because of an error in the program.

✔ Instead of using default error handling, the program provides robust error handling that leaves the operating system in a stable state.

Writing your own error-handling code

Adding an error handler to your program is a two-part process. First, you must tell VBA that you've included an error handler. Otherwise, VBA uses the default error handler, even when error-handler code appears in the program. Second, you must provide the error-handling code. Listing 6-2 shows an example of a Sub that uses error handling. (You can find the source code for this example on the Dummies.com site at http://www.dummies.com/go/mueller.)

Listing 6-2   Defining a Custom Error Handler

```
Public Sub ErrorHandle()
    ' The variable that receives the input.
    Dim InNumber As Byte

    ' Tell VBA about the error handler.
    On Error GoTo MyHandler

    ' Ask the user for some input.
    InNumber = InputBox("Type a number between 1 and " + _
                        "10.", "Numberic Input", "1")

    ' Determine whether the input is correct.
    If (InNumber < 1) Or (InNumber > 10) Then

        ' If the input is incorrect, then raise an error.
        Err.Raise vbObjectError + 1, _
                "ErrorCheck.ErrorCondition.ErrorHandle", _
                "Incorrect Numeric Input. The number " + _
                "must be between 1 and 10."
    Else
        ' Otherwise, display the result.
        MsgBox "The Number You Typed: " + CStr(InNumber), _
```

(continued)

Listing 6-2 *(continued)*

```
                    vbOKOnly Or vbInformation, _
                    "Successful Input"
        End If

        ' Exit the Sub.
        Exit Sub

    ' The start of the error handler.
    MyHandler:

        ' Display an error message box.
        MsgBox "The program experienced an error." + vbCrLf + _
               "Error Number: " + CStr(Err.Number) + vbCrLf + _
               "Description: " + Err.Description + vbCrLf + _
               "Source: " + Err.Source, _
               vbOKOnly Or vbExclamation, _
               "Program Error"

        ' Always clear the error after you process it.
        Err.Clear
    End Sub
```

This example introduces a few new features. Notice the use of the GoTo statement. You can use a number of forms of On Error, but the GoTo form shown
is the most common. Another common form is On Error Resume Next,
which tells VBA to ignore the line of code with a problem and continue with
the next line. The problem with this second form is that you haven't really
handled the error. It remains unreported and could cause a severe crash later.

Never use the On Error GoTo 0 statement. This statement turns error handling off, which means that errors go unhandled, and VBA won't even tell you
about them. This setting can cause a range of problems, including application
failure and data loss.

The InputBox function is an interesting way to get hold of one piece of information. This example uses the InputBox function for testing, which is the
most common way that I've seen it used. In general, you never use the
InputBox function in a program because you normally need more than one
input. The first argument prompts for information, the second contains a
default value, and the third provides a title for the dialog box. You can also
include arguments for placement of the dialog box onscreen and provide a
help context.

Notice the InNumber data type. Using this data type ensures that you can't
input a letter or special character without generating an error. If you try to
input the wrong information, VBA detects the error and generates an error
number 13 (type mismatch). (You can find a standard list of VBA error codes

at `http://www.halfile.com/vb.html`.) The `Byte` data type also limits the acceptable input range. If you overflow the buffer by using a number that is too large, VBA generates error 6 (overflow). You can detect these errors in your error handler and take appropriate action.

The `If...Then` statement performs a special task. This is one method for performing a range check — something that you should do for every input that you receive from a user. The check ensures that the input is within a specific range. If the input isn't within the specified range, the code uses the `Err.Raise` function to generate an error. User-defined errors fall within a specific range, so you should always add your custom error number to `vbObjectError` to ensure that the number is within the proper range. All error numbers must be less than 65,535.

As part of a *custom error* (one that you define), you should tell yourself exactly where the error occurred. I always include the filename, the module name, and the `Function` or `Sub` name. Notice that the description information for this error is complete and descriptive. Just because Microsoft provides ambiguous information doesn't mean that you have to follow its bad example. Always include descriptive error messages so that you have a good idea of what went wrong.

The error handler begins at the `MyHandler` label. The handler shows the various `Err` object properties that you can access to determine the source and cause of an error. The example could easily include a retry feature, but I chose to keep things simple. See the earlier "Recovering from an error" section for details on a retry feature.

The last statement might not look like much, but it's very important. Always clear errors after you handle them by using the `Err.Clear` method. If you don't, VBA might think that the error is still a problem and fail again.

Reporting errors

It's essential to report program errors. You can't overcome problems with your program when you don't know about them. In addition, knowing about errors makes it possible to create a recovery plan. Here are some techniques that you can use to report errors.

- ✔ **Message box:** Many of my examples in this chapter use message boxes, which is the standard method that most programs use.

- ✔ **Text file:** You can create a text file with error information. A formatted text file — one that uses tabs to separate individual entries — can act as input to a database. See Chapter 10 for details on working with disk files.

✔ **Windows Event Log:** You can use a Windows Event Log entry to hold the error information. The Event Log uses a standard format for error messages. It's the place where network administrator looks for errors. See the upcoming "Using the Event Log" section for details on using this technique.

✔ **E-mail:** You can create an e-mail message with error information about your program. See Chapter 17 for details on working with Outlook from a VBA program.

Using the Event Log

VBA doesn't provide an easy or a friendly way to work with the Event Log. In fact, you need to create a connection between VBA and the Windows 32-bit Application Programming Interface (Win32 API). Look in the \Windows\ System32 folder of your machine, and you see a vast number of files with a Dynamic Link Library (DLL) extension (.dll). Each of these files contains code that Windows or your applications use. You can also use features in these DLLs for your own needs.

You can safely skip the code explanation that I present in this section. I provide the code that you need in a form that works with any application that uses VBA. Simply import the code by using the procedure in the upcoming "Importing a module in a program" section and use the function it contains, as shown in the later "Making an Event Log entry" section.

In this section, I describe the essential Event Log code. The example also requires some small pieces of utility code that I don't include in the chapter. You can find the complete source code for this example on the Dummies.com site at http://www.dummies.com/go/mueller.

Understanding the Win32 API function code

To create a connection to a function in an external DLL, you need to tell VBA about it. Defining the function lets you use it within your VBA programs. Listing 6-3 contains the six external functions that you use for this example.

Listing 6-3   Defining the Event Log Functions

```
' **** These three functions work with the Event Log. ****

' This function tells Windows to use a specific Event Log
' for Event Log entries.
Declare Function RegisterEventSource _
        Lib "advapi32.dll" _
```

```
        Alias "RegisterEventSourceA" ( _
            ByVal lpUNCServerName As String, _
            ByVal lpSourceName As String) As Long

' This function creates the report entry within the Event
' Log.
Declare Function ReportEvent _
        Lib "advapi32.dll" _
        Alias "ReportEventA" ( _
            ByVal hEventLog As Long, _
            ByVal wType As EntryType, _
            ByVal wCategory As Integer, _
            ByVal dwEventID As Long, _
            ByVal lpUserSid As Any, _
            ByVal wNumStrings As Integer, _
            ByVal dwDataSize As Long, _
            plpStrings As Long, _
            lpRawData As Any) As Boolean

' This function tells Windows that the program is done using
' the Event Log.
Declare Function DeregisterEventSource _
        Lib "advapi32.dll" ( _
            ByVal hEventLog As Long) As Long

' **** These three functions work with memory used by the
'      event reporting functions. ****

' This function asks Windows to provide memory for use with
' the Event Log functions.
Declare Function GlobalAlloc _
        Lib "kernel32" ( _
            ByVal wFlags As GlobalAllocFlags, _
            ByVal dwBytes As Integer) As Long

' This function copies information from VBA to the memory
' provided by Windows.
Declare Sub CopyMemory _
        Lib "kernel32" _
        Alias "RtlMoveMemory" ( _
            hpvDest As Any, _
            hpvSource As Any, _
            ByVal cbCopy As Long)

' This function tells Windows that we no longer need the
' memory allocated using the GlobalAlloc function.
Declare Function GlobalFree _
        Lib "kernel32" ( _
            ByVal hMem As Long) As Integer
```

You can find documentation for each of these functions at the Microsoft Developer Network (MSDN) Library (`http://msdn.microsoft.com/library/`). Simply type the name of the function in the Search For field and then click Go. You can find a wealth of information about other Win32 API functions at this Web site. A discussion of the entire Win32 API would consume several books, so this book only shows a few of them.

Whenever you want to use an external function, you begin with the `Declare` keyword. This word is followed by the function name that you want to use in VBA and the library (DLL file) where VBA can find the function. The Win32 API might use names that are hard to remember, so you can use a different function name — one that's descriptive and easy to remember. If you use a different name, you must include the `Alias` keyword in your declaration that tells the original name of the function.

The declaration must include the list of variables that Win32 API expects as input. You can find these variables in the Win32 API documentation in the MSDN Library. I use the same names for the variables that the Win32 API documentation does so that matching my functions with the documentation is easier when I need to remember what the functions do later.

The code includes two *enumerations*, which is a list of constants. Chapter 8 shows how to use enumerated constants. When you see the list of buttons and icons for the `MsgBox` function, that's an enumerated constant. The example code includes enumerated constants for the kind of Event Log entry, such as information, warning, and error. It also includes enumerated constants for asking Windows for memory.

Creating an Event Log for your program

When you open the Event Log, you see a number of log files in it. The three common log files are Application, Security, and System. You commonly see other logs when working with a server. Each of these logs contains specific information. Unfortunately, the Application log can fill quickly, and it's easy to miss messages.

A simple change to the Windows Registry lets you use a custom log for your program. Using a custom log has the advantage of making errors easy to find but also means that your setup won't match that of other machines on the network. Use the Application log if you don't plan to make a lot of entries in the Event Log. Create a custom log to make Event Log entries regularly.

You can open the Registry Editor by choosing Start⇨Run. Type **RegEdit** in the Open field of the Run dialog box and then click OK. Figure 6-4 shows an example of the Registry Editor with special entries added for an Event Log.

Figure 6-4:
Registry
entries for
Event Log.

Notice that you need to add two new keys: one for the Event Log and a second for your application. Make sure that you use this application name when creating an Event Log entry. You need to create two values for the application key as shown. The `EventMessageFile` value contains the location of the Visual Basic Runtime file (`D:\WINDOWS\System32\msvbvm60.dll` in this case). The `TypesSupported` value is a `DWORD` (a double word or a 32-bit value) that contains 4 for this version of the Visual Basic Runtime. Look at the `HKEY_LOCAL_MACHINE\SYSTEM\CurrentControlSet\Services\ Eventlog\Application\VBRuntime` key if you have questions about what your application key should contain.

Understanding the Write2EventLog function

The function that you use to create an Event Log entry hides the complexity of performing this task. Using functions to hide complexity makes programming easier. Listing 6-4 shows the `Write2EventLog` function code that you use to interact with the Event Log.

Listing 6-4   Hiding Event Log Entry Complexity

```
Public Function Write2EventLog( _
    Optional LogName As String = "Application", _
    Optional EventType As EntryType = 4, _
    Optional Category As Integer = 0, _
    Optional EventID As Long = 0, _
    Optional Description As String = "None") As Boolean

    ' The address of the open Event Log. A handle is a way
    ' to access the Event Log.
    Dim EventLogHandle As Long

    ' The address of the Windows memory used to store the
    ' event description.
    Dim MessageHandle As Long

    ' This functions writes information to the local
    ' machine Event Log. If you want to write to an Event
    ' Log on a server, then change the first argument in
```

(continued)

Listing 6-4 *(continued)*

```
    ' this call to the name of that server.
    EventLogHandle = RegisterEventSource("", LogName)

    ' Ask Windows for memmory to store the description
    ' string and the raw data.
    MessageHandle = _
        GlobalAlloc(GMEM_ZEROINIT, Len(Description) + 1)

    ' If Windows doesn't have any memory to offer, tell the
    ' user and then exit.
    If (MessageHandle = 0) Then
        MsgBox "Windows ran low on memory, so the " + _
                "program can't create an Event Log entry.", _
                vbOKOnly Or vbExclamation, _
                "Error Getting Memory"

        Exit Function
    End If

    ' Now that we have memory to use, copy the description
    ' and the raw data to the Windows memory.
    CopyMemory ByVal MessageHandle, _
                ByVal Description, _
                Len(Description) + 1

    ' Write the information to the Event Log.
    Write2EventLog = ReportEvent(EventLogHandle, _
                                EventType, _
                                Category, _
                                EventID, _
                                0&, _
                                1, _
                                0, _
                                MessageHandle, _
                                0)

    ' Always free memory that you request from Windows.
    Call GlobalFree(MessageHandle)

    ' Tell Windows the Event Log entry is finished.
    DeregisterEventSource (EventLogHandle)
End Function
```

This function begins with an interesting new feature. When you define an argument for a function, you can make it optional and also assign it a default value. The Write2EventLog function has a number of arguments, all of which are optional. To create an optional argument, use the Optional keyword. When you want to assign the argument a default value, follow the type declaration with the value that you want to assign. Using default values ensures that the function receives some input.

Before you can write to an Event Log, you have to tell Windows which one you want to use. The `RegisterEventSource` function tells Windows which Event Log to associate with your program. The first argument for this function tells which machine to use for the Event Log. Windows uses the local machine when you use a null string, as shown in the code. The second argument contains the log name. This function returns a *handle*, which is a method of accessing the Event Log. Think about a handle like you would a real-world handle. For example, the handle of a pan lets you move the pan from the stove to the sink. You aren't actually touching the pan — the handle simply gives you access to the pan.

The functions in the Win32 API can't access the memory that your VBA program uses. This is a safety feature, but it also causes problems for this example. The `GlobalAlloc` function creates memory that your program can share with the Win32 API. The first task that the code performs is to ask Windows to allocate (provide) some global memory that you can use to store a description of the event (provided by `Err.Description`) that you want to enter in the Event Log. The code ensures that Windows allocated the memory by checking the value of `MessageHandle` on return from the `GlobalAlloc` call. If this call wasn't successful, Windows probably lacked the memory to allocate, and you need to exit this function.

Your program can't simply place information in the memory that it requested from Windows — it must use a special function to copy the information to this memory. The `CopyMemory` function performs this task. Notice that this function doesn't have a return value. Windows assumes that if you've allocated memory properly, the call succeeds. You can always check this assumption by using the `Err.LastDLLError` property.

It's time to write information to the Event Log by using the `ReportEvent` function. This function returns a Boolean value that indicates success or failure that the `Write2EventLog` function passes to the calling program. The `ReportEvent` function accepts several arguments, many of which aren't used for this example. You must provide the `EventLogHandle` received from the `RegisterEventSource` function. The `ReportEvent` function also requires an event type (information, warning, or error), a category, the event identifier (acquired from `Err.Number`), and the event description pointed to by `MessageHandle`. The optional arguments include a user identifier and raw data (see the MSDN Library for details).

After the event appears in the Event Log, the code performs some clean-up. VBA doesn't know about the Windows memory, and it couldn't do anything with it even if it did know. Whenever you allocate memory by using the

GlobalAlloc function, you must free it by using the GlobalFree function. The GlobalFree function accepts the memory handle (MessageHandle) as input. If you don't free the memory, it's lost. This is a *memory leak* and can eventually cause Windows to run out of memory.

The final task is to tell Windows that you don't need the Event Log any longer. The DeregisterEventSource function accepts the EventLogHandle as input and closes the Event Log. If you don't close the Event Log, Windows assumes that you're still using it and could refuse access to other applications.

Exporting a module from a program

When you work with VBA, you might create some modules that you want to use in other places. This means exporting your module to a BAS (BASIC) file. (Forms rely on the FRM file, and class modules rely on the CLS file.) The following steps tell you how to perform this task.

1. **Highlight the module, form, or class module that you want to export from a program in the Project window.**

2. **Right-click the entry and then choose Export File from the context menu that appears.**

   You see the Export File dialog box.

3. **Choose a location for the module, form, or class module and then click Save.**

   VBA exports the file.

Importing a module in a program

The library that you build while you write VBA programs is an important resource because it reduces the need to write new code. Every time that you need to reuse existing code, you can import the module by using the following procedure.

1. **Right-click anywhere in the Project window and then choose Import File from the context menu that appears.**

   You see the Import File dialog box.

2. **Locate the BAS, FRM, or CLS file that you want to import.**

3. **Highlight the file and then click Open.**

   The module appears in the Project window in the appropriate folder.

Making an Event Log entry

Using the Write2EventLog function is easier than writing it initially. The function asks for simple entries that VBA provides for you in many cases. Listing 6-5 shows an example of how to use the Write2EventLog function.

Listing 6-5   Creating an Event Log Entry

```
Public Sub SampleEntry()
    ' Create an object.
    Dim MyObject As Object

    ' Tell VBA about the error handler.
    On Error GoTo MyErrorHandler

    ' Generate an error.
    MyObject = 2

    ' Exit the Sub.
    Exit Sub

MyErrorHandler:
    ' Create an Event Log entry.
    If Write2EventLog("MySpecialProgram", _
                EVENTLOG_ERROR_TYPE, _
                0, _
                Err.Number, _
                vbCrLf + "Source: " + Err.Source + _
                vbCrLf + "Decription: " + _
                Err.Description) Then

        ' Indicate success.
        MsgBox "Event Log entry written.", _
               vbOKOnly Or vbInformation, _
               "Success"
    Else
        ' Indicate failure.
        MsgBox "Error writing Event Log entry.", _
               vbOKOnly Or vbExclamation, _
               "Event Log Error"
    End If
End Sub
```

The code begins by creating an object, which means that it doesn't contain anything. The code then tells VBA to use the custom error handler. Finally, it generates an error.

The error handling code calls the `Write2EventLog` function. It provides the name of a program entry (use `VBRuntime` to place the entry in the Application Event Log). You also need to decide on the type of entry: information, warning, or error. Because this is an error handler, the code uses the `EVENTLOG_ERROR_TYPE` constant. The category argument is normally set to 0 unless you want to create a special category for your custom errors. Finally, the `Err` object provides all the other information for you, including the error number, the error source, and error description. Figure 6-5 shows the output of this example. You can read the detail information by double-clicking the entry and displaying the Event Properties dialog box.

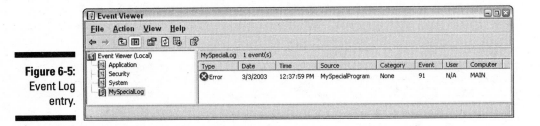

Figure 6-5: Event Log entry.

Time for a Bug Hunt

You aren't alone when you have a bug to find in your program because the VBA IDE provides a special tool called a *debugger*. The debugger is a built-in feature that you access by using a special Debug toolbar. Figure 6-6 shows the Debug toolbar. Add it to your IDE by right-clicking the toolbar area and then choosing Debug from the list of available toolbars.

Figure 6-6: Use the Debug toolbar to access debugger features.

Executing a break

Whenever you open your program in the VBA IDE and execute it from there, the program is in debug mode. Using debug mode lets you stop the program and see what it's doing at any particular moment. Not only can stopping the program help you find bugs, but it can also help you discover more about VBA and how to use it. You could use this feature to view other people's code to see how they perform programming tasks.

Before you can stop execution of your program, you need to tell VBA where to stop. A stop within a VBA program is a *breakpoint*. To add a breakpoint to your code, highlight the stopping point and then click the Toggle Breakpoint button on the Debug toolbar. When you click the Run Sub/User Form button, VBA automatically stops at the point that you selected.

When your program has a natural stop, such as in a form or at an `InputBox` statement, you can also click the Break button on the Debug toolbar to stop the program. (See the earlier "Writing your own error-handling code" section for an example of the `InputBox` statement.) The Break button differs from the Reset button because it only pauses execution. Clicking the Reset button always stops the program, and you have to restart it from the beginning.

Another way to execute a break is to use the `Debug.Assert` method. You can use any Boolean expression with this method. If the expression is true, program execution continues as normal. However, if the expression is false, the program breaks so that you can examine the value. This form of break is helpful when you know that a program should have variables with a certain range of values.

Whenever you execute a break, the program is temporarily stopped. Click the Run Sub/User Form button to start the program from the current stopping point. As far as the program is concerned, it never stopped.

Taking individual steps

Whenever you execute a break in a running program, the debugger enables the Step Into, Step Over, and Step Out buttons. You use these three buttons to take individual steps within the program — to execute one line of code at a time. The reason why you want to do this is to see the effect of each statement on the program data. When you think that a statement changes a string in a certain way, you can prove it to yourself by viewing the effect of that particular statement.

You use the Step Over button in most cases because you want to see the effects of statements in the current Sub or Function. Clicking the Step Over button moves from line to line in the current code. The code still executes in any Function or Sub called from the current Function or Sub, but you don't see it. The code executes in the background.

When you suspect that the called Function or Sub has an error, use the Step Into button to go into that Function or Sub from the current location. The IDE moves the cursor from the current position to the called Function or Sub so that you can see the code while it executes. You still view one line at a time when using this button. The difference is that you see the called code in addition to the Function or Sub of interest.

When you debug a called Function or Sub, you might decide that there really isn't an error in that section of the code. Instead of stepping through one statement at a time until you return to the calling code, you can use the Step Out button to return immediately. VBA still executes all the code in the called function — it just happens in real time rather than one line at a time.

Viewing the data tips

When you execute a program break, you can view the current value of variables in several ways. The easiest way is to use the data tips feature shown in Figure 6-7. (See the upcoming "Using the Locals Window" and "Using the Watch Window" sections for other techniques.) To see this view, simply hover the mouse over any variable, including objects.

Figure 6-7:
Rely on data tips whenever possible to see the value of a variable.

Using the Immediate window to your advantage

The Immediate window is a valuable debugging tool. You can display the Immediate window by clicking the Immediate Window button on the Debug toolbar (refer to Figure 6-6). In Chapter 1, I show how you can actually create a mini-program by using it. The Immediate window can perform simple assignments, and you can use it to determine the value of a variable.

The Immediate window can act as an output screen. The most common way to use the Immediate window as an output is the Debug.Print method. Here in Listing 6-6 is some code showing how to use this valuable debugging method. (You can find the source code for this example on the Dummies.com site at http://www.dummies.com/go/mueller.)

Listing 6-6   Using the Debug Object

```
Public Sub UseDebug()
    ' The variable that receives the input.
    Dim InNumber As Byte

    ' Ask the user for some input.
    InNumber = InputBox("Type a number between 1 and " + _
                    "10.", "Numberic Input", "1")

    ' Print the value of InNumber to the Immediate window.
    Debug.Print "InNumber = " + CStr(InNumber)

    ' Stop program execution if InNumber is not in the
    ' correct range.
    Debug.Assert (InNumber >= 1) And (InNumber <= 10)

    ' Display the result.
    MsgBox "The Number You Typed: " + CStr(InNumber), _
        vbOKOnly Or vbInformation, _
        "Successful Input"
End Sub
```

Notice how this sample uses the Debug.Print and the Debug.Assert methods in combination. The Debug.Print method outputs the current values to the Immediate window, and the Debug.Assert method checks for a specific input range. When the range is incorrect, the program breaks, and you can see the errant value in the Immediate window.

Using the Locals Window

The Locals window shows all the variables that the current code segment can see. This means that you can see variables defined within the current Sub or Function as well as global variables. You display the Locals window by clicking the Locals Window button on the toolbar. Figure 6-8 shows a typical example of the Locals window.

The Locals window displays three kinds of information: variable name, value, and data type. You can see two global variables at the top of Figure 6-8. Immediately below the global variables is FreeSpace, a local Long. The current value is the amount of space on the C drive of my system.

Figure 6-8: Use the Locals window to see visible variables.

Two objects appear next in the list. Normally, just the object name appears in the list. Click the plus sign next to the name, and you see the object properties and their values. Notice that the MyDrive.AvailableSpace property matches the FreeSpace value because I stopped the program immediately after the drive space assignment. (See the earlier "Recovering from an error" section for details.)

Objects can contain other objects. MyDrive is a Drive object that contains a RootFolder object. Notice the plus sign next to RootFolder in Figure 6-8. Click this plus sign, and the Locals window shows the contents of the second object. You can continue looking through a hierarchy of objects until you reach the last one contained within the original object.

The Locals window is also handy for playing "what if" scenarios with your program. The `DriveTest` program always fails because the check value is too high. You can double-click the Value field of the `FreeSpace` entry to change its value to 1,000,000,001. The check passes now because `FreeSpace` is one more than the check value. Try this test; the program exits without error.

Using the Watch window

The Watch window works similarly to the Locals window, but it has a different purpose. The Locals window shows variables in their raw format and only the variables that you can see locally. You might want to see other variables, or you can use a function to change a variable before viewing it. The Watch window helps you perform these kinds of tasks, but it requires a little more work to use. You can display the Watch window by clicking the Watch Window button on the toolbar. Figure 6-9 shows a typical example of the Watch window.

Expression	Value	Type	Context
CStr(FreeSpace)	"152403968"	String	ErrorCondition.DriveTest
FreeSpace < 1000000000	True	Boolean	ErrorCondition.DriveTest
MyDrive.AvailableSpace	152403968	Variant/Long	ErrorCondition.DriveTest
Result	0	Long	ErrorCondition.DriveTest

Notice that this window does add a Context field. This field tells you where a variable is defined. Because you can use variables from any location, knowing where they come from is important.

Adding a new watch expression

The easiest way to add a watch expression is to highlight the expression in your code and then drag it to the Watch window. VBA automatically enters all the correct information for you — you don't need to do anything else but look at the value. You can also highlight the expression and click the Quick Watch button on the toolbar. When you use this method, you see a Quick Watch dialog box that tells you about the new watch expression. Click Add to add the new watch or click Cancel to change your mind.

Using the Add Watch dialog box

A watch expression might be more complex than a single variable or even an expression in your code. Look at the first expression in Figure 6-9. This expression doesn't come from the code — I created it by using the Add Watch dialog box. The Add Watch dialog box (see Figure 6-10) gives you full control over the expression. To display the Add Watch dialog box, highlight any expression in your code, right-click the highlight, and then choose Add Watch from the context menu that appears.

Figure 6-10:
The Add
Watch
dialog box
helps you
modify
existing
expressions
or create
new ones.

You can modify an expression by changing the content of the Expression field. For example, in Figure 6-9, I highlighted the FreeSpace entry in the code and added the CStr part of the expression. You can also use this dialog box to change the context of a watch expression. It might help to have access to global variables in every procedure and not just the current procedure. A common local variable could also appear in more than one Sub or Function.

Notice the three options in the Watch Type group. VBA assumes that you want to create a watch expression. That's what you get when you create a quick watch or use the drag-and-drop method. You can also set a watch to cause the program to break when the value is true or when it changes. Creating a break condition is one of the more interesting ways to use the Watch window.

Chapter 7

Interacting with the User

* *

In This Chapter

▶ Using forms to interact with the user

▶ Creating forms by using controls

▶ Designing forms for specific Microsoft Office applications

* *

*V*BA utility programs can usually perform their jobs without too much input. However, a VBA program that helps you perform a task usually needs some type of input. A *form* provides fields where you can enter additional information or read additional information. You might need a form that asks about the machine environment or how to interact with the data. Forms can also provide formatted output in ways that a message box can't. You can include fields on the form that format data and present it in a useful manner. You use forms constantly in Windows in the form of dialog boxes and data entry windows.

In this chapter, I provide an overview of VBA forms. You can also find forms in most of the remaining chapters of this book. VBA forms can include complex concepts, but the best forms are simple and easy to use. The examples in this chapter concentrate on the idea of simplicity. Other chapters build on this base and demonstrate special kinds of forms.

Understanding Forms

It's easy to think of forms as blobs with controls attached because so many examples of bad form design are available. Well-designed forms consider a number of requirements such as how the information flows from one area to the next. A form also needs prompts that are easy to understand as well as a pleasing presentation. You might think that designing such a form is hard, but if you follow the same strategy that you do with other areas of programming, you can create great forms with relative ease.

Using forms creatively

Good design begins when you consider how your application uses the information that appears on the form and how you want to interact with it. A form that presents every piece of information that you might ever need sounds good until you try to use it. A form should contain focused information that easily fits on any display that you use. You might find that you need to design a series of forms that appear in sequence.

Another consideration is clutter. Even if you create a focused form, it might contain too much nonessential information. That's why you see Details and Properties buttons of various kinds on forms. When you need to see the details, you can click the button to present another form. Otherwise, you can ignore the details and provide just the essentials.

Add informational forms to your program as needed. When a program completes a task, the program should tell you about it. A message box that says, "I'm done" might seem appropriate, but often it's a nuisance. You can include program statistics or other helpful information. I often build statistical forms into my programs so that I can monitor performance. When I see that the program isn't performing as expected, I know that I need to look for potential problems. I often fix the problem long before it becomes a work-stopping issue.

The important thing to remember is that a form is interaction between a person and the program running on the computer. If the form that you design doesn't evoke a response, perhaps you haven't used it creatively enough. You should be able to look at a form and have a good idea of its purpose. Each control (such as a push button) should provide *balloon help* (the little window that pops up when you hover the mouse) that helps anyone using the form to understand the intent of that control. Finally, context-sensitive help and other forms of visual aid should make difficult forms easy to understand.

Designing a form for your application

When you use the Forms Designer, it's easy to get the idea that the VBA Integrated Development Environment (IDE) is somehow performing magic on your behalf by creating forms visually. A form is simply a specialized kind of code, and you use code to perform a number of tasks in the book. Forms are simply an extension of what you do when you perform any other task. The only difference is that a form is visual: It presents information onscreen in a form that the user can see.

To begin this example, you need to add a few references that VBA doesn't provide. Use the Tools⇨References command to display the Reference dialog box. Select the Microsoft Visual Basic for Applications Extensibility 5.3

Library, as shown in Figure 7-1. Make sure that you also have the other references shown selected.

Figure 7-1:
Adding
these
references
can make it
easy to
create your
own
dynamic
forms.

The easiest way to design a form is by using the IDE. In the upcoming "Using the Basic Controls" section of this chapter, I show this traditional method of form design, which is also the method that I use in the other examples in this book. A form that you design using these tools is static — you decide how it looks during the design phase of your program.

However, you can also design forms by using code. A coded form is dynamic because you can change its appearance quite easily while the program is running. No one says that you have to use the IDE. If you want, you can create anything that you need in VBA by using pure code. An interesting way to use this technique is to create custom forms based on criteria that you decide while the program is running. (You can also store this information on disk.) Listing 7-1 shows an example of a simple form created by using the code method. (You can find the source code for this example on the Dummies.com site at http://www.dummies.com/go/mueller.)

Listing 7-1   Creating a Form Dynamically Using Only Code

```
Public Sub ShowFirstForm()
    ' Used to keep track of the lines of code.
    Dim Count As Integer

    ' Create the form object.
    Dim FirstForm As VBComponent
    Set FirstForm = _
        ThisWorkbook.VBProject.VBComponents.Add( _
```

(continued)

Listing 7-1 *(continued)*

```
          vbext_ct_MSForm)

' Give the form a caption.
FirstForm.Properties("Caption") = "Custom Dialog Box"

' Add a command button to the form.
With FirstForm.Designer.Controls.Add( _
          "Forms.CommandButton.1", _
          "btnOK", _
          True)

    ' Configure the command button for use.
    .Left = 156
    .Top = 6
    .Caption = "OK"
End With

' Add some code so btnOK is functional.
With FirstForm.CodeModule

    ' Get the current number of lines of code.
    Count = .CountOfLines

    ' Insert code at the end.
    ' Begin by creating a Private Sub statement.
    .InsertLines Count + 1, "Private Sub btnOK_Click"

    ' Display a message that says "Goodbye!"
    .InsertLines Count + 2, "MsgBox " + Chr(&H22) + _
                      "Goodbye!" + Chr(&H22)

    ' Close the dialog box so the program can end.
    .InsertLines Count + 3, "Unload Me"

    ' End the Sub.
    .InsertLines Count + 4, "End Sub"
End With

' Create a label.
With FirstForm.Designer.Controls.Add( _
          "Forms.Label.1", _
          "lblMessage", _
          True)

    ' Configure the label.
    .Left = 23
    .Top = 60
    .Width = 190
    .Height = 90
    .Caption = "This is a custom form that shows " + _
               "there is no magic in the IDE. " + _
```

```
                              "You can create any form you want " + _
                              "using simple code."
        End With


        ' Display the form.
        VBA.UserForms.Add(FirstForm.Name).Show

        ' Remove the form from the worksheet.
        ThisWorkbook.VBProject.VBComponents.Remove _
             VBComponent:=FirstForm
End Sub
```

The code begins by creating a form. This process might look confusing at first, but it's the same process that you use to add a form. The only difference is that you're using code to perform the task instead of using the IDE. You can also use the vbext_ct_ClassModule to create a class module and the vbext_ct_StdModule constant to create a standard module.

Notice the technique used to access the form properties. The example modifies the Caption property so that you can see a nice form title. This technique appears in several places in the book. It enables you to access elements of a collection. See Chapter 9 for a description of collections.

Forms contain controls such as command buttons and labels. You use these controls in every form that Windows displays. The first control that the example adds is a command button. The first argument is the special identifier used for the control in the Windows Registry. You can find a list of these identifiers in the MSForms Add Method help topic. The second argument is the name of the control. This is the name that you use to access the control. The third argument determines whether VBA makes the control visible.

This code uses the With structure. You can use the With structure as shown in the code to avoid typing the full name of the control every time. Notice how each of the statements within the With structure begins with a period to show that they're part of the control specified by the With expression.

After the code creates the command button control, it changes some of the control properties. The changes give the control a caption and place it in the upper-right corner of the form.

To make the command button functional, you need to add some code. This special code is an *event handler*. See the later "Handling form events" section of this chapter for details. The code must create the Sub dynamically after the control is created so that VBA associates the code with the control. The Sub displays a message box and closes the dialog box every time that you click OK.

The code also adds a label to the dialog box. The label requires a little more formatting but doesn't require any code.

After the form is complete, the code can add it to the list of user forms that VBA maintains by using the Add method. The same statement tells VBA to display the form by using the Show method. The code pauses, at this point, because it waits for you to interact with the form. Figure 7-2 shows what the form looks like when you display it.

The final step removes the form from the document. If you don't include this step, the program keeps creating new forms until the document becomes absurdly large. Always remove the forms that you create.

Figure 7-2:
A dynamic
form
example.

Custom Dialog Box

OK

This is a custom form that shows there is no magic in the IDE. you can create any form you want using simple code.

Considering the form layout

The way that you design your form is important. When you use a well-designed form, you feel good about the program. A form with a good layout is easy to use and understand. Here are some design elements that you should consider for your form (all of which appear in examples in this chapter):

- **Flow:** The controls on a form should naturally flow from one element to the next. For example, you should place the fields on the form so that someone performing a task, such as typing an address, types the name first, the company second, the address third, and so forth.

- **Prompts:** Forms should always have prompts for every field. Some forms in applications that you use probably have blank fields that don't contain any information. Unless you hover the mouse over the field, you don't know the field's purpose.

- **Decoration:** Gaudy forms make people ill, but you can still embellish the forms that you create a little. A company logo or other form of simple decoration makes a drab form nicer to use.

- **Accelerator keys:** You might not like moving your hand from the keyboard to the mouse every time that you want to select a new control. In fact, many people find this requirement difficult or impossible. Using accelerator keys (shown as an underlined letter) lets someone use just the keyboard to access the controls on your form.

✔ **Control choice:** VBA provides you with a good selection of useful tools in the Toolbox. If you find these choices limiting, you can always add new controls to the Toolbox. Always use the right control for the job. Not every data entry task requires a `TextBox`. Some tasks require a `ListBox`, a `ComboBox`, a `CheckBox`, or an `OptionButton` control. (See the upcoming Figure 7-3 for a list of standard controls.)

✔ **Flexibility:** A form requires some level of flexibility to display properly on every system. You might need to use your program on a system with a smaller display, which means that you might have to resize the form. If you use a laptop, you might have to use the high contrast setting to see the display, which means that the characters are larger and that the form might not display correctly.

Using the Basic Controls

VBA provides a good set of basic controls, as shown in Figure 7-3. You might use VBA to create a number of programs and never need anything more than the basic control set. In fact, the basic control set meets just about every need, and you seldom see anything other than these controls used in Windows programs.

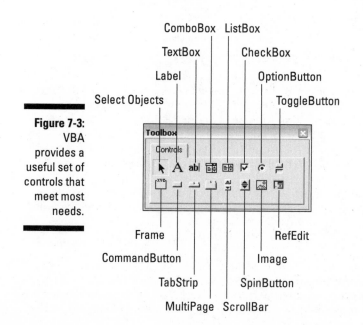

Figure 7-3: VBA provides a useful set of controls that meet most needs.

Click the Select Objects button (refer to Figure 7-3) whenever you want to select any object on a form. VBA selects this button by default. It also picks the Select Objects button after you add a new control to a form.

Adding controls to the form

Before you can add controls to a form, you need a form. Right-click anywhere in the Project window and then choose Insert⇨UserForm from the context menu that appears. After you add the form, make sure that you give it an easily remembered name by changing the `Name` property in the Properties window. Use the `Caption` property to change the text on the title bar.

The easiest and least error-prone method of adding a control to a form is to select the control in the Toolbox and then click the area of the form where you want the control to appear. The mouse cursor points to the upper-left corner of the control. The cross cursor makes it easy to place the control accurately. You might need to organize the controls after you add them because it isn't easy to add the controls precisely. See the upcoming "Making your form pretty" section for details.

Another method for adding controls to a form is to drag the control from the Toolbox and then drop it on the form. The reason why this method is less precise is that you don't always see the control's location. The IDE displays a box showing the outline of the control, so you do see the basic layout when using this method.

Using the Label control to display text

You use the `Label` control to display text onscreen. A `Label` is for informational purposes. Although you can copy the content of a `Label`, you can't change it directly. The most common use for labels is to identify other controls and to provide accelerator key access to them. (See the upcoming "Modifying the form and control properties" section of this chapter for details on adding an accelerator key.) Labels also act as output for read-only text.

Figure 7-4 shows a simple form with two labels. The first label has `Message Text` in the `Caption` property. It uses M as the `Accelerator` property value, so the <u>M</u> in Message Text is underlined. When you press Alt+M, VBA selects the `TextBox` control associated with the first label.

The second label contains `Message Output:` in the Caption property. This label receives the output from the `TextBox` when you click the Test button. Here's some sample code that shows the `btnTest_Click` event handler. (You can find the source code for this example on the Dummies.com site at `http://www.dummies.com/go/mueller`.)

```
Private Sub btnTest_Click()
    ' Move the information from the TextBox input to the
    ' label output.
    lblOutput.Caption = "Message Output: " + vbCrLf + _
                        txtInput.Text
End Sub
```

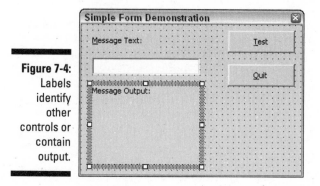

Figure 7-4:
Labels
identify
other
controls or
contain
output.

VBA executes this code whenever you click the Test button. The name of the
control is btnTest, and the name of the event is Click, so the name of the
Sub is btnTest_Click. The result of this code is that lblOutput, the output
label, contains the text that it originally contained plus the contents of the
TextBox control, txtInput.

You might wonder why I begin the control names in this example with lbl,
txt, or btn. The most important reason why I use this naming strategy (or
notation) is that VBA sorts the controls for me so that I can quickly find the
one that I want. For example, Figure 7-5 shows the object list in the Properties
window. Notice that using the notation makes it easy to find the controls.

Figure 7-5:
Use a
standard
notation for
control
names.

Getting user input with text boxes

The TextBox control makes it possible to request information from the user. This control doesn't have a Caption property because it doesn't provide any visual identification. You should always use the TextBox control with a Label control, as shown in Figure 7-4, so that everyone can see what kind of input that the TextBox is supposed to get.

You use the Text property to access the content of the TextBox control. Even if you type a number, the TextBox control treats it like a string. VBA automatically performs a conversion between a numeric variable and the TextBox control for you in many cases. For example, the following code (see Listing 7-2) works just fine. (You can find the source code for this example on the Dummies.com site at http://www.dummies.com/go/mueller.)

Listing 7-2   Using the Text and Caption Properties

```
Private Sub btnTest_Click()
    ' Create the input variable.
    Dim InputValue As Integer

    ' Tell VBA about the error handler.
    On Error GoTo NotANumber

    ' Get the string value and place it in the numeric
    ' variable.
    InputValue = txtInput.Text

    ' Tell the user what they typed.
    lblOutput.Caption = InputValue

    ' Exit the Sub.
    Exit Sub

    ' Handle non-numeric input.
NotANumber:
    MsgBox "You must type a number!"
End Sub
```

The example code places the value contained in the txtInput.Text property into Input. VBA performs the conversion automatically as long as the user types a number. If you use this technique, always provide error handling, as shown in the example code after the NotANumber label. Otherwise, if the user types something other than a number, the program displays an error message.

The conversion process works in both directions. Notice that the `lblOutput.Caption` property accepts `InputValue` as acceptable input. If you decide to add text to the output value, you still need to use the `CStr` function to convert the number to a string. Otherwise, VBA displays a type mismatch error.

Executing tasks with command buttons

Command buttons are the main form of action. The default event (action) is a click. Whenever you click the button, it generates a special message known as an *event*. See the later "Handling form events" section for details on events and how they work.

Like the `Label` control, the `CommandButton` control has a `Caption` property so that you can type text that appears on the button face when you start the program. In addition, you can use the `Accelerator` property to make it easy to access the button by using an Alt+key combination. The example in this section uses three command buttons to perform three different tasks. Figure 7-6 shows the output of the example.

Figure 7-6: Command buttons help you choose actions to perform with your program.

Listing 7-3 shows the code that you need to create this example. (You can find the source code for this example on the Dummies.com site at `http://www.dummies.com/go/mueller`.)

Listing 7-3   Using the Clipboard to Copy Data

```
Private Sub btnCopy_Click()
    ' Create a Clipboard storage object.
    Dim ClipData As DataObject
    Set ClipData = New DataObject

    ' Place the text in lblOutput in the Clipboard.
    ClipData.SetText lblOutput.Caption

    ' Place the object on the Clipboard.
    ClipData.PutInClipboard
End Sub

Private Sub btnQuit_Click()
    'End the program.
    End
End Sub

Private Sub btnTest_Click()
    ' Create a string to hold the data.
    Dim Output As String

    ' Create a document property holder.
    Dim DocProp As DocumentProperty

    ' Handle properties that the application doesn't support.
    On Error Resume Next

    ' Start creating the output string.
    For Each DocProp In _
    ActiveWorkbook.BuiltinDocumentProperties
        Output = Output + DocProp.Name + " = " + _
                 CStr(DocProp.Value) + vbCrLf
    Next

    ' Display the output onscreen.
    lblOutput.Caption = Output

    ' Enable the Copy Data button.
    btnCopy.Enabled = TrueEnd
Sub
```

VBA puts your code in alphabetical order when you work with forms, which changes the appearance of the code but not the actual flow. This technique makes it easier to find a particular Sub. However, it can also make it more difficult to follow the expected flow of the program. The code begins with btnTest_Click because btnCopy is disabled when you start the program.

The "Writing Your First Sub" section of Chapter 3 shows how to retrieve just one value from the BuiltinDocumentProperties collection. This example shows how to use the `For Each...Next` statement to retrieve all the values available for an application.

Notice that `btnTest_Click` uses the `On Error Resume Next` statement. This program shows one of the few times where that statement is the correct one to use. Not every application supports every built-in property. If you try to retrieve the value of a built-in property that the application doesn't support, VBA generates an error. Because there's nothing that you should do to correct the error, resuming with the next statement is the correct error-handling strategy.

After the code retrieves all the built-in document properties, it places the information in the `lblOutput.Caption` property, which displays the information onscreen. The code also enables `btnCopy` by setting its `Enabled` property as true.

The `btnCopy_Click` sub-procedure introduces the `DataObject` type. You might need to interact with the Clipboard when writing an application. This object is what you use to perform the interaction. The `DataObject` methods help you retrieve information from the Clipboard, place information on the Clipboard, and format Clipboard data.

Working with the Clipboard is normally a two-step process. To place data on the Clipboard, the code must place it in the `DataObject` first by using the `SetText` method. The next step uses the `PutInClipboard` method to move the data from the `DataObject` to the Clipboard. To get data from the Clipboard, follow the opposite procedure. Use the `GetFromClipboard` method to place the text on the Clipboard into the `DataObject` and then use the `GetText` method to move the data from the `DataObject` to a variable.

Every program that you create should include some means of ending. A dialog box-based program, like the one in this section, normally includes a Quit or an Exit button. A configuration dialog box normally relies on the OK or Cancel button to perform cleanup and exit. The `btnQuit_Click` sub-procedure for this example performs a simple task — it uses the End statement to end the program.

Saying yes or no with check boxes and toggle buttons

The `CheckBox` and `ToggleButton` controls are Boolean — controls with a true or false value. The implication of each control is different. A `CheckBox` control normally indicates yes or no. On the other hand, a `ToggleButton` indicates an on or off condition. You can use the controls as you see fit, but this is the normal way to work with them.

Both controls use the `Click` event to indicate a change in status. In addition, both controls use the `Value` property to show their status (checked or toggled). Each control maintains its status information automatically — you don't have to do anything special. This feature is useful when creating various types of toggled setups in addition to the more mundane task of providing input to a form. Figure 7-7 shows an example of how you can use both control types for a toggle application.

Figure 7-7:
Use these controls as information input or as toggle switches.

Listing 7-4 shows the code that you need to create this example. (You can find the source code for this example on the Dummies.com site at `http://www.dummies.com/go/mueller`.)

Listing 7-4   Using Check Boxes

```
Private Sub cbChecked_Click()
    ' Verify the checked status.
    If cbChecked.Value Then
        ' Display a message.
        MsgBox "CheckBox Checked"

    Else
        ' Display a message.
        MsgBox "Checkbox Cleared"
    End If
End Sub

Private Sub tbCBEnable_Click()
    ' Check the state of cbChecked.
    If tbCBEnable.Value Then
        ' Disable cbChecked.
        cbChecked.Enabled = True

        ' Change the caption.
```

```
        tbCBEnable.Caption = "CheckBox Enabled"

    Else
        ' Enable cdChecked.
        cbChecked.Enabled = False

        ' Change the caption.
        tbCBEnable.Caption = "CheckBox Disabled"
    End If
End Sub
```

When the program starts, cbChecked is disabled, and tbCBEnable is in the non-depressed state. Click the CheckBox Disabled button, and the code calls tbCBEnable_Click. This sub-procedure checks the status of the tbCBEnable.Value property to determine which course of action to take. In both cases, it changes the state of cbChecked by using the Enabled property and the ToggleButton Caption property. The code doesn't need to consider the Value property because the control changes it automatically.

After the CheckBox is enabled, you can click it. This time, the code calls the cbChecked_Click sub-procedure. The code checks the cbChecked.Value property and displays the appropriate message box. Again, the control automatically changes the value, so you don't have to keep track of it.

You could easily exchange the roles of the controls in this case. There's no reason to avoid using the ToggleButton as a yes/no indicator or the CheckBox as an on/off toggle. However, when you build your application, you need to consider how the visual presentation affects you. Although the two controls work precisely the same, the ToggleButton does present as an on/off switch, and the CheckBox does present as a yes/no indicator.

Making choices with option buttons and frames

You never use the OptionButton control alone. This control always appears in groups. A group of OptionButton controls lets you make one selection from a list of selections. Only one OptionButton control is selected at any given time, so selecting one automatically deselects all the other buttons.

Because the OptionButton controls work in a group, you have to tell VBA which controls belong to which group, especially if a form contains more than one group. You can create groups in one of two ways. The first technique is to add the same string to the GroupName property of each memory of the group. The advantage of using this method is that it requires less space and can make your program work faster. In addition, this method is transparent so that any background image that you use on the form shows through.

The second method is to place the `OptionButton` controls in a `Frame` control. To use this technique, you must create the `Frame` control first and then place the `OptionButton` controls within the `Frame` control. The advantage of using this method is that it's less error prone (the first method depends on you typing the same string each time and not making a typo), and you can visually see which buttons belong in the same group. Frames can also provide special visual effects, such as a sunken control group. Figure 7-8 shows examples of both `OptionButton` group methods.

Figure 7-8:
Use the
`Option`
`Button`
control to
select one
of many
choices.

Unfortunately, a group of `OptionButton` controls still acts as individuals. You have to monitor each control separately.

One way to monitor option button groups is to create a global variable and use the `Click` event of each control to change it. This method provides a slight performance boost because you don't have to determine which `OptionButton` is selected when you want to perform a task — the status is always known. The disadvantage of this method is that it requires slightly more code and a little more memory, and the global variable could be a source of errors. Listing 7-5 shows an example of using the global variable approach. (You can find the source code for this example on the Dummies.com site at `http://www.dummies.com/go/mueller`.)

Listing 7-5   Using Global Variables with Option Buttons

```
Private ColorSelect As String
Private NumberSelect As String

Private Sub btnStatus_Click()
    ' Create an output string.
    Dim Output As String
    Output = "The selected color is: " + ColorSelect + _
             vbCrLf + _
             "The selected number is: " + NumberSelect
```

```
                    "The selected number is: " + NumberSelect


        ' Display the result.
        MsgBox Output
End Sub

Private Sub obBlue_Click()
        ' Change the ColorSelect value.
        ColorSelect = obBlue.Caption
End Sub

Private Sub obGreen_Click()
        ' Change the ColorSelect value.
        ColorSelect = obGreen.Caption
End Sub

Private Sub obOne_Click()
        ' Change the NumberSelect value.
        NumberSelect = obOne.Caption
End Sub

Private Sub obRed_Click()
        ' Change the ColorSelect value.
        ColorSelect = obRed.Caption
End Sub

Private Sub obThree_Click()
        ' Change the NumberSelect value.
        NumberSelect = obThree.Caption
End Sub

Private Sub obTwo_Click()
        ' Change the NumberSelect value.
        NumberSelect = obTwo.Caption
End Sub

Private Sub UserForm_Initialize()
        'Set the initial global values.
        ColorSelect = obRed.Caption
        NumberSelect = obOne.Caption
End Sub
```

Using global variables means that you have to set them to some initial value. The UserForm_Initialize sub-procedure performs this task when you start the program. When you click each OptionButton control, VBA calls the appropriate Click event handler. The event handler changes one of the two global variables, ColorSelect or NumberSelect, as appropriate. Click the Status button, and VBA calls the btnStatus_Click sub-procedure. Notice that this sub-procedure has little work to do because the program tracks the option button status.

Another approach is to use a series of `If...Then...ElseIf` statements to determine which `OptionButton` control is selected by using the `Value` property. Listing 7-6 shows a sample of the selection process that uses this second method.

Listing 7-6   Making Selections with Option Buttons

```
Private Sub btnElseIfSelect_Click()
    ' Create an output string.
    Dim Output As String
    Output = "The selected color is: "

    ' Determine the color value.
    If obRed.Value Then
        Output = Output + "Red"
    ElseIf obGreen.Value Then
        Output = Output + "Green"
    Else
        Output = Output + "Blue"
    End If

    ' Add the number string.
    Output = Output + vbCrLf + "The selected number is: "

    ' Determine the number value.
    If obOne.Value Then
        Output = Output + "One"
    ElseIf obTwo.Value Then
        Output = Output + "Two"
    Else
        Output = Output + "Three"
    End If

    ' Display the result.
    MsgBox Output
End Sub
```

The code begins by determining the status of the color option buttons. It uses the `Value` properties to perform this task. After the code determines the color option status, it creates that part of the `Output` string and moves on to the number values. The code uses the same procedure as before to determine the number option status.

Both of these techniques display the same output. The difference between the two techniques is where they perform their work. If you use the first technique, you write more code to gain a performance advantage. The second method requires just one sub-procedure and no global variables but can result in a performance hit.

Choosing options with list boxes and combo boxes

You use `OptionButton` controls when you want to create a *static* list — one that doesn't ever change. The `ListBox` and `ComboBox` controls help you create *dynamic* lists — lists that can change while the program runs or from session to session. The list of options doesn't have to change, but knowing that you have the option is helpful.

Both controls require that you *populate* (fill) them with information. The easiest method is to use the `AddItem` method. Use this method when you populate the control with the same information each time that the program starts. You can also create an array and add the array to the `List` property. The advantage of this second method is that you can pass different arrays to a function or sub-procedure when the list content requirements change. (See Chapter 9 for details on using arrays.)

You need to consider differences in these two controls when designing an application. The `ComboBox` is smaller, but it only displays the selected option. To see all the options, you have to click the down-arrow. The `ListBox` is a bit more accessible because it displays many (but not necessarily all of the) options at once.

The default `ComboBox` setting also lets the user type in a value other than those presented. This makes the `ComboBox` more flexible, but it also means that you have to deal with input errors. Set the `MatchRequired` property to `True` if you want the `ComboBox` to limit the input to the choices that you provide. A `ListBox` always limits input to the choices that you provide, so there's never a chance for input that causes a program error.

The advantage of using a `ListBox` is that you can set the `MultiSelect` property to allow the user to make more than one choice. This feature lets you limit the input choices while allowing multiple inputs. Use the `Selected` property to determine which entries are highlighted. The `Value` property is always `Null` (set to nothing) when you allow multiple selections.

Both of these controls require less code than the `OptionButton` control to perform approximately the same task. Listing 7-7 shows an example of both the `ComboBox` and the `ListBox` in action. (You can find the source code for this example on the Dummies.com site at `http://www.dummies.com/go/mueller.)`

Listing 7-7   Working with List Boxes and Combo Boxes

```
Private Sub btnStatus_Click()
    ' Create an output string.
    Dim Output As String
    Output = "The selected color is: " + _
             comboColors.Value + vbCrLf + _
             "The selected number is: " + listNumbers.Value

    ' Display the result.
    MsgBox Output
End Sub

Private Sub UserForm_Initialize()
    ' Populate the ListBox control.
    listNumbers.AddItem "One"
    listNumbers.AddItem "Two"
    listNumbers.AddItem "Three"
    listNumbers.AddItem "Four"
    listNumbers.AddItem "Five"
    listNumbers.AddItem "Six"

    ' Select the default value.
    listNumbers.Value = "One"

    ' Populate the ComboBox control.
    comboColors.AddItem "Red"
    comboColors.AddItem "Green"
    comboColors.AddItem "Blue"
    comboColors.AddItem "Yellow"
    comboColors.AddItem "Orange"
    comboColors.AddItem "Purple"

    ' Select the default value.
    comboColors.Value = "Red"
End Sub
```

The code begins in the UserForm_Initialize sub-procedure. You must populate the two controls by using the AddItem method. Setting the Value property to one of the values that you provide selects that value in the list.

The btnStatus_Click sub-procedure retrieves the current selections that use the control's Value property. It displays a message box containing essentially the same information as the OptionButton example in the preceding "Making choices with option buttons and frames" section.

Although this code performs essentially the same task as the OptionButton code, it requires far less code. In fact, this code actually provides more input choices than the OptionButton example.

Adding controls to the Toolbox

You might find that you need other controls to create your program. Windows provides a wealth of controls that you can use. The Toolbox that VBA provides only has a few essential controls in it — you can always add more by using the following procedure:

1. **Right-click anywhere on the Controls page of Toolbox and then choose Additional Controls from the context menu that appears.**

   You see the Additional Controls dialog box as shown in Figure 7-9.

Figure 7-9:
Add
controls to
your
Toolbox by
using the
options in
this dialog
box.

2. **Select the control that you want to add to your Toolbox by placing a check next to its entry.**

3. **Click OK.**

   VBA adds the selected control to your Toolbox.

The Toolbox can get crowded after you add a few controls to it. You can add additional pages to the Toolbox by right-clicking outside the existing pages and then choosing New Page from the context menu that appears. Getting rid of a page is as easy as selecting that page, right-clicking outside the page area, and then choosing Delete Page from the context menu that appears. It's also easy to move and rename pages by using context menu entries.

Using the Forms You Create

Forms are only useful if they're usable. This means modifying the form and control properties to provide a pleasant appearance. You should change certain properties every time that you create a form to ensure that everyone can use it easily. Arranging the content of the form onscreen is important, as is making sure that the form operates correctly. Finally, you need to know how to handle events that the form generates to ensure that you see the expected results.

Modifying the form and control properties

In previous sections of the chapter, I mention properties that you can change on your form or control to get specific results. Whenever you select the form or a control that it contains, the Properties window changes to match the selection.

You might look at the enormous list of properties provided with the form and controls and wonder how you can memorize them all. The fact is that you don't have to memorize any of them. To see what a task a property performs, highlight that property and then press F1. VBA provides property-specific help.

Some properties provide exceptional value from a user perspective. Always define the Accelerator property for your controls. This property lets someone use the keyboard to access the control rather than the mouse. It's an essential property if you want to make your program accessible to those with special needs.

When you use a Label control to provide accelerator key access for a control that doesn't include a Caption property, make sure that the TabIndex property value for the Label is one less than the control that it references. For example, if a TextBox has a TabIndex value of 5, the associated Label should have a TabIndex value of 4. Otherwise, the accelerator key won't work as anticipated.

Another important property is ControlTipText. Type a description of the control's purpose in this property. When you hover the mouse over the control, VBA displays the text that you typed as balloon help. This kind of help is a halfway point between the prompt that you type and the context-sensitive help that your program should provide. It gives additional information without opening the help file.

Every control should have a `Caption` property entry. If the control doesn't provide a `Caption` property (such as a `TextBox` control), make sure that you add a `Label` to act as a prompt for the control.

Making your form pretty

Creating a neat appearance for your form is important. You want to use a form that looks nice because the appearance of the form affects the attitude of those who use it. VBA provides a number of options on the Format menu for making your form look nice. These same options appear on the UserForm toolbar in button form (see Figure 7-10).

Figure 7-10: Make your form look nice by using the Designer window features.

Notice that some of the buttons on the UserForm toolbar have down-arrows associated with them. Click the down-arrow, and you see a list of potential button functions for that button. Select the option that you want to use.

Aligning controls begins when you select two or more controls on the same form, as shown in Figure 7-10. Use a Ctrl+left-click to select each control in turn. The last control that you select acts as the guide for aligning the other controls, so make sure that the last control is in the position that you want to use for the other controls. If you want to align the tops of the controls, select the Format➪Align➪Tops command. You can perform tasks such as centering individual controls by using the Format➪Center in Form menu options.

Displaying the form onscreen

Displaying a form onscreen is easy. Simply use the Show method, as shown in Listing 7-8.

Listing 7-8   Displaying a Form

```
Public Sub ShowAForm()
    ' Use the Show method to show a form.
    ' You can perform other tasks using a modeless form.
    ButtonDemo.Show vbModeless

    ' A modal form requires that you complete the task with
    ' that form before you proceed to other tasks.
    NumericText.Show vbModal
End Sub
```

The problem that many developers have is deciding between a modal and a modeless form. Always use a *modeless* form if you want to display other forms or perform other tasks while the current form is displayed. Use a *modal* form when you want to ensure that any tasks for the current form complete before you display another form.

The example code shows both kinds of forms. You can try to select the ButtonDemo form, but you won't be able to do it. The NumericText form insists that you complete tasks with it before you do anything else. As soon as you finish working with the NumericText form, the program completes. VBA displays modeless forms and essentially forgets about them.

Validating user input

Always validate user input. The main source of security problems and many types of application error is user input. If the user doesn't provide the correct input, your program won't run no matter how much effort you put into it. In addition, many security exploits rely on poor program validation. A *buffer overrun,* one of the well-known causes of security problems, is simply a failure to check input. Validating user input means the following:

- ✓ **Always ensure that the input uses the correct data type.**

- ✓ **Always check the range of numeric information.** If you want numbers between 1 and 5, don't let the user input anything else.

- ✓ **Always check the value of text input whenever possible.** If you're expecting an address, look for elements in the text that make up an address.

> ✔ **Never allow the user to input special characters unless you actually need the special characters to make the input work.**
>
> ✔ **Remember to keep input simple enough so that the user knows what you want and to make it easy to check.** For example, use separate entries for city, state, and ZIP code in a contact management program.

Handling form events

Events are a part of most objects. Whenever the system, a user, or an external input interacts with your program, it's likely to generate an event. For example, when you click a button, it generates a `Click` event. An *event* is simply a way of saying that something has happened.

Forms and every control that they contain support a number of events. Look at the top of the Code window, and you see two Combo Boxes. The first is the Object list. It contains a list of every object associated with the current form. Figure 7-11 shows an example of this list. The UserForm entry is the actual form object.

Whenever you select an object, VBA automatically creates a sub-procedure for the default event that object supports (the `Click` event in many cases). You can remove this entry if you're interested in writing code for some other event.

The second Combo Box is the Procedure list. Figure 7-12 shows an example of this list box. The Procedure list contains a list of events associated with the current object. This list changes when you change entries in the Object list.

Figure 7-11:
Use the
Object list to
select
objects
associated
with the
current
form.

Figure 7-12:
Use the
Procedure
list to select
events
associated
with the
current
object.

When you look through the Procedure list, you notice that some entries are in bold. A bolded entry is one that you've added to the program. The normal text entries are events that you can choose to handle but haven't so far. To add a new event handler to the program, simply select the entry from the Procedure list. VBA adds the event Sub to your code — type your code within this Sub to handle the event.

Part III

Expanding Your VBA Horizons

The 5th Wave   By Rich Tennant

"You ever get the feeling this project could just up and die at any moment?"

In this part . . .

This is the part of the book where you move from knowing the language to using the language for beneficial work.

In Chapter 8, I show how VBA can use objects to model program elements. (For example, VBA sees every document that you create as an object with its own unique features.) Arrays and collections in VBA share similar characteristics to real-world collections. In Chapter 9, I help you understand the value of the individual elements and the collection as a whole.

In Chapter 10, I demonstrate techniques for using disk storage. Microsoft considers XML the next storage technology that everyone will want to use. In Chapter 11, I describe how XML can benefit you and how to use it within VBA.

Chapter 8

Object-Oriented Programming

*I*f you've followed each chapter of this book to this point, you've used objects to perform tasks. For example, forms and all the controls that they contain are objects. The Clipboard also requires use of an object. In short, objects are an essential part of working with VBA because they reduce the amount of code that you have to write.

In this chapter, I describe the underlying mechanisms behind objects. You can create your own objects by using VBA to design classes, which are essential object blueprints. In fact, you can create these objects and share them with other people who might need to use the same features. Using and creating objects by designing classes makes your VBA programming experience better.

Understanding Classes

A *class* is a description of an object: It's the blueprint that VBA uses to build an object when you request one. The class isn't the object; it's merely the building instructions for the object. This is important to remember because many information sources confuse objects and classes. You need to keep them separate to better understand how objects work.

You might want to think of a class as a substitute for a Function or a Sub, but classes are separate. A Function or Sub always describes a *procedure* — a list of steps. A *class* describes a thing. You can visualize a file because it's a thing. That's why VBA uses classes to describe the file system and objects to work with individual file system elements such as a drive. Although you might read that objects are substitutes for procedures, the two kinds of programming have definite places in your programmer's toolbox. Make sure that you work with both as needed.

To build an object, you tell VBA to *instantiate* (create an instance of) the object. All the code required to build the object appears in the class. As a VBA user, you create the class and not the object. Here's a simple example of the two-step process used to instantiate an object.

```
' Create a reference to the file system.
Dim MyFileSystem As FileSystemObject

' Create a reference for the target drive.
Dim MyDrive As Drive

' Fill these two objects with data so they show the
' available space on drive C.
Set MyFileSystem = New FileSystemObject
Set MyDrive = MyFileSystem.GetDrive("C")
```

VBA creates the object, `MyFileSystem`, based on the blueprint provided by the `FileSystemObject` class. Likewise, VBA creates the object, `MyDrive`, based on the `Drive` class.

Telling VBA that you want to create these two objects by using the `Dim` statement is not the same as instantiating them. The `Set` statement instantiates the object. You `Set` an object equal to the blueprint contained within a class.

You can instantiate objects by using a number of techniques — the above example shows two of them. In the first case, `MyFileSystem` is instantiated by using the `New` keyword and the name of the class, `FileSystemObject`. In the second case, `MyDrive` is instantiated based on an existing object contained within the `MyFileSystem` object. The `GetDrive` method tells VBA which `Drive` object to use within the `MyFileSystem` object.

Classes come in two varieties: components and controls. A *component* is a class that describes an object without a user interface. The `FileSystemObject` class is a component. It shows VBA how to create an object that lacks a user interface. You usually create components with VBA. All the examples in this book (such as the upcoming Listing 8-1) show how to create components.

A *control* is a class that describes an object that includes a user interface or affects the user interface. The `CommandButton` class is a control because it includes a user interface. Don't assume that every control provides a view-able piece of the user interface. When you use the Timer class, it's still a control (even if it doesn't have a user interface) because it interacts with the user and affects the user interface. It's very hard to create controls with VBA. You should use another language, such as Visual Basic (not VBA), Visual C++, or Visual C# when you want to create special controls for your VBA program.

Note that the Timer class might not appear with VBA, but you can read about it at http://msdn.microsoft.com/library/en-us/vbcon98/html/vbcontimercontrol.asp. This control is so incredibly useful that you might want to download the version that appears at Programmers Heaven (http://www.programmersheaven.com/zone15/cat872/23271.htm) even if VBA includes the standard Timer control. The Programmers Heaven version provides better control over the timing interval and can provide long-term timing.

Designing a Basic Class

Because a class is a blueprint for an object, you need to have some idea of what you want to build. The best classes are ones that answer a specific need that you have. A class requires a specific look and feel. VBA includes this look and feel as part of the objects that it creates from the class.

It helps to look at existing classes when you think about your own class to see what other people have done. All the controls provided with VBA make a good starting point because you can play with them in code to see how Microsoft designed a particular feature. You should also examine VBA objects, such as the ones used in the examples in this book. Control and component examples are readily available for your use as patterns for your own class. (See the "Locating Just the Right Code" section of Chapter 18 for ideas on where to find examples.) Here's a list of the items that you should consider copying.

- **Property, method, and event names:** Use recognizable (similar) names for properties, methods, and events. For example, don't call your Click event a Pushed event because no one will know what you mean.

- **Mandatory features:** It's easy to forget to include a feature in your class. Existing classes can help you create a complete list of mandatory features, such as a Caption property, so that nothing is left out.

- **Design style:** Your control provides unique features and functionality. However, it helps to look at the way other people design classes, especially the visual elements of the class. For example, something as simple as providing a True/False drop-down list box for Boolean properties is very helpful.

✔ **Visual aids:** A class can provide visual aids such as special dialog boxes for some types of information. Look at other classes for ideas on how you can add visual aids to your class that makes it easier to use.

✔ **Privacy:** You might find it tempting to expose every feature to anyone who might use it. However, that approach can lead to problems because objects are only supposed to expose necessary elements. Use other classes as examples of what you should keep hidden in your own class.

The example in this section shows how to create a simple class. The component encapsulates the MsgBox function and makes it easier to use by helping you see the options clearly. More importantly, the example demonstrates how to construct properties, methods, and events for this simple class.

Defining properties

A *property* describes a feature of the object, such as its color, the caption, a method of presentation (such as sunken or etched), or some other characteristic. Don't assume that a property has to describe a physical characteristic of the object. A filename is a perfectly acceptable property. A property is a special kind of object-specific data.

Property construction methods

VBA provides three kinds of construction methods for properties. You can choose to use one or all three methods. A property requires at least one of the methods that I describe in this list.

✔ **Let:** The Let method helps you set the value of a property. Use it when the property has a standard data type as an input value.

✔ **Set:** Use the Set method when you create objects that contain other objects. For example, a FileSystemObject contains Drive objects. To access these objects, you must use the Set method and not the Let method.

✔ **Get:** The Get method returns the stored property value to the caller. The method that you use for objects is different from other data types, but you can return any property value by using this method.

When you create a property, you decide not only the name and data type, but you also decide its accessibility. The accessibility is read only (using the Get method), write only (using the Set or Let method), or read/write (using the Get method along with the Set or Let method).

Properties have scope, just like everything else in VBA. Beside `Public` and `Private`, a property can also have a special `Friend` scope. The `Friend` scope is a step between `Public` and `Private`. Everything within the current project can see the property but nothing outside the current project can. The `Friend` scope is useful for local configuration. Any part of the local project — the part of the program that controls the functionality of the object — can configure the property, but your other projects can't see it.

You can also add the `Static` keyword to properties. Always add the `Static` keyword when you want the property to maintain its value between calls but not when you want to make sure that the property resets to the default value. The `Static` keyword is important when you want the object to maintain its settings.

Here in Listing 8-1 is an example of two of the read/write properties used for this example. The example actually contains several properties, but these two represent standard data type and object coding. (You can find the source code for this example on the Dummies.com site at http://www.dummies. com/go/mueller.)

Listing 8-1   Creating Object Properties

```
Private UseIcon As VbMsgBoxStyle
Private NewIcon As Image

Public Static Property Let Icon(Value As IconTypes)
    ' Change the value of the message icon based on the
    ' input value.
    Select Case Value
        Case Critical
            UseIcon = vbCritical
        Case Question
            UseIcon = vbQuestion
        Case Exclamation
            UseIcon = vbExclamation
        Case Information
            UseIcon = vbInformation
    End Select
End Property

Public Static Property Get Icon() As IconTypes
    ' Return the value of the message icon.
    Select Case UseIcon
        Case vbCritical
            Icon = Critical
        Case vbQuestion
            Icon = Question
```

(continued)

Listing 8-1 *(continued)*

```
            Case vbExclamation
                Icon = Exclamation
            Case vbInformation
                Icon = Information
        End Select
End Property

Public Static Property Set SpecialIcon(Value As Image)
    ' Set the custom icon value. Make sure the user has
    ' supplied a valid image.
    If Not Value Is Nothing Then
        Set NewIcon = Value
    End If End Property

Public Static Property Get SpecialIcon() As Image
    ' Return the custom icon value.
    Set SpecialIcon = NewIcon
End Property
```

The first property, Icon, uses a standard data type. In this case, it's an enumerated data type that ensures that you provide the correct values. See the "Using enumerated constants" section later in this chapter for details on using enumerated types. Notice that the code transfers the input value to the private UseIcon variable only after it checks the input for correctness. When you work with a non-enumerated data type, it pays to include an Else Case clause that displays a message with correct input values. Using an enumerated type means that you don't have to include this feature.

The second property, SpecialIcon, requires an object as input. This means that you must use the Set and Get methods rather than the Let and Get methods that the first property uses. Data-type checking is less intense in this case because VBA always provides a type mismatch error message if you provide the wrong value.

Notice that you still have to check for empty objects that don't contain anything. The code shows how to perform this task by using the Is Nothing keyword sequence. When you require specific kinds of input for objects, you need to check object property values as well. This example doesn't perform this task, but it's something that you should consider for complex properties. For example, an image should have a valid Picture property value.

Property conversion considerations

When you choose to encapsulate a function to make it easier to use, you can run into situations where there isn't a direct conversion between the function and the object version. The MsgBox function includes the vbMsgBoxHelpButton style. This feature works better as a Boolean property, so you use the following code to create a property for it.

```
Public Static Property Let HelpButton(Value As Boolean)
    ' Should the example use the vbMsgBoxHelpButton style?
    UseHelpButton = Value
End Property

Public Static Property Get HelpButton() As Boolean
    ' Return the vbMsgBoxHelpButton value.
    HelpButton = UseHelpButton
End Property
```

The code for this property is very simple. It simply passes the UseHelpButton value back and forth. Notice that the comment for the Let method includes a reference to the vbMsgBoxHelpButton style. Whenever you convert a function or other real-world entity into an object, try to preserve the original information in the comments that you write. This comment helps you remember that this property replaces the vbMsgBoxHelpButton style.

Property naming considerations

You normally want to use the same names for properties in your object that other programmers use for their objects. This technique makes it easier for you to remember the purpose of a property. However, you also want to avoid confusion. If a property doesn't provide precisely the same functionality, it's better to use a different name. For example, the MsgBox function provides the vbMsgBoxRight style to allow flush-right text alignment. You might think that you should use the TextAlign property found in other objects such as the Label control. However, the TextAlign property allows left, center, and right text alignment, so using this name for the example could prove confusing because the MsgBox function doesn't allow center alignment. The example uses a Boolean value and a different name for the property as shown here.

```
Public Static Property Let RightAlignText(Value As Boolean)
    ' Should the example use the vbMsgBoxRight style?
    UseRightAlignment = Value
End Property

Public Static Property Get RightAlignText() As Boolean
    ' Return the vbMsgBoxRight value.
    RightAlignText = UseRightAlignment
End Property
```

Notice that the property name is very specific. The name makes it clear that left alignment is the default and that you can only choose right alignment as an option.

The MsgBox Context argument does precisely match the HelpContextID property used by many existing objects, so the example does use that name for the property. I ran into a problem with the MsgBox Prompt and Title arguments. Theoretically, both arguments should appear as part of the

Caption property. When you set the Caption property of a UserForm, you set the title bar text. Likewise, the Caption property sets the text that appears in a Label control. The example uses the Caption property for the Prompt argument and a Title property for the Title argument. Because you use the Prompt argument more often, setting it equal to the Caption property makes sense.

Defining methods

Methods help you interact with an object by defining the form of interaction. The example in this chapter only has one method, Show. After you configure a message box for use, you want to show it onscreen, so the name is appropriate. The UserForm control also uses this name for the same purpose.

A method can rely on a Public Sub if it doesn't return a value or a Public Function if it does. You call a method by using the same technique that you would with a Sub or Function. The difference is that a method is associated with a specific object and relies on the property values contained within that object. This difference means that when you call a method, you don't have to supply every value that the method needs to perform a task — the object supplies many (if not all) of the required arguments. Listing 8-2 contains the Show method code for this example.

Listing 8-2   Creating an Object Method

```
Public Function Show() As VbMsgBoxResult
    ' Create a variable to hold the message box result.
    Dim Result As VbMsgBoxResult

    ' Create and build the option list.
    Dim Options As VbMsgBoxStyle
    Options = UseIcon
    Options = Options Or UseButtons
    Options = Options Or UseDefault
    Options = Options Or UseModal

    ' Each of the Boolean values require conversion to a
    ' style equivalent.
    If UseForeground Then
        Options = Options Or vbMsgBoxSetForeground
    End If
    If UseRightAlignment Then
        Options = Options Or vbMsgBoxRight
    End If
    If UseRightToLeft Then
        Options = Options Or vbMsgBoxRtlReading
```

```
        End If

        ' The help button requires special handling.
        If UseHelpButton Then
            ' Verify the user has supplied all required
            ' help information.
            If TheHelpFile = "" Then
                ' If the help filename is missing, the message
                ' box can't display help. Raise an error to tell
                ' the user about the problem.
                Err.Raise vbObjectError + 1, _
                        "SpecialMsg.Show", _
                        "You must provide a HelpFilename " + _
                        "property value to use the Help " + _
                        "button in a message box."
            Else
                ' The user has provided all required help
                ' information, so set the help button option.
                Options = Options Or vbMsgBoxHelpButton
            End If
        End If

        ' Determine if the message box will display help.
        If ((TheHelpFile = "") And (Not UseHelpButton)) Then
            ' Display a message box without help.
            Result = MsgBox(ThePrompt, Options, TheTitle)
        Else
            ' Display a message box that includes help.
            Result = MsgBox(ThePrompt, Options, TheTitle, _
                    TheHelpFile, TheHelpContext)
        End If

        ' Raise the Click event so the caller can react to it.
        RaiseEvent Click(Result)

        ' Return a result.
        Show = Result
End Function
```

The MsgBox function provides access to a number of styles. It's easy to forget how many styles until you start looking at code like this. The code creates an Options variable that contains all the style options that you've set up through object properties. It selects an icon, button set, default button, and modality type (application or system). These options always appear in the list, and the Class_Initialize method sets them to default values. (See the upcoming "Defining initialization" section for details.) The Options variable can also contain a number of optional settings. The code checks the Boolean values, such as UseForeground, to determine whether you want to include these optional styles. It then adds the actual style to the Options variable.

Notice that the `UseHelpButton If...Then` statement includes error handling. See the upcoming "Adding Error Handling to Classes" section for a description of class error handling. In this case, the class determines whether you've assigned a help file to the message object. If not, clicking the Help button causes an error. The `MsgBox` function doesn't protect you from this error, but the `SpecialMsg` class does.

The code uses one of two methods for displaying the message box. When you haven't defined help, it passes just the prompt, the style options, and the title to the `MsgBox` function. If you do define help, the code also passes the help filename and the help context to the `MsgBox` function.

At this point, the `Show` method pauses. It waits for you to click one of the buttons on the message box. After you click one of the buttons, control returns to the `Show` method.

The code calls the `RaiseEvent` method next. See the following "Defining events" section for more information about events. In this case, the code raises the `Click` event to show that you've clicked a button. Notice that the `Click` event receives the return value from the `MsgBox` function call. Finally, the `Show` method also returns the result to the caller. Using this approach lets you react to a message box return value as either a method call return or as an event, which increases the flexibility of the `MsgBox` function. You can also choose to ignore the return value, if desired.

Defining events

Events are an essential part of most classes. They signify that you've done something to the control. The example provides two kinds of events, but the actual number that you can create is unlimited. Anytime that an action occurs, you can *fire* (raise) an event. However, most classes limit their events to a user action or a change in data.

The example code in the preceding "Defining methods" section shows one way to fire an event. You use the `RaiseEvent` method to perform this task. Before you can fire an event, you must define it. Events are always public, but you should include the `Public` keyword to ensure that your event works with future versions of VBA and that you avoid making the code hard to read. Here are some examples of event declarations.

```
' Define an event that occurs when the user clicks a button.
Public Event Click(Result As VbMsgBoxResult)

' Define events for various property changes.
Public Event ChangeButton(Result As ButtonTypes)
Public Event ChangeIcon(Result As IconTypes)
```

The event declarations always includes the Event keyword and the event name. The example uses Click as an event name because that's what other VBA objects use for this particular event. Arguments are optional. All three of the declarations use single arguments in this case. I prefer to include information that I think I might need later as part of the event declaration rather than get that information by using other means.

Monitoring data change is an important event. You might need to perform verification or to modify other object settings when a data change occurs. For example, when you decide to change the button style, you also need to check the default button setting to ensure that it falls within the desired range. Listing 8-3 shows a typical example of a data modification event.

Listing 8-3   Creating an Object Event

```
Public Static Property Let Buttons(Value As ButtonTypes)
    ' Change the value of the message button based on the
    ' input value.
    Select Case Value
        Case OKOnly
            UseButtons = vbOKOnly
        Case OKCancel
            UseButtons = vbOKCancel
        Case AbortRetryIgnore
            UseButtons = vbAbortRetryIgnore
        Case YesNoCancel
            UseButtons = vbYesNoCancel
        Case YesNo
            UseButtons = vbYesNo
        Case RetryCancel
            UseButtons = vbRetryCancel
    End Select

    ' Raise an event to show the button type has changed.
    RaiseEvent ChangeButton(Value)
End Property
```

Notice that in the code in the earlier "Defining methods" section and in this code, the RaiseEvent method isn't called until after the action takes place. Always raise the event after you verify that the event has occurred. Otherwise, you might react to an event that hasn't taken place yet (and might not take place at all).

Using enumerated constants

The example uses a number of enumerated constants. These constants serve to limit the number of acceptable input values. They also act as reminders of the acceptable inputs. Listing 8-4 contains an example of a public enumeration.

Listing 8-4   Using Constants in an Object

```
' This enumeration shows the button types.
Public Enum ButtonTypes
    OKOnly = 0
    OKCancel = 1
    AbortRetryIgnore = 2
    YesNoCancel = 3
    YesNo = 4
    RetryCancel = 5
End Enum
```

You assign values to each of the constants within the enumeration. The values don't have to follow any particular order, and you don't have to start with 0. It helps to order the enumeration in some way. The example uses the help topic order to make it easier to compare values that the code contains with the help files. You can also order the entries alphabetically or in order of usage frequency. When a class uses an enumeration for a particular value, VBA displays the acceptable values, as shown in Figure 8-1.

Figure 8-1:
Define
enumerated
constants
to act as
memory
aids.

Look at the `MsgObj.Buttons` line of code. When you type = at this line, you see the dialog box shown in Figure 8-1. The list contains the acceptable button values for the example. The advantage of this technique is that you don't have to remember the individual values, and the probability of providing an incorrect value drops dramatically. Always use enumerated constants when you can to reduce errors and typing time.

Defining initialization

Every class should provide property and local variable initialization. Adding initialization ensures that your class won't fail because of a lack of input. In addition, initialization can help you create objects with less code because many of the values are already defined. The `Class_Initialize` method performs all the initialization tasks for any class. See Listing 8-5 for the initialization code used for the example.

Listing 8-5   Initializing a Class

```
Private Sub Class_Initialize()
    ' Set the initial prompt.
    ThePrompt = "Hello World"

    ' Define a simple title.
    TheTitle = ""

    ' Don't include a default help file or context.
    TheHelpFile = ""
    TheHelpContext = 0

    ' Initialize the variables.
    ' Use the Information icon.
    UseIcon = vbInformation

    ' Display only the OK button.
    UseButtons = vbOKOnly

    ' Make the first button the default button.
    UseDefault = vbDefaultButton1

    ' Ensure the message box is application modal. The user
    ' must clear the message box before doing anything else
    ' with the application.
    UseModal = vbApplicationModal

    ' Don't display a help button.
    UseHelpButton = False

    ' It's not essential that the message box always appear
    ' in the foreground.
    UseForeground = False
    ' Left align the message box text.
    UseRightAlignment = False

    ' Display the text in left to right order.
    UseRightToLeft = False

    ' Initialize the special icon, but don't load a picture.
    Set SpecialIcon = New Image
End Sub
```

The code shows that initialization is simply the task of assigning values to every variable. However, the code also demonstrates some subtleties that you should consider. The MsgBox function has only one required input: a prompt. The code defines a value for ThePrompt because it's a required input. The Show method works even when you simply instantiate the object and make the method call.

The title, help filename, and help context are all optional MsgBox function arguments, so the code doesn't define a value for them. The empty string ensures that the variable is usable but nothing else.

Variables such as UseIcon must use one of the enumerated values. In this case, the initialization process sets the variable to use the default value that the MsgBox function uses or the value that you use most often. For example, the MsgBox function doesn't require that you provide an icon, but the object does provide one for the sake of onscreen appearance.

Setting the Instancing property

You can create two kinds of classes for your program: private and public. The default setting is private, which means that no one outside the program can see the class or create objects from it. When you create a class that's so special that there's no chance that you can use it outside the current program, this is the setting that you should use.

You'll use most of the classes that you create in multiple programs. You should set the Instancing property of these classes to Public. Figure 8-2 shows the Instancing property in the Properties window.

The not-creatable portion of this property value means that other VBA programs can use objects contained within your class, but only if your class creates them. In the case of the example, this means that other programs can use the SpecialIcon object, but they can't create the SpecialIcon object directly. The SpecialMsg class must create the SpecialIcon object, and then the caller can assign a value to that object.

Figure 8-2:
Modifying the Instancing property for class usage.

Creating useful classes

You might wonder why a class that encapsulates the MsgBox function would be useful. This class is useful for a number of reasons. The most important is that it makes using the MsgBox function less of a memory teaser. The MsgBox function provides a wealth of style options, but trying to memorize them all is a waste of time. Creating a class that eliminates the memory gymnastics for you saves time and effort.

Using the class also reduces the chance of error. Each property provides access to mutually exclusive styles. You can combine multiple icon types when using the MsgBox function like this:

```
MsgBox "Hello", vbCritical Or vbInformation
```

The result is a message box that doesn't display any icon. The class version eliminates this problem. You can only choose one icon, and you don't have to remember the icon choices.

The class form of the MsgBox function also makes setups easier. You can use this class to set up certain types of message boxes that you use regularly at the beginning of the program. For example, you can use it to set up an error message box. When an error occurs, you can quickly set the Caption property and use the Show method to display the message box. The idea is that the error message box is consistent and easy to use.

The example class in this chapter shows the three reasons to encapsulate functions and also the three things that you should consider when creating new objects. The following list summarizes these three elements.

- ✔ **Ease of use:** A class should always make coding easier. Useful classes reduce the programming burden rather than increase it.

- ✔ **Reduced learning curve:** A class should reduce the need to memorize things or to figure out odd programming techniques. A class should provide easy to understand methods, properties, and events.

- ✔ **Enhanced reliability:** A well-designed class provides error handling not found in a function. The class should sensibly restrict actions that result in coding errors. It should also check inputs to ensure that the information is correct.

Using Your New Object in an Application

The SpecialMsg class is ready for use in an application. You can use it in place of the MsgBox function . . . and in some places where the MsgBox function simply won't work. For example, you can't ask the MsgBox function to generate events, but the SpecialMsg class does. The following code in Listing 8-6 shows an example of the SpecialMsg class in action.

Listing 8-6   Testing the New Object

```
Private WithEvents MsgObj As SpecialMsg

Private Sub btnTest_Click()
    ' Instantiate the special message box.
    If MsgObj Is Nothing Then
        Set MsgObj = New SpecialMsg
    End If
    ' Assign some property values.
    MsgObj.Caption = "This is a message object."
    MsgObj.Title = "Special Message"
    MsgObj.Buttons = YesNoCancel
    MsgObj.Icon = Question

    ' Display the message box.
    MsgObj.Show
End Sub

Private Sub MsgObj_ChangeButton(Result As ButtonTypes)
    ' Show the new button type.
    lblButtonType = Result
End Sub

Private Sub MsgObj_Click(Result As VbMsgBoxResult)
    ' Show the return value.
    lblReturnValue = Result
End Sub
```

Notice that the example declares the MsgObj object as Private WithEvents. The WithEvents statement is important because it tells VBA that you want the object to handle events. When you leave out this statement, the object won't respond to any events declared in the class.

The example uses a standard form with a Test and a Quit button to test the class. The form also contains two labels for displaying output values from the class. The btnTest_Click sub-procedure instantiates the object, performs all the required setups, and then displays the message box by using the Show method.

Changing the button type automatically generates a ChangeButton event. The example handles this event by displaying the new button type in lblButtonType. Like with most event handlers, the sub-procedure is private and uses a combination of the object name and the event, MsgObj_ChangeButton.

The example also handles the Click event. The MsgObj_Click sub-procedure produces the same result as the output of the Show method. Which technique you use in your code depends on the results that you want to achieve.

Adding Error Handling to Classes

Classes have to provide exceptionally robust error handling so that they're reliable. The earlier "Defining methods" section shows one type of error handling that you can add to a class. Keeping track of property interactions before you perform a task such as displaying the message box is important.

You can add other forms of error handling to your class. Tracking actual input values is another good form of error handling when you can't use enumerated constants. It's also important to monitor property values based on other input values. Here's an example of code (see Listing 8-7) that monitors the DefaultButton property based on the number of buttons that the message box has. The code ensures that the default button is a button that actually exists on the message box.

Listing 8-7   Providing Error Handling in an Object

```
Public Static Property Let DefaultButton(Value As
        DefaultButtonTypes)
   ' Change the value of the message icon based on the
   ' input value.
   Select Case Value
       Case Button_1
           UseDefault = vbDefaultButton1
       Case Button_2
           If ((UseButtons = vbOKOnly) And _
               (Not UseHelpButton)) Then
               ' Can't have a single button setting if
               ' there is no Help button, so raise an
               ' error.
               Err.Raise vbObjectError + 2, _
               "SpecialMsg.DefaultButton", _
               "The selected default button value is " + _
               "incorrect. Choose a default button " + _
               "that matches the message box settings."
           Else
               ' Set the default button value.
               UseDefault = vbDefaultButton2
           End If
       Case Button_3
           If ((UseButtons = vbOKOnly) Or _
               (((UseButtons = vbOKCancel) Or _
               (UseButtons = vbRetryCancel) Or _
```

(continued)

Listing 8-7 *(continued)*

```
                    (UseButtons = vbYesNo)) And _
                    (Not UseHelpButton))) Then
            ' This setting doesn't support a single
            ' button option at all. It also doesn't
            ' support any of the double button options
            ' if there is no Help button. Raise an error
            ' if any of these conditions is true.
            Err.Raise vbObjectError + 2, _
            "SpecialMsg.DefaultButton", _
            "The selected default button value is " + _
            "incorrect. Choose a default button " + _
            "that matches the message box settings."
         Else
            ' Set the default button value.
            UseDefault = vbDefaultButton3
         End If
      Case Button_4
         If Not UseHelpButton Then
            ' Can't have four buttons if there is no
            ' Help button, so raise an error.
            Err.Raise vbObjectError + 2, _
            "SpecialMsg.DefaultButton", _
            "The selected default button value is " + _
            "incorrect. Choose a default button " + _
            "that matches the message box settings."
         Else
            ' Set the default button value.
            UseDefault = vbDefaultButton4
         End If
   End Select
End Property
```

The logic that you use for error handling can become quite complex. There's no error handling for a `DefaultButton` value of `Button_1` because you can't create a message box with no buttons (every message box has at least one button). Only one setting results in a message box with just one button. When you create a message box with `vbOKOnly` and leave out the Help button, there's only one button on the message box. The `Case Button_2` clause checks for this possibility and generates an error when you ask for the second button as a default on a message box with only one button.

The `Case Button_3` error handling logic is especially complex. When you encounter a situation where the logic becomes this complex, it pays to take the problem apart, solve the individual pieces, and then put the pieces together. A message box has three buttons when you request the `vbYesNoCancel` option. The message box also has three buttons when you request the `vbYesNo` option and a Help button. The message box never has three buttons when using the vbOKOnly option — even adding the Help button increases the number of buttons only to two. The code uses all these criteria to look for situations where the message box won't have three buttons. When the message box lacks the proper number of buttons, the code produces an error.

The Case Button_4 error handling logic demonstrates a situation where you can turn something very complicated into something very simple. None of the button options has more than three buttons. Therefore, the only time when you can set the default button to the fourth button is when there's a Help button. The code looks for this button. When you don't include it, the code generates an error.

Using the With Statement

VBA does provide an interesting feature that makes it easier to write code for an object. The With statement tells VBA that you plan to perform a number of tasks by using the same object. Every dotted statement within the structure applies to that object. Using this technique reduces the amount of code that you have to type and can reduce the chance of typos. Listing 8-8 shows an example of the With statement in use.

Listing 8-8   Using an Alternative Object Testing Technique

```
Private Sub btnTest2_Click()
    ' Instantiate the special message box.
    If MsgObj Is Nothing Then
        Set MsgObj = New SpecialMsg
    End If
    ' Assign some property values.
    With MsgObj
        .Caption = "This is a message object."
        .Title = "Special Message"
        .Buttons = YesNoCancel
        .Icon = Question

        ' Display the message box.
        .Show
    End With
End Sub
```

Notice that this code is similar to the code in the earlier "Using Your New Object in an Application" section. The only difference is that you don't have to type MsgObj so many times. The code works precisely the same as before, and you get the same prompts as before. This is a personal-taste coding technique. You don't lose anything by not using it, and you don't gain anything significant when you do.

Adding a Digital Signature to Your Creation

You might eventually want to send your class to someone else. In some cases, this means sending the entire project to them. Whenever you send your project to someone else, make sure that you sign it so that the recipient knows that you actually created it. Use the following steps to sign your creation:

1. **In the VBA Integrated Development Environment (IDE), choose Tools⇨Digital Signature.**

   You see a Digital Signature dialog box like the one shown in Figure 8-3.

Figure 8-3: Verify the signature status of your project.

2. **Click the Choose button.**

   You see a Select Certificate dialog box.

3. **Highlight a certificate in the list and then click OK.**

   VBA signs the target project using your certificate.

4. **Click OK to close the Digital Signature dialog box.**

Chapter 9

Working with Arrays and Collections

In This Chapter
▶ Using arrays within a program
▶ Using collections within a program
▶ Creating new data types
▶ Defining collections within a program

To this point in the book, all the data types you've used have one thing in common — they store a single data element. When you create an integer, it holds a single number. Placing a new number within the integer removes the old value. However, the real world doesn't work this way. A computer can have more than one disk drive. Your contact database contains more than one name. A mailbox can contain more than one piece of mail. You need a method of storing more than one piece of information in a single variable so that you can model the real world in your programs. VBA provides two methods of doing this: arrays and collections.

Arrays provide a way for your programs to store more than one item in a single container. Think of the array as a large box with a bunch of small boxes inside. Each small box can store a single value. You decide how many small boxes the array can hold when you create the array. Use arrays when you need to store a number of related items of the same data type.

Collections always relate to objects. In most cases, a main object contains one or more sub-objects. For example, an Excel Application object contains a Workbooks collection, and a Workbook object contains a Sheets collection. The Application can contain one or more Workbooks, and an individual Workbook can contain one or more Sheets. A Word Section object can contain a HeadersFooters collection. Microsoft Office and many third-party products are packed with object collections that you can access from VBA.

In this chapter, I also demonstrate how you can create your own data types. A *data type* is a way to mark information so that you can understand it better. The computer doesn't care about data types. VBA uses data types to enforce certain data behaviors, but it doesn't really understand them. The use of a data type is for your benefit so that you can understand the information better.

Using Arrays for Structured Storage

An *array* is a list of items. When you write a list of tasks to perform for the day, you create an array. The piece of paper is a single container that holds a number of strings, each of which is a task that you have to perform. Likewise, you can create a single piece of paper in your VBA program — an array — and use that array to hold multiple items.

Understanding array usage

You can define arrays by using several techniques. However, all these techniques use the same basic approach. Listing 9-1 contains an example that demonstrates the essential array usage process. (You can find the source code for this example on the Dummies.com site at http://www.dummies.com/go/mueller.)

Listing 9-1   Creating and Using an Array for String Data

```
' Tell VBA to start all arrays at 0.
Option Base 0

Public Sub SingleDimension()
    ' Define an output string.
    Dim Output As String

    ' Define a variant to hold individual strings.
    Dim IndividualString As Variant

    ' Define the array of strings.
    Dim StringArray(5) As String

    ' Fill each array element with information.
    StringArray(0) = "This"
    StringArray(1) = "Is"
    StringArray(2) = "An"
```

```
    StringArray(3) = "Array"
    StringArray(4) = "Of"
    StringArray(5) = "Strings"

    ' Use the For Each...Next statement to get each array
    ' element and place it in a string.
    For Each IndividualString In StringArray

        ' Create a single output string with the array
        ' array elements.
        Output = Output + IndividualString + " "
    Next

    ' Display the result.
    MsgBox Trim(Output), _
           vbInformation Or vbOKOnly, _
           "Array Content"
End Sub
```

Notice that the code begins with an `Option Base 0` statement. This statement tells VBA whether you want to start counting array elements at 0 or 1. The default setting is 0. Most programming languages use 0 as the starting point, which is why Microsoft made 0 the default for VBA. However, older versions of Visual Basic (including VBA) use 1 as the starting point. When you want to ensure that your program works in every environment, include the `Option Base` statement.

The code for `SingleDimension` begins with some variable declarations. Notice the `StringArray` declaration. When you want to create an array, you follow the variable name with a pair of parentheses that contains the number of elements. You can also create an empty array by leaving the number out, but then you need to use the `ReDim` statement to set the number of elements later. See the upcoming "Understanding the array types" section for details.

Because the array begins at 0 and not at 1, you can actually store six items in an array that is defined as having five elements. The number that you include in the declaration is always the top element number of the array and not the actual number of elements.

The code that follows fills each of these elements with a string. Notice the use of numbers in the statement. This number is an *index*. The statement `StringArray(1) = "Is"` places the word `Is` in the second array element by using an index of 1. You can always access an individual element by using its index.

This example shows how to use a `For Each...Next` statement to access each array element in turn. Notice that you don't need to use an index in this situation because the `For Each...Next` statement keeps track of it for you. The `IndividualString` variable is a `Variant` — the only acceptable type when using a `For Each...Next` statement. You don't have to convert `IndividualString` when you add it to `Output` because VBA tracks it as a `Variant/String`. Check this statement out in the Debugger, and you can see how it works.

The final statement displays a message box containing the value of `Output`. This message box presents the list of the strings originally added to the array as a single string.

Understanding the array types

You can classify arrays in several ways. The first method is by the kind of data that the array holds. A `String` array is different from an `Integer` array. An array always keeps the array data type unique. Using a `Variant` data type lets you mix data types within an array. You should use this technique carefully because it can lead to bugs that are difficult to debug.

A second method is to define the number of array dimensions. A *dimension* is the number of directions in which the array holds information. A simple list such as the one in the earlier "Understanding array usage" section is a single-dimensional array. A table that consists of rows and columns is a two-dimensional array. You can create arrays with any number of dimensions.

Listing 9-2 shows an example of a two-dimensional array that holds the result of a calculation. Note that this is also the first example to mix forms into the program, and it also shows how to use the `ReDim` statement. (You can find the source code for this example on the Dummies.com site at `http://www.dummies.com/go/mueller.`)

Listing 9-2   Creating and Using a Two-Dimensional Array

```
' Define some data exchange values for the
' GetArrayDimensions form.
Public Input1Value As Integer
Public Input2Value As Integer
Public ClickType As VbMsgBoxResult

Public Sub TwoDimension()
    ' Create an array to hold the calculation results.
```

```
    Dim CalcResult() As Integer

    ' Create some loop variables for the calculation.
    Dim Loop1 As Integer
    Dim Loop2 As Integer

    ' Create an output string for the display.
    Dim Output As String

    ' Display a form to obtain the array dimensions.
    GetArrayDimensions.Show

    ' Determine which button the user clicked.
    If ClickType = vbCancel Then

        ' If the user clicked Cancel, exit.
        Exit Sub
    End If

    ' Redimension the array.
    ReDim CalcResult(Input1Value, Input2Value)

    ' Perform the calculation.
    For Loop1 = 1 To Input1Value
        For Loop2 = 1 To Input2Value
            CalcResult(Loop1, Loop2) = Loop1 * Loop2
        Next
    Next

    ' Create a heading.
    Output = "Calculation Results" + vbCrLf + _
             "In Tabular Format" + vbCrLf + vbCrLf

    ' Define the column heading values.
    For Loop1 = 1 To Input2Value
        Output = Output + vbTab + CStr(Loop1)
    Next

    ' Define the rows.
    For Loop1 = 1 To Input1Value
        Output = Output + vbCrLf + CStr(Loop1)
        For Loop2 = 1 To Input2Value
            Output = Output + vbTab + _
                     CStr(CalcResult(Loop1, Loop2))
        Next
    Next

    ' Create a message box to show the result.
    MsgBox Output, vbInformation Or vbOKOnly, "Results"
End Sub
```

The program declares three public variables. These variables hold the results from the dialog box created to ask you how many values to compute. This technique is regularly used to get information.

The TwoDimension sub-procedure begins by declaring some variables. Notice that it doesn't define the number of elements in CalcResult — the code only tells VBA that it's an array.

The code displays the dialog box shown in Figure 9-1 using the GetArrayDimensions.Show method. The program uses this dialog box to get the array dimensions.

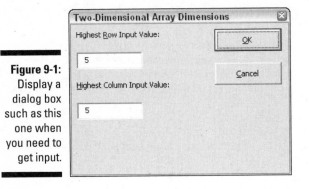

Figure 9-1:
Display a dialog box such as this one when you need to get input.

This dialog box has several interesting features to consider. First, unlike the standalone dialog boxes in Chapter 7, this dialog box interacts with a sub-procedure. Consequently, you can't simply end the dialog box — the code within the dialog box has to report back to the calling sub-procedure in some way. This is the reason for creating the global Input1Value, Input2Value, and ClickType variables. Listing 9-3 shows the essential code from the Two-Dimensional Array Dimensions dialog box.

Listing 9-3 Creating a Form to Interact with a Two-Dimensional Array

```
Private Sub btnOK_Click()
    ' Change the click type.
    ArrayTypes.ClickType = vbOK

    ' Check the two input values.
    txtInput1_Change
    txtInput2_Change

    ' End the form.
    Me.Hide
```

```
End Sub

Private Sub txtInput1_Change()
    ' Verify the user has input a number greater than 1.
    If Val(txtInput1.Text) = 0 Then
        ' If not, display an error message box.
        MsgBox "Type a numeric value greater than 1."

        ' Return the text to an acceptable value.
        txtInput1.Text = "5"
    Else
        ' Otherwise, store the numeric value.
        ArrayTypes.Input1Value = CInt(txtInput1.Text)
    End If
End Sub
```

The txtInput1_Change sub-procedure monitors any change to the txtInput1 control. (The txtInput2 control has a similar event handler associated with it.) The If...Then statement verifies that you have input a number by using the Val function to compare the number with 0. You can't use the CInt function because it generates a type mismatch error when you type a letter or special character. Typing an incorrect character generates an error message and returns the value to something correct. A correct entry places the integer value into the Input1Value variable in the ArrayTypes module (the one with the sub-procedure).

The btnOK_Click sub-procedure sets the ClickType variable in the ArrayTypes module to vbOK. Likewise, clicking Cancel sets the ClickType variable to vbCancel. The code then calls Me.Hide. The special keyword Me refers to the current object. The Hide method removes the form from sight but not from memory.

When you want to remove an object from memory, you use the Unload method and supply the object name. This method only works if VBA is done using the object. Likewise, when you want to load an object into memory (but not display it), use the Load method. This method only works when VBA has memory and other resources available to load the object.

When the GetArrayDimensions UserForm completes (you click OK or Cancel), control returns to the TwoDimension sub-procedure. The code checks the ClickType value. Click Cancel, and the sub-procedure exits.

At this point, the code has the information needed to *dimension* the array (that is, make it a certain size), so it uses the ReDim statement to change the CalcResult dimensions. Changing the dimensions erases the content of the array unless you include the Preserve keyword. A double loop serves to address the two dimensions of the CalcResult array. The calculation is a simple multiplication, but you can perform any task in the loop.

After the array is filled with data, it's time to create an output string. The code uses simple assignment to create a heading, generates the row heading using a single loop, and then uses a double loop to create the output information. The final statement displays an output message box containing a table of the information. Figure 9-2 shows typical output from this program.

Results

Calculation Results
In Tabular Format

	1	2	3	4	5
1	1	2	3	4	5
2	2	4	6	8	10
3	3	6	9	12	15
4	4	8	12	16	20
5	5	10	15	20	25

OK

Copying data from one array to another

You might need to copy data from one array to another. For example, you can base a new array on the content of an existing array. It's also safer to make changes to a copy of an array rather than to change the original and potentially damage the data. Listing 9-4 shows an example of code that you can use to copy one array to another. (You can find the source code for this example on the Dummies.com site at http://www.dummies.com/go/mueller.)

Listing 9-4   Copying an Array

```
Public Sub ArrayCopy()
    ' Create a loop variable.
    Dim Counter As Integer

    ' Create an orignal array of strings and a copy.
    Dim OriginalArray(4) As String
    Dim CopiedArray(5) As String

    ' Create an output variable.
    Dim Output As String

    ' Fill the array with data.
    OriginalArray(0) = "This"
    OriginalArray(1) = "is"
    OriginalArray(2) = "the"
```

```
    OriginalArray(3) = "original"
    OriginalArray(4) = "array!"

    ' Copy the data.
    For Counter = 0 To UBound(OriginalArray)
        CopiedArray(Counter) = OriginalArray(Counter)
    Next

    ' Modify some data elements.
    CopiedArray(3) = "copied"
    CopiedArray(4) = "array"

    ' Add a new element.
    CopiedArray(5) = "too!"

    ' Create the first part of the output string.
    Output = "The first string:" + vbCrLf
    For Counter = 0 To UBound(OriginalArray)
        Output = Output + OriginalArray(Counter) + " "
    Next

    ' Create the second part of the output string.
    Output = Output + vbCrLf + "The Second String:" + vbCrLf
    For Counter = 0 To UBound(CopiedArray)
        Output = Output + CopiedArray(Counter) + " "
    Next

    ' Display the results.
    MsgBox Output, vbInformation Or vbOKOnly, "Results"
End Sub
```

The code begins by creating two arrays and filling the original array with information. Copying the OriginalArray elements to the CopiedArray elements comes next. Follow this process in the Debugger, and you see that the two arrays are the same except that the CopiedArray has one extra element. Notice how the code uses the UBound function to determine the last element of the array. Use the LBound function to determine the lower boundary of the array subscripts.

At this point, the code modifies CopiedArray. First, it changes the content of two of the elements. Second, it adds information to the last element. These changes don't affect the original array. If an error occurs, you can always reconstruct CopiedArray by using OriginalArray as a starting point. The message box that the code constructs shows that the original array is the same, but the copied array is different. You should see a message box like the one shown in Figure 9-3 when you run this program.

Figure 9-3:
Copy an
array and
change the
copy.

```
Results                              ☒
   ⓘ    The first string:
        This is the original array!
        The Second String:
        This is the copied array too!

            ┌──────────────┐
            │      OK      │
            └──────────────┘
```

Using Collections to Create Data Sets

You can view a collection as an advanced form of an array. Like an array, a collection maintains a list of items in one package. Because these items are related in more than a superficial way, such as a group of worksheets, many people refer to the list of items as a *data set*. Using a collection is different from an array, however, and you might find that you like using them better than arrays. A collection has some advantages, such as not requiring the ReDim statement, but is a little more complicated to use. This section explains these differences in detail and shows how to use collections in a program.

Understanding collection usage

If you've followed the book to this point, you've used collections in previous chapters. For example, the "Recovering from an error" section of Chapter 6 relies on a collection to retrieve information from a specific hard drive. The FileSystemObject object contains a collection of Drive objects. The example in the "Designing a form for your application" section of Chapter 7 also relies on collections. This example adds control objects to the Controls collection of the UserForm object. VBA uses a lot of collections — you can't escape their use.

The easiest way to understand a collection is to create one of your own. You can create collections and add them to a class that you create or use them by themselves. VBA doesn't place any restrictions on how you use collections. Listing 9-5 shows an example of a simple collection. It creates the collection and then provides the means for adding, removing, and listing elements in the collection. (You can find the source code for this example on the Dummies.com site at http://www.dummies.com/go/mueller.)

Listing 9-5 Creating and Using a Simple Collection

```
' Declare the collection.
Private MyCollection As Collection

Private Sub btnAdd_Click()
    ' Add a new item.
    MyCollection.Add _
        InputBox("Type a new item.", "Add Item", "Hello")

    ' List the items.
    ListItems
End Sub

Private Sub btnDelete_Click()
    ' Define variables to hold the selection.
    Dim UserInput As String
    Dim Selection As Integer

    ' Define an error handling result variable.
    Dim Result As VbMsgBoxResult

    ' Get the input from the user.
RetryInput:
    UserInput = InputBox("Type an existing item number.", _
                         "Remove Item", _
                         "1")

    ' Validate the input.
    If Val(UserInput) > 0 And _
       Val(UserInput) < MyCollection.Count + 1 Then

        ' Use good input to delete a value.
        Selection = CInt(UserInput)
    Else
        ' Display an error message.
        Result = MsgBox("Type a number greater than 1 " + _
                        "and less than or equal to the " + _
                        "number of elements.", _
                        vbExclamation Or vbRetryCancel, _
                        "Input Error")

        ' Allow for a retry.
        If Result = vbRetry Then
            GoTo RetryInput
        Else
            Exit Sub
        End If
    End If
```

(continued)

Listing 9-5 *(continued)*

```
        ' Delete the existing item.
        MyCollection.Remove Selection

        ' List the items.
        ListItems
End Sub

Private Sub UserForm_Initialize()
        ' Initialize the collection.
        Set MyCollection = New Collection
End Sub

Public Sub ListItems()
        ' Create the listing variable.
        Dim Element As Variant

        ' Clear the current list.
        lblCollection.Caption = ""

        ' Display each element in turn.
        For Each Element In MyCollection
            lblCollection.Caption = lblCollection.Caption + _
                                    Element + vbCrLf
        Next

        ' Determine whether to enable the Delete button.
        If MyCollection.Count > 0 Then
            btnDelete.Enabled = True
        Else
            btnDelete.Enabled = False
        End If
End Sub
```

This is a standalone form program. The code declares `MyCollection` as a private global variable so that all the sub-procedures can access it. The `UserForm_Initialize` sub-procedure initializes the collection.

The example provides two `CommandButtons` for changing the collection: Add and Delete. The Delete button is disabled at program start because you can't delete a non-existent element from the collection without producing an error. Consequently, the first button that you click is Add. The `btnAdd_Click` event handler displays an `InputBox` that requests string input. After making the addition by using the `Add` method, the code calls the `ListItems` sub-procedure.

The `ListItems` sub-procedure provides a convenient place to put common code for the event handlers. You should use this type of sub-procedure with common code for programs that you create. The code begins by creating a `Variant` to hold individual collection members. It also sets the `lblCollection.Caption` to `""` (nothing) in order to erase the current content from the display. Notice the use of the `For Each...Next` statement to fill the `lblCollection.Caption` property with new data.

It's important to check the status of the collection to ensure that the program enables or disables `btnDelete` as appropriate. The `If...Then` statement compares the number of collection items using the `Count` method with 0. When true, the collection is empty, and the code disables `btnDelete`. Otherwise, the code enables `btnDelete`.

The `btnDelete_Click` event handler requires some error handling to ensure that the program operates as expected. You can add any string desired to the collection, but you can't enter just any information during a deletion because incorrect input causes an error.

The `InputBox` places the information that it receives in `UserInput`. An `If...Then` statement compares the `UserInput` with specific numeric values. When you type a character or a special symbol, it's the same as typing a 0 — the `Val` function returns a 0 for non-numeric input. The `If...Then` statement also compares the `UserInput` with the upper limit of the collection entries by using the `Count` method. If the input meets the criteria, the code places the integer part of the input into `Select` by using the `CInt` function.

When an input error occurs, the code displays a message box that tells you about the correct input and asks whether you want to try again. An `If...Then` statement compares your button click with `vbRetry` and takes appropriate action.

The deletion process relies on the `Remove` method. You must supply an integer value that reflects the index of the entry that you want to remove. A collection can also use *keys* — strings that stand in for the actual value. You can see a demonstration of this technique in the upcoming "Adding keyed data to the collection" section. The event handler ends with a call to `ListItems`.

Knowing when to use a collection

Throughout this chapter, I show examples of both arrays and collections. The examples demonstrate that the techniques for using each storage technique are different, but the results can be the same in many cases. For example, you can store strings equally well in a collection or an array. You can also access the information by using similar techniques. It might be difficult to determine which method to use. In some cases, it doesn't matter — it's a matter of personal taste.

There are advantages and disadvantages to consider when you make your decision. Here's a list of the things that you should consider.

- ✔ Arrays have a slight performance advantage and use less memory to store the same information.

- ✔ Collections are more flexible than arrays — they can grow and shrink as needed.

- ✔ Arrays are easier to conceptualize, and you might find them easier to use.

- ✔ Collections excel at storing objects, and they work well with complex data types.

- ✔ Arrays can appear in multiple dimensions — there's no limit. (Collections are limited to a single list.)

- ✔ Collections are self contained, so you don't have to memorize a list of external functions to work with them.

Although you can use either an array or a collection in some situations, you must use a specific option in other cases. For example, arrays are the only solution when you need to perform complex matrix math because collections are simple lists and don't include the concept of dimensions. On the other hand, when you want to include a list of objects within an object, you must use a collection. However, you can use either solution when you want to create a list of simple items, such as names.

Adding keyed data to the collection

You can normally create collections without keys, and they work fine. A collection that relies on user input is an exception. It's easier to get string input from users rather than ask them to count down a row of entries to provide a number. Database collections also provide an opportunity to use keyed entries. In fact, many predefined collections use keyed entries to make it easier for you to develop programs with them.

This example shows an Access contact database. It uses keys to make finding an entry easier. The database only contains three fields: a contact name, the telephone number, and the last date of contact. To use this example, you must add a reference to the Microsoft DAO 3.6 Object Library. Listing 9-6 shows the code for this example. (You can find the source code and associated database for this example on the Dummies.com site at http://www.dummies.com/go/mueller.)

Listing 9-6   Using Keyed Data with a Collection

```
Public Sub DisplayContacts()
    ' Create a loop counter variable.
    Dim Counter As Integer
    Counter = 1

    ' Create a recordset object.
    Dim CurrentData As DAO.Recordset

    ' Create the collection variable.
    Dim ContactList As Collection
    Set ContactList = New Collection

    ' Create the output variables.
    Dim Element As Variant
    Dim Output As String

    ' Get the current data.
    Set CurrentData = _
        Application.CurrentDb.OpenRecordset("Contacts")

    ' Create the collection from the data.
    While Not CurrentData.EOF

        ' Get the information and place it in the user
        ' data type.
        ContactList.Add _
            CurrentData.Fields("Name").Value, _
            "Name" + CStr(Counter)
        ContactList.Add _
            CurrentData.Fields("Telephone").Value, _
            "Telephone" + CStr(Counter)
        ContactList.Add _
            CurrentData.Fields("LastContact").Value, _
            "LastContact" + CStr(Counter)

        ' Update the Counter.
        Counter = Counter + 1

        ' Move to the next database record.
        CurrentData.MoveNext
    Wend

    ' Create an output string by getting the values from
    ' the collection.
```

(continued)

Listing 9-6 *(continued)*

```
    For Counter = 1 To (ContactList.Count / 3)

        ' Access the collection elements by name.
        Element = ContactList("Name" + CStr(Counter))
        Output = Output + Element

        Element = ContactList("Telephone" + CStr(Counter))
        Output = Output + vbTab + Element

        Element = ContactList("LastContact" + CStr(Counter))
        Output = Output + vbTab + CStr(Element) + vbCrLf
    Next

    ' Create the message box.
    MsgBox Output, vbInformation, "Contact List"
End Sub
```

The code begins by defining and initializing some variables. Notice the `CurrentData` declaration. It's a `DAO.Recordset`, not the default `ADODB.Recordset` object. When you use the default, the program fails with a type mismatch error. This example points out one of the problems that you can encounter when working with objects. Make sure that you use specific object references as necessary.

You can use a number of methods to get hold of the Contacts table in the example database. The easiest method is to use the `Application.CurrentDb.OpenRecordset` method. This method includes constants that determine how VBA opens the recordset. For example, you can tell VBA that you only want to read the recordset by using the `dbReadOnly` constant. See the OpenRecordset Method help topic for additional information.

The code uses a `While...Wend` structure to retrieve the individual data elements. Notice the use of a string to access the `Fields` collection, which acts as the first argument for the `ContactList.Add` method. The second argument for the `Add` method used to add a new item to the `ContactList` collection is the string key that you can use to access it. When you look at `ContactList` in the Debugger, you see that it contains a single list of entries. Make sure that you use the `CurrentData.MoveNext` method to select the next record at the end of the loop, or the database never reaches the end of file (`EOF` property set to `True`).

In this case, the code relies on a `For...Next` loop to create the output string. The collection isn't in a configuration where one element equals one database record — the code requires three elements for each database record. The code shows how you can create a loop to compensate for this fact.

The For...Next loop expression isn't actually optimal in this case. I use this presentation to make the example clearer. Notice the ContactList. Count / 3 portion of the expression. VBA has to calculate that value during every loop. Calculating the value outside the loop would save time and make this program faster.

Accessing predefined collection items

VBA uses collections quite often. For example, the Fields collection of a database is a collection of Field objects. Likewise, the Drives collection contains multiple Drive objects. You should notice something interesting about the relationship between collections and objects. Microsoft usually uses an s at the end of the name to denote a collection, such as the Drives and Fields collections.

The balloon help that you see when you type an object name normally contains methods and properties for that object. It can also contain other objects and collections. When you look through the list of items, anything plural is normally a collection.

You see another clue when you double-click a property and then press F1 to display help. VBA help not only tells you that the item is a collection, but it usually displays a hierarchical chart to show where the collection fits within the object hierarchy and what types of items that the collection can contain.

The Debugger can also help you ferret out collections. The Watches window shown in Figure 9-4 shows how the CurrentData Recordset object holds the Fields collection (highlighted in figure), which contains multiple Field objects. You can click the plus signs next to each item to see each field and its current content. Look especially in the Type column where you can see the data type used for each item in the collection.

Another place to acquaint yourself with collections is the Object Browser. The Help file is only useful when you know what you're looking for. The Debugger is also problematic because you have to build something to see what it contains. The Object Browser is different. When you know what you need but not what to call it, you can select the library in question and browse.

Figure 9-5 shows the DAO library used for the example in the preceding "Adding keyed data to the collection" section. This figure shows three collections and the objects that they contain: Errors, Fields, and Groups. When you find something interesting, highlight it, and then press F1. When you know what you're looking for, help can be useful.

Figure 9-4:
Use the
Debugger
to see
predefined
collections.

Figure 9-5:
Browse
for the
collections
that you
need to use
in your
program.

Defining Your Own Data Types

A VBA *user-defined data type* is nothing more than a list (collection) of data elements that you want to use together. You aren't really creating a new data type — at least not one that you could identify as a unique entity such as a

`String` or an `Integer`. In this section, I show how to benefit from user-defined data types and demonstrate their use.

Understanding user-defined data types

Creating a user-defined type means defining the data that you want to use together and deciding which native data types work best. The example in the earlier "Adding keyed data to the collection" section uses a database connection to get hold of data and place it in a collection. The implementation (the actual coding) in that example is difficult because you have to make three entries in the collection for each database record. Here's a user-defined type that places all the information in one entry. (You can find the source code for this example on the Dummies.com site at `http://www.dummies.com/go/mueller`.)

```
' Define a user type.
Public Type APerson
    Name As String       ' The person's name.
    Telephone As String ' The contact telephone number.
    LastContact As Date ' The date of last contact.
End Type
```

You create a user-defined type by using the `Type` keyword, followed by the name of the new data type. The structure contains native data types. Each variable also has a name. VBA helps you create user-defined types of any complexity. They can include arrays, other user-defined types, and even objects. However, you always want to make the user-defined type as simple as possible and document it fully so that you remember what it does later.

Knowing when to create your own data type

Before you create a user-defined data type, always ask whether any existing type (including objects and collections) can fulfill your need. After you know that you have to create a user-defined type, make sure that you think about the purpose that the user-defined type fulfills.

A user-defined data type can save time and effort by letting you declare all the data elements that you normally use together for a task in one place. It can also group data so that you don't have to perform finger gymnastics to locate your data. However, the main reason to create a user-defined type is to make your program easier to understand. A well-defined data type can make your code simpler and keep the number of code lines to a minimum.

Accessing and manipulating data

The example in the earlier "Adding keyed data to the collection" section works well because it doesn't have to work with complex data. A program that modifies multiple tables and 20 or 30 fields might not work so well by using the technique shown in that section. (It would work, but it wouldn't be fun to program.) By using the new data type that you just created, you can make the programming example in the "Adding keyed data to the collection" section easier to understand.

The example in this section relies on a user-defined data type. It builds an object on that data type and then adds the object to a collection. This example shows how to create your own collections to make working with your data faster and easier.

Defining an individual contact

When you decide to create your own collection, begin with the individual object. Make sure that you know what one copy of an object looks like before you create multiple copies of it. See Chapter 8 for a complete object creation demonstration.

```
' Create an instance of this type.
Private ThePerson As APerson

Public Property Get Name() As String
    ' Get the current user name.
    Name = ThePerson.Name
End Property

Public Property Let Name(Value As String)
    ' Set the new user name.
    ThePerson.Name = Value
End Property
```

The object for this example essentially maintains a reference to the user-defined data type and exposes the individual elements as properties. The listing shows the user-defined type declaration. Notice that the declaration doesn't vary from that used for native data types.

The code consists of three pairs of property declarations — one for each variable in the APerson data type. Each property provides both read and write capabilities. Although this is an object, the individual variables aren't objects, so you use the Let and Get method of exposing them.

Defining a collection of contacts

After you have a single object to use, it's time to create a collection of them. A collection doesn't have to implement the methods and properties found in the Collection class, but it helps if it does. It pays to look at the collections in VBA for ideas on which methods and properties that you can implement. Always implement the Item property because you need it for most of your code. Listing 9-7 shows an example of a typical collection.

Listing 9-7   Manipulating Data in Collections

```
' Declare the collection.
Private PersonCollection As Collection

Public Sub Add(Item As Person, _
               Optional Key As String, _
               Optional Before As Integer, _
               Optional After As Integer)

    ' Determine whether there is a Key.
    If Not Key = "" Then

        ' Determine whether there is a Before value.
        If Before > 0 Then

            ' Add an entry with a Key and Before value.
            PersonCollection.Add Item, Key, Before

        ' Determine whether there is an After value.
        ElseIf After > 0 Then

            ' Add an entry with a Key and After value.
            PersonCollection.Add Item, Key, , After

        Else

            ' The entry is just an Item and Key.
            PersonCollection.Add Item, Key
        End If
    Else
        ' Determine whether there is a Before value.
        If Before > 0 Then

            ' Add an entry with a Before value.
            PersonCollection.Add Item, , Before

        ' Determine whether there is an After value.
```

(continued)

Listing 9-7 *(continued)*

```
        ElseIf After > 0 Then

            ' Add an entry with an After value.
            PersonCollection.Add Item, , , After

        Else

            ' The entry is just an Item.
            PersonCollection.Add Item
        End If
    End If
End Sub

Public Property Get Count() As Long
    ' Return the current collection count.
    Count = PersonCollection.Count
End Property

Public Sub Remove(Index As Variant)
    ' Remove the requested item.
    PersonCollection.Remove Index
End Sub

Public Property Get Item(Index As Variant) As Person
    ' Return the requested item.
    Set Item = PersonCollection.Item(Index)
End Property

Private Sub Class_Initialize()
    ' Initialize the collection.
    Set PersonCollection = New Collection
End Sub
```

Notice that the code begins by creating a `Collection` object. You could also use the `Implements` statement to implement the `Collection` class, but this technique is easier. The `Class_Initialize` method initializes `PersonCollection` so that other methods can use it.

The `Add` method is the most complex sub-procedure that you write for a collection in most cases. The reason for the complexity is that this method has so many optional arguments. In addition, when you supply a `Before` argument, you can't supply an `After` argument — the two are mutually exclusive. The code divides the task of determining what to do into a `Key` or no `Key` decision. It then decides whether you supplied `Before`, `After`, or neither argument and takes the appropriate action. Look through the `Add` method code, and you see that each decision results in a different `Add` method-calling syntax.

The `Count` property returns the `PersonCollection.Count` property. You never need to add error-handling code to this property because it's read only. Never make this property read/write. You don't want someone using the collection to change the count.

The `Remove` method makes a direct call to the `PersonCollection.Remove` method. You could add range checking to this method by using the same techniques that I use in previous examples. The `PersonCollection.Remove` method raises an error when you supply an incorrect value. Notice the use of a `Variant` for this method so that it can accept a string or an integer as input.

The `Item` property is also read only. Again, you should never make this property read/write. Always use the `Add` method to add new entries to the collection. Notice that this method returns an object, so you have to use the `Set` statement.

Creating a default property

No matter which collection you look at, `Item` is the default property or function. Figure 9-6 shows that `Item` uses a special symbol. The explanation for `Item` in the lower pane of the Object Browser window also says that this is the default property of the `Fields` collection. The only problem is that VBA doesn't provide a direct method for you to create a default property or method for your class.

You have to use a little-known and somewhat undocumented method of adding a default property to the example. When you look at the `Persons.cls` file in the source code, you see that code actually looks like the code in Listing 9-8.

Figure 9-6: Create a default `Item` property or method to ensure that your collection works properly.

Listing 9-8   Creating a Default Property Declaration

```
Public Property Get Item(Index As Variant) As Person
' Tell VBA this is the default property.
Attribute Item.VB_UserMemId = 0

    ' Return the requested item.
    Set Item = PersonCollection.Item(Index)
End Property
```

However, the first line of code doesn't appear in the IDE. VBA forces you to use a simple but odd procedure to add this line of code. Simply use the following procedure to add this line of code.

1. **Right-click the** Persons **entry in the Project window and then choose Export File from the context menu that appears.**

    You see the Export File dialog box.

2. **Click Save to save the file as** Persons.cls.

    VBA exports the file.

3. **Open the file in any text editor such as Notepad.**

    Never use Word for this task because it can add control characters.

4. **Type** Attribute Item.VB_UserMemId = 0 **as the first entry for the** Item **property.**

5. **Save the** Persons.cls **file and then exit the editor.**

6. **Right-click the** Persons **entry in the Project window and then choose Remove Persons from the context menu that appears.**

    VBA asks whether you want to export Persons before you remove it.

7. **Click No.**

    VBA removes the class module.

8. **Right-click anywhere in the Project window and then choose Import File from the context menu that appears.**

    VBA displays the Import File dialog box.

9. **Highlight the** Persons.cls **file and then click Open.**

    VBA imports the updated file. It appears that nothing has changed. The code looks the same as before. However, the unseen Attribute entry has changed.

10. **Open Object Browser and view the updated** Persons **class.**

    You notice that Item is now the default property for this class.

Developing the test program

The test program in Listing 9-9 is similar to the one used for the earlier "Adding keyed data to the collection" section (see Listing 9-6). You can find it in the source code as DisplayContacts2. The new example in Listing 9-9 still begins by creating variables, and it opens the same recordset. Here are the essential differences between the two test programs:

Listing 9-9   Updating the Key Data Collection Example

```
' Create the collection from the data.
While Not CurrentData.EOF

    ' Define a new element.
    Set Individual = New Person

    ' Get the information and place it in the user
    ' data type.
    Individual.Name = _
        CurrentData.Fields("Name").Value
    Individual.Telephone = _
        CurrentData.Fields("Telephone").Value
    Individual.LastContact = _
        CurrentData.Fields("LastContact").Value

    ' Add the information to the collection.
    ContactList.Add Individual, Individual.Name

    ' Move to the next database record.
    CurrentData.MoveNext
Wend

' Create an output string by getting the values from
' the collection.
For Counter = 1 To ContactList.Count
    ' Get the current element.
    Set Individual = ContactList(Counter)

    ' Access the collection elements by name.
    Output = Output + Individual.Name + _
            vbTab + Individual.Telephone + _
            vbTab + _
            CStr(Individual.LastContact) + vbCrLf
Next
```

The code is easier to understand now because you can quickly identify the data elements, and each collection entry is equal to a single database record. Notice that you create a single `Person` object (`Individual`) to store the information. A single call to the `Persons` collection object, `ContactList`, adds all the information at once.

Creating the output is also easier. A single call to `ContactList` places the information in `Individual`. The `Output` string uses information from this single object to create an entry for the message box. Notice that you don't need any strange math for the expression in the `For...Next` loop.

Chapter 10

Working with Disk Files

*Y*ou use disk storage every time that you work with an application. Disk storage is the most convenient and least expensive means of permanently saving data on a computer system. Permanent storage means that the information on the disk drive remains there after you turn the computer off.

Disk storage can hold several kinds of information. The program that you use to write VBA code is an executable file — it contains information but not user data. The documents that you save are user data. The program that you use to work with VBA already supports the documents that you want to use. However, you might want to save information in other formats, which is one reason to write a VBA program that works with disk storage.

A third kind of disk storage is settings. Older versions of Windows use the initialization (INI) file exclusively. Newer versions of Windows rely heavily on the Registry for setting storage, and some use server storage in the form of Active Directory. All three forms of settings storage are viable, but the INI file is the easiest method to use from VBA.

This chapter demonstrates various methods for working with disk files. You might find that you want to store data in a new format or save program settings after you see how easy it is to work with disk files.

Using Disk Storage

Placing information on disk is an essential task for most applications. The data that an application creates is the main reason why you have an interest in it. However, the application already handles data storage for you, so you don't need to consider this use for disk files in your program. You might think that's the end of the data storage needs for your program, but it isn't. Your program also has valuable data that it must maintain.

Application configuration information

When you interact with the user of your program, you might want to retain any settings that the user has made. It's always a good idea to store the user interface settings so that they are restored every time that you start the program.

You can also store usage information. For example, when you open a Word document, you can press Shift+F5 to return to your previous editing location in the document. Microsoft stores that information between writing sessions so that you can resume your work quickly.

The easiest place to store these settings is on disk in an INI file. However, you can also use a plain text file if you want. You might find the text file easier to understand and use than an INI file. It's important to choose a convenient location for the information. Here are places that you should consider:

- **User folder:** Place user-specific information in the user's folder, which is normally the `\Documents and Settings` directory of the machine. Every user has a personal directory, and you can create a subdirectory in that folder for your program. Using this technique lets users have their own settings.

- **Document folder:** When a series of settings apply to a specific document and not to a particular user, it pays to use a document folder for configuration storage. Using this technique ensures that any custom document settings are stored with the document.

- **Project folder:** A setting could affect all documents in a particular project. You can store the configuration with the project to ensure that everyone working with the project can access them. Using a project folder also ensures the settings remain safe because the same security settings that keep the data safe will keep your configuration file safe.

- **Workgroup folder:** Your program could affect how the members of a workgroup interact. When everyone uses the same settings, you want to be sure that they are in a central place. The question to ask yourself in this case is whether the settings are truly necessary. You might want to consider writing your program so that it uses those settings by default rather than storing the settings in a file.

Data translation

Data translation is a task that you might have to perform from time to time. You might have to transfer information to another system, or you might simply require the information in another form. Before you break out the VBA Integrated Development Environment (IDE), though, make sure that the application doesn't provide the required translation for you. Most applications install with just the most popular data conversion choices and support many others. In addition, vendors often create new translation options for their application that you can download from a Web site.

After you know that you need to translate the data, try to choose an easy format. Pure text is the easiest method of transferring information between two programs. Unfortunately, pure text lacks formatting information. The content is still intact, but notes and other information that you added in the application might not appear with the data. In some cases, transferring the content is the best you can hope to achieve, but you should look for other options.

Data storage

You might find that you have program data storage needs. This is information outside of the data that the program normally tracks. For example, you might want to create a log file that contains activities performed by your program so that you can detect errors or security problems. It also helps to create performance logs when you suspect that your program doesn't work as fast as it could.

Program data storage should appear in a format that's convenient for you because you're the only one who will see it. You should try to store the information by using the program itself. This is relatively easy to do with a program such as Word or Excel. In some cases, you might want to go to the extra trouble of creating the document by using indirect programming of another application. See Chapter 17 for details on this technique. Finally, you could use an informational Event Log entry to store the information. See the "Using the Event Log" section of Chapter 6 for details on using this technique.

When no other technique will work (or other techniques are just too inconvenient), you can always rely on a simple text file to store the program information. The problem with text files for complex data is that you can't format them, and they can't contain information in easy-to-use formats such as graphs. The best reason to use a text file is that it's an easy and convenient method for storing text information.

Gaining Access to Data Storage

The "Recovering from an error" section of Chapter 6 demonstrates a technique for working with drives by using the FileSystemObject. This same object proves very useful for working with data storage. You can create, delete, read, and write text files by using the TextStream object associated with the FileSystemObject.

Writing to the file

Before you can do anything with disk storage, you need to have data to work with. Writing to a file is the first task that you perform in most cases because you need to create the data that you use later in your program. The example relies on the FileSystemObject, so you need to add a reference to the Microsoft Scripting Runtime by using the Tools➪References command. Listing 10-1 shows a typical example of writing code to a file. (You can find the source code for this example on the Dummies.com site at http://www. dummies.com/go/mueller.)

Listing 10-1   Writing Data to a File

```
Public Sub WriteFile()
    ' Define the path variable.
    Dim DataPath As String

    ' Create a path string for the file. Start with the
    ' default program settings path. Add a special folder
    ' for this program.
    DataPath = Application.UserLibraryPath + "FirstFile\"

    ' Create a file system object.
    Dim FS As FileSystemObject
    Set FS = New FileSystemObject

    ' Verify the path exists.
    If Not FS.FolderExists(DataPath) Then
        ' If not, create it.
        FS.CreateFolder DataPath
    End If

    ' Create a text file object.
    Dim Output As TextStream
```

```
      Set Output = FS.CreateTextFile(DataPath + "Config.txt")

      ' Write information to the file.
      Output.WriteLine "Hello"
      Output.Write "World"

      ' Close the file.
      Output.Close
   End Sub
```

This example assumes that you want to write personal configuration information for a user. The code begins by creating a DataPath variable by using the Application.UserLibraryPath property and a special folder for the application information.

After the code creates a FileSystemObject named FS, it checks for the existence of the output folder. You must perform this task each time because you don't know whether this is the first time that the program has run or whether the user has removed the folder. The code creates the folder by using the CreateFolder method if it doesn't exist.

After the code knows that the data folder exists, it can create the TextStream object that writes data to the file. Use the CreateTextFile method if you're not sure whether the file exists. This method normally *overwrites* (erases the content) any existing file, but one of the optional arguments lets you *append* (add to the end) information to an existing file.

The code uses the WriteLine method to output the first line of text. This is the same as using Write and adding a vbCrLf constant to the end of the text. Using WriteLine for multiple lines of text is more convenient because you don't have to remember to add the constant.

Always use the Close method to close the file before the code ends. Otherwise, VBA won't write the information to disk, and you'll lose any information still located in memory.

Reading from the file

Storing information on disk means reading it into memory at some point so that you can use it. You use the FileSystemObject for this task, just as you use it to write the file. Listing 10-2 shows a typical example of reading a file from disk.

Listing 10-2   Reading Data from a File

```
Public Sub ReadFile()
    ' Define the path variable.
    Dim DataPath As String
    DataPath = Application.UserLibraryPath + "FirstFile\"

    ' Create a file system object.
    Dim FS As FileSystemObject
    Set FS = New FileSystemObject

    ' Determine whether the file exists.
    If Not FS.FileExists(DataPath + "Config.txt") Then

        ' Tell the user there are no config settings.
        MsgBox "The Configuration file is missing!", _
               vbCritical, _
               "Missing File Error"

        ' Exit the Sub without reading the file.
        Exit Sub
    End If

    ' Create a text file object.
    Dim Output As TextStream
    Set Output = FS.OpenTextFile( _
        DataPath + "Config.txt", ForReading)

    ' Determine whether there is data in the file.
    If Output.AtEndOfStream Then

        ' Tell the user the file is empty.
        MsgBox "There is no configuration file data!", _
               vbExclamation, _
               "Data Missing Error"

        ' Exit the Sub without reading the file.
        Exit Sub
    End If

    ' Create a variable to hold the information.
    Dim ReadData As String

    ' Write information to the file.
    ReadData = Output.ReadLine()
    ReadData = ReadData + " " + Output.ReadLine()

    ' Display the result.
    MsgBox ReadData, vbInformation, "File Content"

    ' Close the file.
    Output.Close
End Sub
```

This example demonstrates the usefulness of the `Application.UserLibraryPath` property. Whenever new users logs onto the system, the value of this property changes automatically to their personal settings directory. All users have their own directory — and, therefore, their own settings. However, your application doesn't have to care about this real-word concern if you write the code carefully because VBA automatically tracks it for you.

You still don't know whether a file exists when you need it — the user could have erased it or might not have used your program before. The `FileExists` method returns `True` when the file exists. You don't have to tell the user that the file is missing — I provide this feature for this example so that you would know. Normally, you can exit the sub-procedure at this point and simply use the default program settings.

Next, the code opens the file by using the `OpenTextFile`. This method also works when you want to write to the file. You know that that files exists, so this task won't generate an error. However, you don't know whether the file contains any information. A system error or user intrusion could leave the file blank. The `AtEndOfStream` property tells you whether a freshly opened file contains any information because a file with 0 bytes will set this property to `True`.

After you know that the file contains data, you can choose to read all the information by using the `ReadAll` method, a single line of information by using the `ReadLine` method, or a series of bytes from the file by using the `Read` method. VBA doesn't return the `vbCrLf` constant at the end of the line when you use the `ReadLine` method.

The code extracts the information from the file. It displays the information by using a message box. Finally, the code closes the file. You must also close the file when you read it. Otherwise, the file could become truncated or experience other damage.

Working with Settings

Many applications, including Windows, use INI files to store information. The INI file has a standard format that is easy to work with. View any of the INI files in the Windows folder, such as `Win.INI` or `System.INI`, and you see two kinds of entry. The first is the section entry, which is surrounded by square brackets, such as the `[fonts]` section in the `Win.INI` file. The second entry is a key and value pair. The key comes first and is separated from the value by an equals sign.

You might need to create an INI file for your program. The INI file provides the means for storing settings and restoring them later. The `Dictionary` object provides the perfect means for working with INI settings because it uses a key and value pair for storing information. The example in this section shows how to read and write an INI file.

Writing an INI file

It pays to create one `Dictionary` object for each section of your INI file. Using the objects in this way makes it easy to quickly locate the information that you need. The tradeoff is that you have more objects to work with, and your program will experience a small performance hit. Listing 10-3 contains the code that you need to use a `Dictionary` object to write to an INI file. (You can find the source code for this example on the Dummies.com site at `http://www.dummies.com/go/mueller`.)

Listing 10-3   Using a Dictionary Object

```
Public Sub WriteDictionary()
    ' Create a variable to hold the data.
    Dim DataString As Variant

    ' Create the dictionary for user settings.
    Dim UserSetting As Dictionary
    Set UserSetting = New Dictionary
    UserSetting.Add "Greeting", "Hello"
    UserSetting.Add "Language", "English"

    ' Create the dictionary for application configuration.
    Dim AppConfig As Dictionary
    Set AppConfig = New Dictionary
    AppConfig.Add "ShowHelpMenu", "True"
    AppConfig.Add "AllowChanges", "True"

    ' Create the configuration file.
    Dim TheConfig As TextStream
    OpenWriteConfig "DictionaryDemo", "Data.INI", TheConfig

    ' Write the UserSetting Dictionary.
    TheConfig.WriteLine "[UserSetting]"
    For Each DataString In UserSetting
        TheConfig.Write DataString
        TheConfig.Write "="
        TheConfig.WriteLine UserSetting.Item(DataString)
    Next

    'Write the AppConfig Dictionary.
    TheConfig.WriteLine "[AppConfig]"
```

```
      For Each DataString In AppConfig
          TheConfig.Write DataString
          TheConfig.Write "="
          TheConfig.WriteLine AppConfig.Item(DataString)
      Next

      ' Close the configuration file.
      TheConfig.Close
  End Sub
```

The code begins by creating two `Dictionary` objects — one for each section of the INI file. It fills these objects with data for the example. In your program, you fill the `Dictionary` objects with your program settings or other data.

The code calls the `OpenWriteConfig` sub-procedure next. This is a special function that I wrote that looks almost exactly the same as the beginning code for the earlier "Writing to the file" section. When this call returns, `TheConfig` points to a `TextStream` that the code can use for writing.

It's important to provide a section header for each of your `Dictionary` objects, or you won't be able to parse the file later. The code writes this heading first, and then it writes the individual key/value pairs by using a `For Each...Next` statement. You could create a single routine to perform this task, but using the technique shown in the code is actually easier to understand and is self documenting to a point. As always, make sure that you close the configuration file before you exit the sub-procedure.

Reading an INI file

Reading the INI file is a little more difficult than writing to it. The problem is that you have straight text and don't know whether someone has changed the file in some way. Parsing straight text means reading key values and acting upon them. (*Parsing* is the act of reading each word individually and determining what that word means in context of the task at hand.) Listing 10-4 contains the code that you need to read an INI file.

Listing 10-4   Reading an INI File with a Dictionary

```
Public Sub ReadDictionary()
    ' Create an individual data element.
    Dim DataElement As String

    ' Create a dictionary selector.
    Dim Selector As Dictionary

    ' Create a string indexer.
```

(continued)

Listing 10-4 *(continued)*

```
    Dim Index As Long

    ' Create the dictionary for user settings.
    Dim UserSetting As Dictionary
    Set UserSetting = New Dictionary

    ' Create the dictionary for application configuration.
    Dim AppConfig As Dictionary
    Set AppConfig = New Dictionary

    ' Try to open the configuration file.
    Dim TheConfig As TextStream
    If Not OpenReadConfig("DictionaryDemo", "Data.INI", _
            TheConfig) Then

        'Exit the sub if not successful.
        Exit Sub
    End If

    ' Read the file into the dictionaries.
    While Not TheConfig.AtEndOfStream

        ' Read the data element.
        DataElement = TheConfig.ReadLine

        Select Case DataElement
            ' Set the selector for AppConfig.
            Case "[AppConfig]"
                Set Selector = AppConfig

            ' Set the selector for UserSetting.
            Case "[UserSetting]"
                Set Selector = UserSetting

            'Fill the selected dictionary with data.
            Case Else
                Index = InStr(1, DataElement, "=")
                Selector.Add Left(DataElement, Index - 1), _
                        Mid(DataElement, Index + 1)
        End Select
    Wend

    ' Close the configuration file.
    TheConfig.Close
End Sub
```

The code begins by creating the two `Dictionary` objects that you need to
hold the information. It also creates a special `Dictionary` object named
`Selector` and a few variables that it needs to parse the file content.

The program begins by opening the configuration file and creating the TextStream by using the OpenReadConfig function. This function is very similar to the beginning code for the example in the earlier "Reading from the file" section. When the function returns, it's True if it opened the file. If the return value is False, the ReadDictionary sub-procedure exits because there's no file information to parse.

Notice how this example uses the AtEndOfStream property. This use is more common than the use shown in the earlier "Reading from the file" section. The While...Wend loop continues reading data until there's no more data to read. Each iteration of the loop selects an action based on the content of DataElement.

Notice the Set Selector = AppConfig statement. This statement does more than you might think. It actually makes Selector and AppConfig equal so that any changes made to Selector also appear in AppConfig. This technique provides a generic reference when parsing the key/value pairs in the file. The routine doesn't have to do anything special because the correct Dictionary object is already selected.

The final piece of coding to consider is the key/value pair parsing. The INI file stores them as two strings separated by an equals sign. The information appears on a single line. Using the string manipulation functions shown separates the two values so that the code can add them to the appropriate dictionary.

Chapter 11

VBA Programming with XML

*T*he *eXtensible Markup Language* (XML) is a special way of marking text so that it contains both information and context. Using this technique means that the recipient not only knows the information but also the meaning behind the information. For example, if you see *12.99* in a text file, you wouldn't know what it meant. It's a number, but that's all you know. However, by adding context to the number, you can say that the number means 12 dollars and 99 cents.

XML is a relatively new technology that began on the Internet to help make information exchange possible. You can use it to exchange data with others, even if they don't have the same program or even the same operating system that you do. The only requirement is that both machines can read text and that you have a program that can understand the XML.

This chapter describes XML and how you can use it to enhance the documents that you create with Office. Although you can manually perform many of the tasks that I describe in this chapter, using VBA to perform them makes sense because the actions are both lengthy and repetitive. In addition, you must perform some XML tasks, such as defining precise output content, with VBA because there is no manual alternative. The chapter also discusses methods for viewing the XML and taking it apart so that you know how it works. More importantly, you see how to write programs that can interpret the XML. This final task is important because you can then use XML to send information in any format needed.

Understanding XML

This section describes the basics of XML and how to construct simple XML files. In many cases, this is all that you need to know to use XML in a VBA program. A simple file can help you store configuration settings for a program or transfer information from one machine to another. If you want to discover more about XML, you can find an excellent tutorial at http://www.w3schools.com/xml/.

Viewing an XML file

XML files contain formatted text. You can open an XML file in Notepad and see everything that the file contains. If you've ever viewed the HyperText Markup Language (HTML) used for a Web page, XML looks very similar. Here's an example of a simple XML document like you would see it in Notepad. (You can find the source code for this example on the Dummies.com site at http://www.dummies.com/go/mueller.)

```
<?xml version="1.0"?>
<Root_Element>
    <!--This is a comment.-->
    <Element1 Attribute1="This is an attribute.">
        <ChildElement1>This is a child element.</ChildElement1>
    </Element1>
    This is some text.
    <Element2>This is the second element.</Element2>
</Root_Element>
```

However, using Notepad to view an XML file isn't the best approach because there's no explanation of the various parts of the XML. You can view XML files by using Internet Explorer. Figure 11-1 shows a typical example of how an XML file looks. The various components of the XML file appear in different colors. You can expand and collapse the parts of the XML file as needed. The hierarchical display works just like the one in the left pane of Windows Explorer. Internet Explorer makes it easy to see just what you need.

Unfortunately, Internet Explorer doesn't allow you to edit the XML file, and you can't really work with the XML information. Microsoft understands that you need to work with XML files, so it created a free program named Microsoft XML Notepad (see Figure 11-2). You can download this program from http://www.webattack.com/get/xmlnotepad.shtml or http://msdn.microsoft.com/library/en-us/dnxml/html/xmlpadintro.asp. Another good free XML editor is the XRay2 XML Editor at http://www.architag.com/xray/. There are also third-party programs such as xmlspy (http://www.xmlspy.com) that you might want to consider. This chapter uses XML Notepad for description purposes.

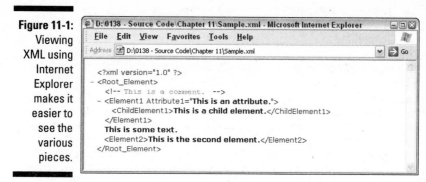

Figure 11-1:
Viewing
XML using
Internet
Explorer
makes it
easier to
see the
various
pieces.

Figure 11-2 shows that each piece of the XML file appears on a different line. Like with Internet Explorer, you can collapse or expand the hierarchy as needed. To edit an entry, select the line. The selected line indents slightly so that you know when you can edit it. You can use the editor to change part names as well as values.

A few of the editing controls work similar to those found in the Outline view of Word (or any other outline program that you might have used). To change the location of an entry, highlight it and then drag it to a new location. The cursor changes to a thick line that shows where the change places the selection part.

Figure 11-2:
Get a better
view of
XML files
with XML
Notepad.

Working with elements

The hierarchy of an XML document depends upon elements. From a code perspective, an element looks like the tags that you find in HTML. An element provides context information for the values and attributes that you create. In many cases, an element acts like a variable would in your VBA program.

Every XML document that you create must have a *root element* — the base element for all other parts of the hierarchy. You must provide precisely one root element — not two or three. Think of the root element like the container that holds all the other elements in place. The root element uses a special icon in XML Notepad so that you can easily see it. (See the `Root_Element` entry in Figure 11-2.)

Elements can contain other elements. Other than the root element, elements that contain other elements use a folder icon, as shown in Figure 11-2. These are *node* elements. An element that is at the end of the hierarchy and that doesn't contain any other element is a *leaf* element. Leaf elements use a red slash icon. An element that appears below another element in the hierarchy is a *child element*.

To add a new element to an XML document by using XML Notepad, right-click the location that you want to use for the element. If this element is at the same level as the place that you clicked, choose Insert⇨Element from the context menu that appears. Otherwise, choose Insert⇨Child Element from the context menu. If you make a mistake, you can simply move the new element to the right location in the hierarchy.

Working with attributes

Only elements can contain information. One of the two common forms of information is the attribute. You normally use an *attribute* to modify the meaning of the element. It's also convenient to use attributes when an element has more than one value, but you should avoid this use if possible because a value is not the same as an attribute, even when there are multiple values to consider.

Think of attributes the same way that you think of properties for a method because they're often used in the same way. Every attribute includes a name, an equals sign, and some value. An element can have as many attributes as needed to describe the element. In fact, you don't have to include any attributes at all.

Attributes appear as purple diamonds in XML Notepad. They always appear as children of the element that they affect. Consequently, `Attribute1` in Figure 11-2 affects `Element1` and not `ChildElement1`. To add an attribute to an XML document by using XML Notepad, right-click the element that you want to use and then choose Insert⇨Attribute from the context menu that appears.

Working with values

Values are the second type of information an element can contain. A *value* appears between a beginning and ending tag like this:

```
<ChildElement1>This is a child element.</ChildElement1>
```

The value is the content that you normally see in a text file. It's the information that the element describes. Only leaf elements can have values, so you need to construct your XML document in a way that allows the leaves to hold the information that you want to transfer to another machine.

Don't confuse this kind of value with the values used for comments, text entries, or attributes. This value always appears as part of a leaf element and is always the content that you want to transfer.

Working with comments

Comments can document your XML file. Generally, you keep comments to a minimum in an XML file because you seldom read the file directly. Using too many comments increases the size and the transmission time of the document. A comment should describe some essential characteristic of the document that might not seem obvious. You can use these comments as programming reminders.

XML Notepad uses a blue exclamation point for comments. To add a comment, right-click the element that you want to document and then choose Insert⇨Comment from the context menu that appears. Comments in an XML document use the same form as comments in an HTML document — they appear like this:

```
<!--This is a comment.-->
```

Comparing WordML with Saved XML

When you save a Word document either manually or programmatically, you can save it as an XML document. However, not all XML documents are created equal. Figure 11-3 shows a Word Save As dialog box set up to save a document as XML.

This dialog box shows the default setup, which is to save the document by using WordML and not as standard XML. Using WordML preserves the information in your document in an XML file that Word can understand. Figure 11-4 shows an XML Notepad view of the information in a simple Word document.

You might think this document is complex, but it isn't too hard to understand if you take it apart one piece at a time. For example, if you open the W:DOCINFO element, you see a list of document information entries such as the name of the author and the company. Every entry that appears in the

Document Properties dialog box also appears as part of this element. You can also see elements devoted to the document properties (such as the document view and default tab stop settings), fonts, and styles.

Figure 11-3:
Save your
document
as XML by
using the
Save As
dialog box.

Figure 11-4 shows part of the W:BODY expanded. This element contains the content for the document. Every heading begins a new WX:SUB-SECTION element. Contained within this element is the name of the style and the text associated with the entry.

Figure 11-4:
Use XML
Notepad to
discover
important
information
about your
WordML
file.

When you try to save a standard Word document as pure XML by selecting the Save Data Only check box (bottom-right of Figure 11-3), Word doesn't generate WordML; instead, it generates standard XML. Unfortunately, your Word template file probably doesn't include the entries required to create standard XML. As a result, the output is going to be 0 bytes long. That's right: Nothing is saved because your document isn't tagged for use with standard XML. See the upcoming "Creating a Simple Word XML Document" section for details on creating a template that saves your data to standard XML.

When you don't need to save all the information provided by WordML and you don't want to create a special template to do the job, you can rely on eXtensible Style Language Transformation (XSLT) to transform your data into standard XML. The benefit of using this technique is that it's faster than using a specialized template. The problem of using this technique is that you can't rely on it to provide complete data translation if you don't use the correct tags or if the XSLT file isn't formatted correctly. See the upcoming "Saving your Word document by using XSLT" section for details on using this technique.

Manipulating XML Data

Microsoft is making it easier to create, change, delete, import, and export XML by using Office products. XML makes it easier to manage data on the Internet and also to exchange data with other people. This section demonstrates several ways to work with XML data by using Office.

Writing the data to disk

The easiest way to export your data to disk is to save it as an XML document by using the SaveAs method. Here's an example of this method.

```
Public Sub OutputInventory()
    ' Use the standard SaveAs method to export XML.
    Sheet1.SaveAs "ExcelXML.XML", xlXMLSpreadsheet
End Sub
```

You can also accomplish this task by choosing the File➪Save As command. The advantage of this method is that you can concentrate on a single worksheet, set of records, or an area of a document instead of saving the whole document. The first argument is the filename. The second argument varies by Office application. Excel uses the xlXMLSpreadsheet to create XML output, and Word uses the wdFormatXML constant.

The only problem with this technique is that it only saves the content and information about the content. Figure 11-4 shows typical output for Word when using this method. This method works best if you plan to manipulate the data outside Office by using another program, interpret the data by using XSLT, or require portions of the data where interpretation isn't required.

Defining a schema

A *schema* is a definition of the structure of your data. You can look at the data and figure out the structure, but the computer can't — it needs additional information. Database managers such as Access always use a schema (you define it when you create a table), but other Office applications don't because you normally don't need to organize the information by using a schema. Figure 11-5 shows a typical worksheet. The data structure is probably obvious to you because each of the columns is named, but the computer doesn't have a clue as to what that data means.

Figure 11-5: Understanding data formats is easy for you but hard for the computer.

An *XML Schema Definition* (XSD) file contains a description of the information that you want to export from or import to an Office application. It doesn't matter which application you use because at some point, you have to create an XSD file to perform pure XML data transfers. Listing 11-1 shows an example of an XSD file that describes the data shown in Figure 11-5. (You can find the source code for this example on the Dummies.com site at http://www.dummies.com/go/mueller.)

Listing 11-1   Creating an XSD Description

```xml
<?xml version="1.0"?>
<xs:schema xmlns:xs="http://www.w3.org/2001/XMLSchema">

<xs:element name="Items">
  <xs:complexType>
    <xs:sequence>
      <xs:element name="Item" maxOccurs="unbounded">
        <xs:complexType>
          <xs:sequence>
            <xs:element name="Name" type="xs:string"/>
            <xs:element name="Value" type="xs:decimal"/>
            <xs:element name="Total" type="xs:decimal"/>
          </xs:sequence>
        </xs:complexType>
      </xs:element>
    </xs:sequence>
  </xs:complexType>
</xs:element>

</xs:schema>
```

This is yet another XML file, so it begins with the standard XML processing instruction. The second line contains the URL for the XSD file definitions. You must include this line in all your XSD files. You can include other information as part of this header such as a personal namespace, but it's all optional. See the tutorial at http://www.w3schools.com/schema/default.asp for additional information.

The structure of your information comes next. Chapter 9 describes how VBA collections work. The tags that XSD relies on to define your data act much like a collection. The top element, Items, defines the collection name. The <xs:complexType> tag tells the XSD parser that you are defining something other than a string or an integer. You use the <xs:sequence> tag to tell the XSD parser that the next set of elements must appear in the order shown and that it can't skip any of the elements.

The <xs:element name="Item" maxOccurs="unbounded"> tag shows how to create an individual item within an XSD collection. The two things that set this tag apart from the <Items> tag is that it appears within the <Items> tag and also uses the special maxOccurs attribute. Notice that the maxOccurs attribute is defined as unbounded (unlimited) so that the Items collection can contain as many individual Item elements as needed.

The <Item> tag is also a complex type and requires elements in a specific sequence. This time, the individual elements are simple types. The <Name> tag is a string, but the <Value> and <Total> tags are both decimal. XSD doesn't currently support a currency type, so your best choice is to use decimal to ensure that the XSD parser preserves the accuracy of the data that you transfer.

Defining XSD to worksheet linkage

Writing the XSD file creates a definition that you can use to work with data in Excel. However, you still haven't created linkage between the XSD file and the Excel document. (You should perform this task by using a document template in Word — see the upcoming "Creating a Simple Word XML Document" section for details.) Here's how to create linkage in Excel.

1. **Open Excel and load the document that you want to export.**

2. **Use the Data⇨XML⇨Design command.**

   Excel displays the XML Structure task pane.

3. **Click Workbook Maps in the XML Structure task pane.**

   Excel displays the Select XML Source dialog box.

4. **Highlight the XSD file that you want to use (ExcelXMLSchema.XSD for the example) and then click Open.**

   Excel displays the content of the XSD file in the XML Structure task pane, as shown in Figure 11-6.

5. **Right-click the top-level element (Items) and then choose Map Element from the context menu that appears.**

   Excel displays an XML List dialog box.

Figure 11-6:
Use the XML Structure task pane to manage your XSD files.

6. **Highlight or type the range of data that you want to use for the exported list and then click OK.**

Excel displays the selected range as a list.

Exporting the data to disk

After you create a schema and link it to an Office document, you can perform a true export of the information as XML. There are two separate methods to perform this task. The first, `ExportXml`, creates a string that you can manipulate by using various XML features built into Office. The second, `Export`, performs a standard export to a file. Listing 11-2 shows examples of both methods.

Listing 11-2   Two Methods for Exporting XML Data

```
Public Sub OutputInventory2()
    ' Use the ExportXml technique to save data and the data
    ' interpretation.
    MsgBox Workbooks(1).XmlMaps("Items_Map").ExportXml()

    ' Use the standard Export method to create a file.
    Workbooks(1).XmlMaps(1).Export "ExcelXML2.XML", True
End Sub
```

In both cases, you rely on collections to obtain the information. Notice that you can use a number or a string to reference the particular XML map that you want to use for export purposes. Both the `ExportXml` and `Export` methods include an optional argument that forces the parser to check the XML for proper form prior to export. When using the `Export` method, you must supply a string, and you should tell the method to overwrite any existing file of the same name.

Importing the data from disk

Importing data from disk varies in difficulty based on the kind of XML file that you want to import. Excel normally does a good job of figuring out how to import well-formed XML. Listing 11-3 shows the code that you need to import a standard XML file.

Listing 11-3   Importing XML from Disk

```
Public Sub ImportInventory()
    ' Obtain the XML from disk using the XmlImport.
    ThisWorkbook.XmlImport "ExcelXML2.XML", _
                           True, _
                           Sheet2.Range("A1")
End Sub
```

The `XmlImport` method requires three arguments. The first is the name of the file that you want to import. The second indicates whether you want to overwrite any existing data. Finally, you must supply a location to hold the data.

When you run this program, you see an Error in Schema dialog box. The data exported with the example doesn't include an XSD reference. Excel doesn't know how to interpret the data because it has no data definition. In this case, you can safely click the Infer button to get the correct result.

Creating a Simple Word XML Document

Word automates the process linking an XSD file to your document by adding this feature through the document templates. When you create a document by using a properly designed template, the XML tags are automatically added according to the XSD schema that you create.

You might want to create searchable letters. One way to do this is to export the letters as XML and to use a standard search engine. Start by creating a letter template file. The example includes the usual features such as To and From addresses, the date that the letter was written, a greeting, the letter body, and a closing element. Listing 11-4 shows the XSD file used to describe this document. (You can find the source code for this example on the Dummies.com site at `http://www.dummies.com/go/mueller`.)

Listing 11-4   Creating an XSD File to Export a Letter

```
<?xml version="1.0"?>
<xs:schema xmlns:xs="http://www.w3.org/2001/XMLSchema"
 targetNamespace="http://www.mysite.com"
 xmlns="http://www.mysite.com"
 elementFormDefault="qualified">

<xs:element name="MyLetter">
 <xs:complexType mixed="true">
  <xs:sequence>
    <xs:element name="FromAddress" type="xs:string"/>
    <xs:element name="Sent" type="xs:string"/>
    <xs:element name="ToName" type="xs:string"/>
    <xs:element name="ToCompany" type="xs:string"/>
    <xs:element name="ToAddress" type="xs:string"/>
    <xs:element name="ToCity" type="xs:string"/>
    <xs:element name="ToState" type="xs:string"/>
    <xs:element name="ToZIP" type="xs:string"/>
```

```
        <xs:element name="Greeting" type="xs:string"/>
        <xs:element name="Body" type="xs:string" maxOccurs="unbounded"/>
        <xs:element name="Closing" type="xs:string"/>
    </xs:sequence>
  </xs:complexType>
</xs:element>

</xs:schema>
```

This example doesn't require a collection of items such as those found in a database, so it doesn't require a complex structure. Each of the elements only appears one time except the Body element, which can appear once for each paragraph in the letter. Notice that this XSD file includes a targetNamespace. Think of this as the default namespace for the XSD file. Word requires this entry. Word also requires that you include the mixed="true" attribute for the <xs:complexType> tag. Otherwise, it continually reports that the MyLetter element can't contain text.

After you create the template and the XSD file, you need to link the two. The procedure for accomplishing this task is different from working with an individual file. Here are the steps that you need to follow.

1. **Use the Tools⇨Templates and Options command.**

   Word displays the Templates and Options dialog box.

2. **Select the XML Schema tab.**

3. **Click the Add Schema button.**

   Word displays an Add Schema dialog box.

4. **Highlight the schema that you want to add (WordLetterSchema.XSD for this example) and then click Open.**

   Word asks whether you want to make this schema available to all users. You must click Yes if you want everyone to use this schema — click No only if you want to use this personally.

5. **Click No.**

   Word adds the new schema to the XML Schema tab.

6. **Select the check box of the new item to attach it to the template and then click OK.**

   Word displays the XML Structure task pane.

7. **Highlight an item and then click the schema entry at the bottom of the task pane.**

   Word asks whether you want to apply the schema to the entire document.

8. **Click Yes.**

   Word applies a beginning and an ending tag for the schema to the template.

9. **Highlight each element in turn and click its schema entry in the XML Structure task pane.**

   Word applies individual element tags to each field in the template.

10. **Save the new template.**

After you create a document by using the new template, you can use the Save Data Only check box of the Save As dialog box as shown in Figure 11-3. The new document contains just the data that you created in a true XML format. Figure 11-7 shows an example of the sample letter provided with the source code.

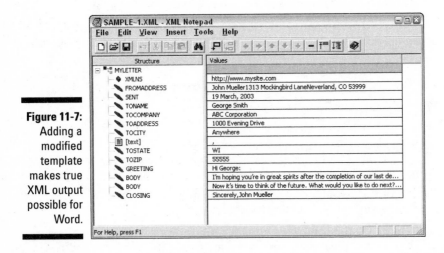

Figure 11-7: Adding a modified template makes true XML output possible for Word.

Changing the Face of XML with XSLT

Looking at Figures 11-1 and 11-2 shows you that XML by itself is a little tough to read. You might also find that some XML files contain too much information. XSLT helps correct both of these problems. It can format the information so that it's easier to read, and you can also use XSLT to limit the amount of information that you see. XSLT transforms XML into something usable.

Note that you might see two definitions for XSLT: eXtensible *Style* Language Transformation and eXtensible *Stylesheet* Language Transformations. Both definitions refer to the same technology. I prefer the first form because it better describes how XSLT works.

This section describes how you can use XSLT to change the way that the output from your applications looks. After you save your document as XML, you can present it on a Web site for someone else to see. XSLT can transform the XML into HTML so that other people can enjoy your work.

XSLT can perform other kinds of transformations, so don't limit yourself to the techniques that you see demonstrated in this chapter. For example, you can use XSLT to create another XML document or even a text file. XSLT is all about transforming your data into the form that you want rather than forcing you to accept data in a less-than-optimal form. There's an excellent XSL tutorial at `http://www.w3schools.com/xsl/default.asp`. You can also find a good XSLT reference at `http://www.zvon.org/xxl/XSLTreference/Output/index.html`.

Understanding XSLT

An *XSLT file* is just a specially formatted XML file that can contain HTML tags and text as well. Whenever a program sees an XSLT file, it calls on the XSL *parser* (the program responsible for working with XSLT files) to read the file and interpret it. XSLT works by matching an element or attribute in an XML file. When the XSL parser finds a match, it uses a template to convert the information that it finds into something else, such as an HTML tag, some text, content, or even different XML. The idea is to transform the data into something useful.

The `Sample.XML` file shown in Figures 11-1 and 11-2 is interesting, but it's hard to read. Listing 11-5 shows an XSLT file that transforms those XML tags into something more useful. (You can find the source code for this example on the Dummies.com site at `http://www.dummies.com/go/mueller`.)

Listing 11-5   Using XSLT to Transform XML Data

```
<?xml version='1.0'?>
<xsl:stylesheet version='1.0'
xmlns:xsl='http://www.w3.org/1999/XSL/Transform'>
<xsl:output method="xml" indent="yes" />
<xsl:template match="/">

<!-- Create the HTML Code for this stylesheet. -->
<HTML>
<HEAD>
    <TITLE>Sample2.XML File Output</TITLE>
</HEAD>

<BODY>
<H1>Sample2.XML File Output</H1>
<xsl:apply-templates select="//Element1"/>
```

(continued)

Listing 11-5 *(continued)*

```
<xsl:apply-templates select="//Element2"/>
<xsl:apply-templates select="//comment()"/>
<H2>Text:</H2>
<xsl:apply-templates select="//text()"/>

</BODY>
</HTML>

</xsl:template>

<!-- XSL template section that describes XML content. -->

<xsl:template match="Element1">
    <H2>Element1 Content</H2>
    <xsl:value-of select="@Attribute1"/>
    <BR/>
    <xsl:value-of select="ChildElement1"/>
</xsl:template>

<xsl:template match="Element2">
    <H2>Element2 Content</H2>
    <xsl:value-of select="."/>
</xsl:template>

<xsl:template match="comment()">
    <H2>Comment:</H2>
    <xsl:value-of select="."/>
</xsl:template>

<xsl:template match="text()">
    <xsl:value-of select="."/>
        <BR/>
</xsl:template>

</xsl:stylesheet>
```

An XSLT document begins like any other XML document with the XML version number. The next line defines the XSL version number and also provides a pointer to the XSL namespace. A *namespace* is a special place on the Internet that defines XSL terms such as stylesheet, output, and template so that Internet Explorer can understand them. Every time that you use a special XSL term in the XSLT file, you must precede it with the special `xsl:` namespace indicator.

The `<xsl:output>` tag tells Internet Explorer what kind of output to create. In this case, the code uses the XML method and indents the output so that you can read it easier.

The actual transformation process begins with the `<xsl:template>` tag. This tag begins the matching process at the very beginning of the XML document. You can process just a part of a document when desired.

The template begins creating the HTML output with the usual list of tags, including the `<HTML>`, the heading, and the body tags. Things change when it comes to the content. Each of these items is an `<xsl:apply>` tag. The first XML file content matched is the `<Element1>` tag shown in Figure 11-1.

Notice the `</xsl:template>` tag at the end of the HTML output. This tag determines where the template specific code begins and where the HTML tags end. When the XSL parser sees the `<xsl:apply>` tag in the HTML section, it looks for a corresponding `<xsl:template match="Element1">` entry in the template section. The XSL parser adds the information found in this template to the content in the HTML section.

The `<xsl:value-of>` tag tells the XSL parser how to use the XML information that matches the criteria that you provide. The `select` attribute defines what to output. For the `<Element1>` tag, the template outputs the value of `Attribute1`, followed by a `<BR>` HTML tag, and the value of `ChildElement1`. XSL uses the @ (each at) sign to designate an attribute, as shown in the code.

When you want to output the value of the matched value, you use a period character as the `select` value. Look at the code for the `Element2` template, and you can see how this feature works.

XSL supplies a wealth of functions to match special values. The example code shows two of them. The first is the `comment()` function, which tells the XSL parser to work with a comment in some way. The second is the `text()` function, which works with text values in some way. The example code uses both functions to match entries in the XML file and output them to the HTML page.

Before you see the results of the transformation, you have to create a connection between the XML file and the XSLT file. There are a number of ways to do this, but the most direct route is to add a processing directive immediately after the `<?xml version="1.0"?>` entry. Here's a processing directive that tells Internet Explorer to find the `Sample2Format.XSLT` file and use it to format the content of the `Sample2.XML` file.

```
<?xml-stylesheet type="text/xsl" href="Sample2Format.XSLT"?>
```

This processing directive is the only difference between the `Sample.XML` and `Sample2.XML` files found in the source code. Figure 11-8 shows the output from this example.

Sample2.XML File Output - Microsoft Internet Explorer

File   Edit   View   Favorites   Tools   Help

Address D:\0138 - Source Code\Chapter 11\Sample2.xml   ⌄ → Go

Sample2.XML File Output

Element1 Content

This is an attribute.
This is a child element.

Element2 Content

This is the second element.

Comment:

This is a comment.

Text:

This is a child element.
This is some text.
This is the second element.

Figure 11-8:
Use XSLT
to convert
XML files
into
readable
HTML
output.

Saving your Word document by using XSLT

You can use XSLT to work with any XML file generated by an Office application — even the WordML documents created by default with Word (see the earlier "Comparing WordML with Saved XML" section for details). When you use the Save As dialog box shown in Figure 11-3 to save a Word document as XML, you can choose to use an XSLT file to modify the output. You might only want the document information or only the document content. It's even possible to build a list of all the fonts used in every Word document on your machine. Any information that WordML provides is available.

The example in this section helps you overcome one of the problems with the output options provided with Word. By using XSLT, you can create an HTML page containing any information about your document. This example shows document information, but the technique works with fonts, options, or the content of the file as well. The main reason why I chose document information is that this particular technique works well if you want to create a Web site with a listing of all the documents that you've created. Using this technique creates a searchable Web site that's infinitely easier to mine for data than using the Word documents directly.

Before you can export data from Word by using XSLT, you need an XSLT file containing the proper code. Listing 11-6 shows the XSLT code for this example. (You can find the source code for this example on the Dummies.com site at http://www.dummies.com/go/mueller.)

Listing 11-6   Using XSLT to Save a Word Document

```
<?xml version='1.0'?>
<xsl:stylesheet version='1.0'
xmlns:xsl='http://www.w3.org/1999/XSL/Transform'
xmlns:w="http://schemas.microsoft.com/office/word/2002/8/wordml">
<xsl:output method="html" indent="yes" />
<xsl:template match="/">

<!-- Create the HTML Code for this stylesheet. -->
<HTML>
<HEAD>
   <TITLE>Word Document Properties</TITLE>
</HEAD>

<BODY>
<CENTER><H3>Word Document Property Values</H3></CENTER>

<TABLE BORDER="2">
   <TR>
      <TH>Property</TH>
      <TH>Value</TH>
   </TR>
      <xsl:apply-templates select="//w:title"/>
</TABLE>

</BODY>
</HTML>
</xsl:template>

<!-- XSL template section that describes table content. -->

<xsl:template match="w:title">
   <TR>
      <TD>
         Title
      </TD>
      <TD>
         <xsl:value-of select="@w:val"/>
      </TD>
   </TR>
</xsl:template>

</xsl:stylesheet>
```

The code shows only one of the `W:DOCINFO` values. This document begins with the standard XSL tags. Notice that it includes a special namespace entry, `xmlns:w="http://schemas.microsoft.com/office/word/2002/8/wordml"`. You must include this namespace to transform WordML documents. Otherwise, you can't interpret them by using XSLT.

Notice that the `<xsl:output>` tag uses the `method="html"` attribute to ensure that the output is in pure HTML. The result displays as HTML in Internet Explorer even if you use the `method="xml"` attribute. However, you experience fewer problems with other browsers if you use the `method="html"` attribute.

The `<xsl:apply-templates>` tag is the first place where you notice the effect of working with WordML. This tag references the new namespace added at the beginning of the file. If you don't include the namespace, none of the entries in the WordML file matches, and there isn't any output in the XSLT file.

Look at the template. It also includes the WordML namespace. You must also include it for entries such as attributes. Many `W:DOCINFO` values rely on the `@w:val` attribute to store their content.

To use the XSLT file to translate a Word file, simply select the Apply Transform check box (bottom-right of Figure 11-3) and select the XSLT file by clicking the Transform button (shown grayed out in Figure 11-3). The output that you create has an XML extension. Simply change it to HTM, and you can view the information as a Web page. Figure 11-9 shows the output from this example.

Figure 11-9:
Creating specialized Word output is easy by using XSLT.

Automating the Word XML process

You can easily automate the task of saving your Word document by using various XSLT files. All you need is a form of the program shown in Listing 11-7.

Listing 11-7   Automatically Saving a Word XML Document

```
Public Sub SaveXMLDocumentInfo()
    ' Create a File Open dialog box.
    Dim GetFile As FileDialog
    Set GetFile = Application.FileDialog(msoFileDialogOpen)

    ' Modify the settings to show XSLT files.
    GetFile.Filters.Clear
    GetFile.Filters.Add "XSLT File", "*.XSLT"
    GetFile.Show

    ' Make sure the save process uses the template.
    ThisDocument.XMLSaveThroughXSLT = _
        GetFile.SelectedItems (1)

    ' Recreate GetFile as a File Save dialog box.
    Set GetFile = Nothing
    Set GetFile = Application.FileDialog(msoFileDialogSaveAs)

    ' Modify the settings to show HTM files.
    GetFile.FilterIndex = 4
    GetFile.Show

    ' Save the document.
    ThisDocument.SaveAs GetFile.SelectedItems(1), _
                    wdFormatXML
End Sub
```

The code begins by creating a `FileDialog` object. You use this object to let the user select files during program execution. When you create a file Open dialog box, you can change the filters to meet specific needs. Use the `Clear` method to remove the default filters and the `Add` method to create new filters. A *filter* consists of a description and the file extension that you want to support in the dialog box. A file Save dialog box doesn't allow you to modify the filters, but you can choose a default filter to help the program user choose the correct save file type quickly.

This example shows the two essential steps that you must perform to save a file by using XSLT. They include setting the `XMLSaveThroughXSLT` property to the name of the template that you want to use and using the Save As dialog box to save the document. Notice the new `wdFormatXML` file format option. This option doesn't appear in older versions of Word (and isn't documented as of the time of writing). The example code forces a save to an HTM document, so you don't even need to rename the file afterward.

Part IV
Programming for Applications

The 5th Wave   By Rich Tennant

"Hey Philip! I think we're in. I'm gonna try linking directly to the screen, but gimme a disguise in case it works. I don't want all of New York to know Jerry DeMarco of 14 Queensberry, Bronx NY, hacked into the 'Times Square video screen.'"

In this part . . .

In this part of the book, I get into the details of using VBA with specific applications. In fact, you discover that VBA can cross application boundaries and perform useful work with more than one application at a time. Office, in general, provides many customization opportunities. Although you can make most Office changes manually, it helps to know how to make them automatically, too. In Chapter 12, I show technique for changing the Office environment to meet changing requirements.

In Chapters 13 through 15, I demonstrate how to add functionality to Word, Excel, and Access, respectively. Each of these host applications provides a unique environment where you can change data and create new information at a click of a button.

When you become more proficient with VBA, you want to build better programs that save you more time. In Chapter 16, I demonstrate how to work with more than one Office application at a time, but you can easily apply what you learn to work with applications from other vendors, too.

Chapter 12

VBA Programming in Office

- -

- -

*Y*ou have the skills required to write any program that you want for your copy of Office. However, there's no program that will do more to improve efficiency than one that affects the user environment. A ten-fold increase in computer performance is of little consequence if you can't employ that performance productively. Yet a small change in the user interface that does nothing to improve computer performance can net huge gains in your productivity by enhancing efficiency.

Microsoft tuned the Office interface to meet the needs of faceless crowds of people. It's hardly the personalized interface that helps you become more efficient and productive. Microsoft provides options that help you modify the interface manually, but that's time consuming. You might find that you need a custom interface to perform each task most efficiently, so manual methods are just counterproductive. VBA is the answer to making these changes automatically as you move from document to document.

This chapter demonstrates two things. First, by using VBA you can modify the Office user interface to meet your specific needs and not those that Microsoft thinks that you might have. Second, VBA helps you perform these interface changes automatically so that you can have a customized environment for every task that you perform.

I also include a section about Office Assistant in this chapter. Judging by the material that I read, people either really dislike Office Assistant, or they think that it's the best feature in the world. In fact, Office Assistant (and its attendant technology, Microsoft Agent) is so successful that you can find other characters to use online (see `http://www.msagentring.org/chars/` for details).

Office Assistant can be entertaining and helpful, but I agree that it's probably not the tool of choice for helping power users. Whether you use Office Assistant depends on the kind of user that you're trying to help with your program. The "Adding Help by Using the Office Assistant" section emphasizes helpful use of Office Agent in your program.

Working with the User Environment

The user environment is where you spend most of your time. It's the visible part of any application. Because it's the visible part of any application, the user environment is the basis on which you make a decision about the application. First impressions are important to how you view an application.

Think of a user environment as *immersive* — as a package of features that present you with a view of the application as a whole. Don't assume that the user environment is the same as the user interface. The user environment includes several features:

- **User interface:** The active portion of the user environment, the *user interface* includes the controls that make the application functional.

- **Graphics:** The physical appearance of the environment affects how you feel about your program. Helpful graphics can direct your attention to specific application features. Some graphics add aesthetic appeal to the application without making it harder to use.

- **Colors and aesthetics:** The use of color can affect your mood. If you use the wrong colors, you can also make some program elements difficult for anyone with certain forms of color blindness to see. A program can really be a thing of beauty.

- **Accessibility:** The difficulty that you encounter using an application affects the way that you view it. An application should include context-sensitive help in addition to the main help. It should also include features that make each control easy to use with either the keyboard or mouse.

- **Logic and flow:** The work required to locate, evaluate, modify, add, and delete data affects your view of an application. Controls should always flow in a logical order to make typing information easy. Data fields should be large enough to include all the information that you need to see at a glance but not so large that you have to move the cursor to see the entire field.

Beneficial changes that you can make

You can make your program a work of art. The beneficial changes that you make to the user environment mean the difference between a program that makes you efficient and one that actually requires more time to use. When you look at your program initially, you think of practical matters — getting the code to work and some essential elements in place. After you get past that stage in development, you need to consider the user environment. Here are some beneficial changes that you should consider:

- **Menus and toolbars:** Create a special menu for features that you use during every session. Note that a feature isn't necessarily a VBA program. For example, it could also be a shortcut to a document template so you can simply click a button to start a new document that requires a certain template. You could also use toolbar buttons for quick access to special symbols, such as the § symbol used for legal abbreviations. Menu entries are always visible and quite easy to use. Use a special toolbar for features that you use during some sessions but not others. Toolbars are easy to hide. Use both a menu and a toolbar for features that you always use and that require quick access.

- **Balloon help:** Every control should have a `ControlTipText` property entry. This includes any toolbar entries that you add. The balloon help text is helpful for anyone who needs additional information about your program features. It's also the only method that ensures that someone who is using a screen reader or other accessibility aid can use your program successfully.

- **Helpful graphics:** A graphic can prove more helpful than text in some cases, especially if the graphic clearly illustrates the intent of a feature better than text can explain (a graphic that's worth a thousand words). You might also want to combine graphics with text to ensure complete understanding.

- **Simplified displays:** You might find that a display becomes too complex after you add the special features that you need to the features that Microsoft thinks that you want. A program that configures a display with features needed to perform a specific task is helpful because reduced complexity makes it easier to find what you need. In fact, a series of task buttons, such as one for letters, another for notes, and still another for lists, can be quite helpful.

- **User settings:** Any time that you can involve the people using your program in the configuration process, you've provided a way for them to express their needs.

Problems that you should consider

Whenever you change something in the user environment, you should consider the problems that such a change can create. The user environment can make or break any program that you create. It might be tempting to add every feature to a menu, drown the display in color, or add graphics to dress up the display.

✔ **Increased training costs:** Whenever you change the user environment, you add a certain amount of confusion. The new features might cause the user to pause to think, or the user might not understand them at all. Training helps users understand the new features and use them efficiently, but training isn't free.

✔ **Update incompatibility:** A new feature that you introduce might cause compatibility problems with future versions of a product. You need to consider how the change will affect the future use of the program.

✔ **Reduced efficiency:** Too many features, controls, display elements, graphics, and other distractions tend to reduce efficiency. It doesn't matter how skilled you are at using a program, too many display elements slow you down because you have to look for what you need. The most efficient program is one that contains just the features that you use and no others.

✔ **Security holes:** Any change that you make to an application can create security holes that the original vendor didn't anticipate and you can't see because you don't have the application code. The very act of turning on macro support in an application opens it to certain types of virus attack. Adding a feature could also make it easier to circumvent security measures such as data encryption and password. Complete testing is usually the only way to ensure that you haven't introduced a security problem.

Manipulating Toolbars and Menus

No matter what program you create, you need to provide a way to run it. Using the Tools⇨Macro⇨Macros command to display the Macros dialog box works fine for a program that you don't use very often, but you want to make some programs easier to access. Manually adding a favorite program to a toolbar or menu works fine if you always want to have it available, but sometimes you don't want to see this option.

This section describes how you can change the toolbar and menu content of an Office application to meet your needs. You can modify existing menus and toolbars as well as add new entries for your custom programs. These changes can occur automatically as the result of environmental conditions, as the result of actions on your part, or on command. Office applications change their appearance to match conditions anyway — this is simply an extension of that idea to meet your specific needs.

Displaying or hiding toolbars and menus

It's helpful to hide or display menus or toolbars as needed. Keeping the display free from clutter is always helpful in improving efficiency and reducing confusion. Both menus and items use the same technique. Working with menus is a little more cumbersome because you have to figure out the name of the menu bar first. It would be nice if Microsoft used the same name for the menu bar in every Office application, but that's just not the case. For example, Excel's menu bar is named Worksheet Menu Bar, but Word uses just Menu Bar. To learn the name of the menu bar for your Office application, simply drag the menu bar from the top and place it somewhere in the editing pane. The name appears on the title bar, as shown in Figure 12-1 for the Word Menu Bar.

Figure 12-1:
The Word
Menu Bar.

After you know the name of the menu or toolbar that you want to change, you can use that information to show or hide it. Listing 12-1 is an example that shows how to work with the Edit⇨Cut menu option. (You can find the source code for this example on the Dummies.com site at `http://www.dummies.com/go/mueller`.)

Listing 12-1   Hiding the Edit⇨Cut Menu Option

```
Public Sub HideAndShowEditCutMenu()
    ' Create the menu command bar.
    Dim TopMenu As CommandBar
    Set TopMenu = _
        Application.CommandBars("Worksheet Menu Bar")

    ' Access the Edit menu control.
    Dim EditControl As CommandBarControl
    Set EditControl = TopMenu.Controls("Edit")

    ' Use the control to access the command bar.
    Dim EditMenu As CommandBar
    Set EditMenu = _
        TopMenu.Controls(EditControl.Index).CommandBar

    ' Access the Cut submenu.
    Dim EditCut As CommandBarControl
```

(continued)

Listing 12-1 *(continued)*

```
        Set EditCut = EditMenu.Controls("Cut")

        ' Change the visible state according to the current
        ' setting.
        EditCut.Visible = Not EditCut.Visible

        ' Display the current setting.
        If EditCut.Visible Then
            MsgBox "The Cut option is visible."
        Else
            MsgBox "The Cut option isn't visible."
        End If
End Sub
```

This code shows that you need to work your way down to the menu that you want to change. Begin by getting the top-level menu by using the `Application.CommandBars` collection. This collection accepts the name of the toolbar or menu that you want to work with as in index. Because this is an Excel example, the code uses `Worksheet Menu Bar` as input. You can use precisely the same code in Word by using `Menu Bar` instead.

After the code can access the top-level menu, it has to drill down to the Edit⇨Cut option. Don't assume that the person who is using your program hasn't changed things around. You need to ask for the various menu entries by name instead of by using a numeric value. Consequently, the code must retrieve the Edit menu `CommandBarControl` by using the `Controls` collection. A `CommandBarControl` is the actual menu entry and not the list of items that it contains.

To get the Edit menu `CommandBar`, which is the object that contains the list of items on that menu, the code uses the `EditControl.Index` property. This property contains a number that indicates the position of the Edit menu on the main menu. VBA won't return the `CommandBar` unless the code supplies this number. It's a subtle point that will likely cause a lot of errors.

The code can access the `Cut` option of the Edit menu at this point by using the `EditMenu.Controls` collection. The code uses the `Visible` property to hide or show the option as a toggle.

Modifying the toolbar or menu content

Toolbars and menus have a lot of properties that you can change. Anything that you can change with the Customize feature of the Office application is also available from code. For example, you might want to provide better tooltips for your program or change the wording of the prompt. Here's an example of code that modifies a ToolTip associated with the **B** (bold) button on the Formatting toolbar. (You can find the source code for this example on the Dummies.com site at http://www.dummies.com/go/mueller.)

```
Public Sub ChangeBoldToolTip()
    ' Get the Formatting toolbar.
    Dim FormatBar As CommandBar
    Set FormatBar = Application.CommandBars("Formatting")

    ' Get the Bold control.
    Dim BoldControl As CommandBarControl
    Set BoldControl = FormatBar.Controls("&Bold")

    ' Change the tooltip.
    BoldControl.TooltipText = "Make the text bold!"
End Sub
```

I purposely selected the TooltipText property because it's one of the few that's difficult or impossible to change manually. If you want to add ToolTips to common menu or toolbar entries, you have to do it with a program. It's a shame that you have to go to this extreme because many accessibility devices rely on the ToolTips to tell those with special needs about the control. For example, most screen readers used by those with special visual needs rely on these ToolTips, so not adding a ToolTip means that someone with special needs will have difficulty using your program.

The code for this example works much like the earlier "Displaying or hiding toolbars and menus" example. Instead of accessing the menu, the code accesses the Formatting toolbar that appears in every Office program (so you can move this example to Word or Access unaltered).

After it gains access to the toolbar, the code accesses the **B** button. Notice that the FormatBar.Controls collection uses &Bold and not just Bold. You need to know the Name property value of the button that you want to change. Use this procedure to obtain the value:

1. **Right-click anywhere in the toolbar area and then choose Customize from the context menu that appears.**

   The Office application displays the Customize dialog box.

2. **Right-click the menu entry or toolbar control of interest.**

   The Office application displays a list of properties associated with the entry.

3. **Note the Name property value and then click Close in the Customize dialog box.**

Creating specialized graphics

Adding graphics to toolbars and menus can dress up your program and provide valuable input as well. For example, you might decide to leave the Format⇨Style command in place but mark it with a special icon that shows that using this command in place of a stylesheet isn't recommended.

The first task is finding a graphic that you want to use. Drawing a graphic is an option. However, you don't have to be an artist to add interesting graphics to your program. Windows comes with a wealth of standard graphics that you can use. The difficulty is figuring out where they are. The three \Windows\ System32 folder Dynamic Link Library (DLL) files that you should check out first are

- ✔ Shell32.dll: 46 bitmaps, 5 cursors, 239 icons
- ✔ User32.dll: 7 bitmaps, 27 cursors, 6 icons
- ✔ MorIcons.dll: 113 icons

Note that a DLL file normally contains code that a number of programs can use. Windows automatically loads the DLL when an application requests the code it contains. However, a DLL file can also contain resources such as icons, bitmaps, and cursors.

The only problem is that you need a program to extract the graphics that you want to use because VBA doesn't provide a method for performing this task directly. To avoid this problem, use a product such as IconForge (http:// www.cursorarts.com/ca_if.html) to read the file and present you with a list of images that you can use. The vendor provides a demonstration version of this product that you can try out. Use the File⇨Acquire Icon from Resource command to open the DLL that you want to work with. Figure 12-2 shows a typical example from the User32.dll file that you can use for this example.

Save any graphic that you want to use to a common folder. I normally use the program folder or the user's personal folder, depending on how the graphic is used. You could also use a central folder on the network or the Windows folder.

After you have one or more images that you want to use, you can load them into the Office application. Listing 12-2 shows code that you use to add an icon to the Format⇨Style command. (You can find the source code for this example on the Dummies.com site at http://www.dummies.com/ go/mueller.)

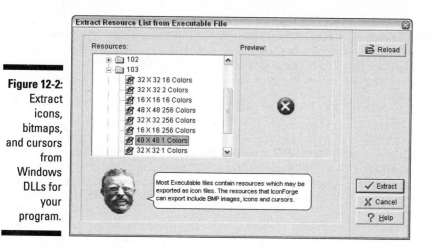

Figure 12-2:
Extract
icons,
bitmaps,
and cursors
from
Windows
DLLs for
your
program.

Listing 12-2   Loading an Icon into a CommandBar Button

```
Public Sub AddIconToFormatStyle()
    ' Create the menu command bar.
    Dim TopMenu As CommandBar
    Set TopMenu = _
        Application.CommandBars("Worksheet Menu Bar")

    ' Access the Format menu control.
    Dim FormatControl As CommandBarControl
    Set FormatControl = TopMenu.Controls("Format")

    ' Use the control to access the command bar.
    Dim FormatMenu As CommandBar
    Set FormatMenu = _
        TopMenu.Controls(FormatControl.Index).CommandBar

    ' Access the Style submenu.
    Dim FormatStyle As CommandBarButton
    Set FormatStyle = FormatMenu.Controls("&Style...")

    ' Load the picture.
    Dim NewPict As IPictureDisp
    Set NewPict _
        = stdole.StdFunctions.LoadPicture( _
            ThisWorkbook.Path + "\Stop.BMP")

    ' Place the picture in the menu.
    FormatStyle.Picture = NewPict
End Sub
```

The code begins by accessing the Format⇨Style menu by using the same technique used in the earlier "Displaying or hiding toolbars and menus" section. Notice that the index for the `FormatMenu.Controls` collection includes an ellipsis (...; three periods). This is another demonstration that the index must precisely match the name of control that you want to access.

Loading the graphic comes next. The `IPictureDisp` object holds the picture for you during loading. To load the picture, the code uses the special `stdole.StdFunctions.LoadPicture` function. You'll receive the best results by using a BMP file because other file formats can be hard to load or might not include compatible color selections. Notice how the code uses the `ThisWorkbook.Path` property to load the picture from the program folder.

The final step is to place the picture on the menu item by using the `Picture` property. When you run this code, you can see that the Format⇨Style menu option now has the red stop sign indicator next to it. To get rid of the picture, use the `FormatStyle.FaceId = 0` statement.

Adding and removing toolbars and menus

You might want to add custom toolbars and menus to hold entries for your programs. Using custom setups means that you can show or hide custom programs as needed. This technique also keeps your code separate from the entries that Microsoft has made to ensure that there's little chance of compatibility problems. Listing 12-3 shows one technique for adding a new toolbar. (You can find the source code for this example on the Dummies.com site at `http://www.dummies.com/go/mueller`.)

Listing 12-3   Adding a New Toolbar

```
Public Sub AddToolbar()
    ' Add the toolbar.
    Dim MyToolbar As CommandBar
    Set MyToolbar = _
        Application.CommandBars.Add("My Toolbar")

    ' Add a control to the toolbar.
    Dim SayHello As CommandBarButton
    Set SayHello = _
        MyToolbar.Controls.Add(msoControlButton)

    ' Configure the control.
    With SayHello
        .Caption = "Say Hello"
        .DescriptionText = "This button displays a message."
```

```
                .OnAction = "DoSayHello"
                .TooltipText = "This button displays a message."
                .Visible = True
                .Style = msoButtonIconAndCaption
                .FaceId = 59
        End With

        ' Make the toolbar visible.
        MyToolbar.Visible = True
End Sub
```

The entire toolbar structure in Office applications consists of collections. Like any collection, you use the Add method to add a new entry. Because there's only one main menu, any new CommandBar object that you add is treated as a toolbar. When adding a new menu entry, you must retrieve the main menu first and then add your menu to that.

Microsoft supplies a number of controls that you can add to a toolbar. The most common option is a CommandBarButton object. You can also choose the CommandBarComboBox, CommandBarControl, or CommandBarPopop object. The Help file doesn't even begin to tell you how many kinds of CommandBarControl objects that you can create. Look at the MsoControlType enumeration in Object Browser. However, if you want to stick to the controls that Microsoft recommends, use the msoControlButton, msoControlEdit, msoControlDropdown, msoControlComboBox, or msoControlPopup types.

After you add a control to your new toolbar, you need to configure it. The new button is blank. The entries that you should always include appear in the code. Make certain that you define an OnAction member that reflects an existing Office application command or a Public Sub that you've defined. The FaceId value, in this case, is the standard smiley face. You do have access to a number of other icon values that are, unfortunately, not documented. Notice also that you must make the individual controls visible by using the Visible property as well as the toolbar.

Removing a toolbar isn't nearly as difficult as creating it. Here's the code that you need.

```
Public Sub RemoveToolbar()
    ' Remove the custom toolbar.
    Application.CommandBars("My Toolbar").Delete
End Sub
```

This single command removes the toolbar permanently. Unfortunately, there isn't a good way to save completed toolbars to disk, so hiding the toolbar by using the Visible property or deleting it completely are the only two options.

Adding Help by Using Office Assistant

This section of the chapter discusses Office Assistant. You don't have to like this feature to use it effectively. This technology does have a place, and it grows on you after a while.

It pays to keep up with current Microsoft Agent developments if you plan to use this technology in your applications. You'll find the main Microsoft Agent site at `http://www.microsoft.com/msagent/`. All the user-related downloads for Microsoft Agent appear at `http://www.microsoft.com/products/msagent/downloads.htm`. Any developer's tools that you need for working with Microsoft Agent are at `http://www.microsoft.com/products/msagent/devdownloads.htm`.

Understanding the kinds of help that you can add

When I communicate with folks by using e-mail, I sometimes find that they misunderstand me. It's not that my words are confused or that I don't know how to write. The problem is that the body language that the people normally see when I talk to them in person is missing. Body language in the form of gestures is an important communication method.

Help files are somewhat like e-mail in a way. You can communicate your ideas by using text. Fortunately, you can easily add graphics and have the advantage of time to let someone else review what you say for clarity. In the end, however, you're still relying essentially on words to communicate your ideas, and this can be problematic.

When folks view help created with Office Assistant, they get back a little of the body language missing from other forms of help. In addition, the often silly-looking characters make them laugh and present information in a cheerful environment instead of the stark reality of an Office environment. The consequence of using this approach is that some people better understand what they see than if they had seen the words alone.

Office Assistant works best in tutorial situations where you want to present a series of steps that the program user must accomplish. The gestures communicate ideas and help lead the user each step of the way. You should consider using the character as a kind of pointer because the user's attention will naturally focus wherever the character appears onscreen.

It's also possible to use Office Assistant in situations where you want to show the user something. For example, the user might leave a field on a form blank.

Rather than simply highlight the field, you could have a character appear, show the user which field is blank, and provide suggestions on how to fill the field with information.

Help is only useful if it communicates well with the person using it. This means that you need to consider spoken as well as textual help. Some people might not be able to see the display, or they might want to listen while the character demonstrates a sequence. Spoken help is different from written help in that the person can combine the two and understands better because two senses are employed.

Knowing when Office Assistant is more annoying than helpful

Because you're very knowledgeable about Office, you might find Office Assistant more annoying than helpful. Many power users find Office Assistant very annoying, and many of them have complained about it. On the other hand, many beginning users find the characters delightful and helpful. I've seen more than a few people smile when they learn something new. It's a matter of perception and need.

The first thing that you need to consider is who will use the program that you write. If you write a program for just your needs or the needs of other power users, adding Office Assistant might be a bad idea. In fact, you'll probably want to avoid using it if you don't want hordes of angry power users assaulting your office. If the program is primarily used to help novice user, you might want to add Office Assistant to help things along.

Problems arise when you don't know who will use your program. When that happens, you have to make a good guess or try to find out by performing a survey. Microsoft handles this problem in newer versions of Windows by showing the Microsoft Agent character initially. If you don't like the character, you can simply shut it off and never see it again. This approach will work fine in most cases.

You should always provide a menu option for turning Office Assistant off because even a novice user will get tired of it at times. In addition, the user might be in a location where the noise created by Office Assistant is unwelcome, such as in a crowded office or in some types of public area. (Although you can use Office Assistant without sound, the sound effects are part of the fun of using this feature, and they do add some essential cues about the current event.) You don't want Office Assistant popping up during a meeting with your boss.

Finally, consider the situation. I know of a few people who think the Office Assistant characters are so cute that they must use them everywhere and for every purpose. They even run Microsoft Agent continually (there are programs for that purpose). Even if you consider Office Assistant the best thing that ever happened to you, don't assume that everyone else feels the same. Use Office Assistant in situations where it can really help and leave it off the rest of the time.

Working with characters

Some people are under the impression that you can use only Office Assistant files for your program. The reality is that you can use any Microsoft Agent character that has the correct animations. Here's the problem. Not all the characters have a full set of animations. A default installation will only have the characters contained within the Office folder. Make sure that any character that you use has the proper Office animations.

Creating a script

Office Assistant requires a script. You have to think about the sequence of steps that you want the character to perform. It might help to write down the sequence of events. Listing 12-4 shows a typical example of a scripted Office Assistant session. (You can find the source code for this example on the Dummies.com site at http://www.dummies.com/go/mueller.)

Listing 12-4   Using Office Assistant in a Scripted Session

```
Public Sub ShowAssistant()
    ' Create a variable for balloons.
    Dim SayIt As Balloon
    Set SayIt = Assistant.NewBalloon

    ' Determine whether Assistant is On.
    Dim IsOn As Boolean
    IsOn = Assistant.On

    ' Configure Assistant for use.
    With Assistant
        ' Turn Assistant on if necessary.
        .On = True

        ' Load a Microsoft Agent file.
        .Filename = "F1.ACS"

        ' Move to a new location.
        .Move 40, 40

        ' Make the Assistant visible.
        .Visible = True
```

```
    End With

    ' Perform some task.
    With Assistant

        ' Greet the user.
        .Animation = msoAnimationGreeting
        Application.Wait Now + TimeValue("0:00:5")

        ' Move to a new location.
        .Move 200, 200
        Application.Wait Now + TimeValue("0:00:2")

        ' Say something to the user.
        SayIt.Heading = "Greeting"
        SayIt.Icon = msoIconAlertInfo
        SayIt.Text = "Hello " + Application.UserName
        SayIt.Show

        ' Say goodbye.
        .Animation = msoAnimationGoodbye
        Application.Wait Now + TimeValue("0:00:5")
    End With

    ' Stop using the Assistant.
    With Assistant
        ' Make the Assistant invisible.
        .Visible = False

        ' Set the Assistant setting to its previous value.
        .On = IsOn
    End With
End Sub
```

Notice how the code is blocked into sections by using the With...End
With statements. Using this technique can help you see elements in your
script easier.

The code begins by creating two variables. The first holds anything that
you want the character to say. Because the character can say only one
thing at a time, a generic Balloon variable works fine — you don't need
one for each statement. The second variable holds the state of Office
Assistant when you start it so that you can return it to that state when
you finish.

The first block of code turns on Office Assistant, loads a character, and
moves it to a starting position. Only after you perform these three steps
can you make the character visible. Always perform the steps in this order
to ensure that the character acts as anticipated.

The second block of code contains the actions that the character performs. The character begins by performing a greeting animation. Notice the use of the `Application.Wait` method. Office Assistant tends to run amok if you don't control it with wait states. You have to experiment to find the correct wait periods for each animation.

The `SayIt` balloon is an object, and you use it like any other object. (See Chapter 8 for a discussion of objects.) Set the heading, icon, and text for the balloon and then use the `Show` method to display it. The balloon remains displayed until the user dismisses it.

The example ends with the character saying goodbye. The third and final code block makes the character invisible and then sets the `On` state to its previous value.

Chapter 13

VBA Programming in Word

*W*ord is the Microsoft Office application that you use to create and edit text, which means spending hours typing. All that typing takes time. However, you have a personal secretary at your disposal that can type thousands of words per minute (without error), and you might not even realize it. The programs that you create for Word can do more than simply change the user environment, convert data to text or eXtensible Markup Language (XML), and perform other helpful, nontyping tasks. The fastest typist that you'll ever know is the Word program that you create by using VBA.

Creating a document is more than just typing, though. You also have to consider the formatting of the text and how to divide it into pieces so that it's easy to read. A document might require graphics, and you might want to add special features to make some sections easier to find. Word programs can handle all these needs, too. Simply decide what you want Word to do and write a program to handle the task.

This chapter demonstrates VBA programming techniques that you can use to make your next Word session more enjoyable and productive. Instead of typing the same material over and over again, you can concentrate on the creative part of the document. In addition, formatting can become a thing of the past (except for unique situations). A VBA program lets you rely on Word to do the formatting for you.

Understanding the Word-Related Objects

If you've followed the book to this point, you've already created a number of programs by using objects. In fact, you've even looked at Word-specific objects in a few cases. (See the "Creating a Simple Word XML Document" section of Chapter 11 as an example.) Word has three special collections (Documents, Templates, and Windows) that you can use to access the details of the Word environment, which includes any documents that you create.

Using the Documents collection

Documents are the essence of working with Word. They contain the data that you create, format, and print for the world to see. Consequently, the Documents collection is the one that you use most when manipulating content.

The Documents collection contains one copy of each Document object currently opened in Word. If you have more than one copy of the same document open, Word will include a single Document object for each copy.

A Document object isn't the same as a Template object. Word keeps these two object types separate. See the upcoming "Using the Templates collection" section for details on working with templates. A document can include content imported from other files. If you open a TXT or an XML file, Word treats it as a Document object.

The Documents collection is most useful when you don't know the name of the document that you want to manage. For example, you might create a program that adds contractions to all documents that use the XYZ template. You don't know how many documents use this template or what the user named them, but you know that you need to make the same change to all open documents. Listing 13-1 shows an example that demonstrates how to use a For Each...Next statement to get information about each document that uses the Normal.dot template. (You can find the source code for this example on the Dummies.com site at http://www.dummies.com/go/mueller.)

Listing 13-1   Getting Word Document Information

```
Public Sub MyDocuments()
    ' Create a variable to hold the individual documents.
    Dim MyDocs As Document

    ' Create a variable to hold information about selected
    ' documents.
    Dim Output As String

    ' Look at each document in the Documents collection.
```

```
For Each MyDocs In Application.Documents

    ' Check for the appropriate template name.
    If UCase(MyDocs.AttachedTemplate) _
        = "NORMAL.DOT" Then

        ' Create a list of information about the
        ' document.
        With MyDocs
        Output = Output + "Name: " + vbTab + vbTab + _
            .Name + vbCrLf + _
            "Window Caption: " + vbTab + _
            .ActiveWindow.Caption + vbCrLf + _
            "Document Type: " + vbTab + _
            IIf(.ActiveWindow.Creator = wdCreatorCode, _
                "Word Document", _
                "Other Document") + vbCrLf + _
            "Writing Style: " + vbTab + _
            .ActiveWritingStyle(wdEnglishUS) _
            + vbCrLf + "Characters: " + vbTab + _
            CStr(.Characters.Count) + vbCrLf + _
            "Words: " + vbTab + vbTab + _
            CStr(.Words.Count) + vbCrLf + vbCrLf
    End With
    End If
Next

' Output the result.
MsgBox Output, _
    vbInformation Or vbOKOnly, _
    "Documents that Use the Normal Template"
End Sub
```

The example shows just a few of the properties available with the Document object. It begins by creating the Document object, MyDocs, and a String, Output that the code uses to hold the document information. The For Each structure retrieves one Document object at a time from the Documents collection and works with it.

Notice that the template comparison relies on the UCase function. You don't know how the user or Word will capitalize the name of the template, normal.dot, so using the UCase function is the safest way to perform the comparison. The property used, in this case, is MyDocs.AttachedTemplate, which is the individual template used for each document. Word always uses the entry found in the Document Template field on the Templates tab of the Templates and Add-ins dialog box for this property even when a document has more than one template attached to it.

The code gathers various kinds of input from the document. Some information, such as `.ActiveWindow.Caption`, is already in text format, so the code doesn't do much more than record the value in `Output`. Notice the use of the `IIf` function to perform the `.ActiveWindow.Creator = wdCreatorCode` inline comparison. Excel uses a similar constant for its documents, `xlCreatorCode`. The creator code can tell you what kind of document that you're working with.

A few of the properties require special handling. For example, because Word is internationalized, you must provide a constant for some properties to ensure that you see the correct value. The `.ActiveWritingStyle` property value varies by language, so you have to tell VBA which language value to retrieve by using the constant for your country. Because I live in the United States, I used the `wdEnglishUS` constant.

Many applications maintain statistics for the documents that they maintain, and Word is no exception. The `Document` object contains a number of statistics that it maintains over the life of the object. The example shows the `.Characters.Count` and `.Words.Count` statistics. Figure 13-1 shows the output from this program.

Figure 13-1: Uncover the mysteries of your data by using the Document object.

```
Documents that Use the Normal Template                          [x]
  (i)   Name:              WordML Example (XSLT).xml
        Window Caption:    WordML Example (XSLT).xml
        Document Type:     Word Document
        Writing Style:     Grammar & Style
        Characters:        81
        Words:             19

        Name:              Temp.txt
        Window Caption:    Temp.txt
        Document Type:     Word Document
        Writing Style:     Grammar & Style
        Characters:        44
        Words:             11

        Name:              WordObjects.doc
        Window Caption:    WordObjects.doc
        Document Type:     Word Document
        Writing Style:     Grammar & Style
        Characters:        467
        Words:             94

                        [   OK   ]
```

You should notice a few interesting features about this example. First, all the files listed have different extensions, yet the code lists them all as Word documents. Imported files count as Word documents because Word performs a conversion on them. The file on disk remains the same until you save it, but the file in memory is a Word document.

Second, notice that each of the documents has the same writing style value. This value can vary if you import documents from older versions of Word. You can also set this value programmatically. The default action is to use the value found in the Writing Style field on the Spelling & Grammar tab of the Options dialog box.

Using the Templates collection

Word users know that templates provide the information required to give a set of documents the same look and feel. For example, a letter template could include special formatting for the heading and body text. It might include all the text that is the same for each letter, such as your name and address. Specialized templates often include automatic setups so that the initial document is as close to the final product as possible. Templates always use the DOT file extension.

The Templates collection contains a list of all the templates in use by your document. Each Template object corresponds to a single template file. If you open several documents that rely on the same template, Word creates only one Template object. No matter which document you open, Word opens a copy of the Normal template in addition to any special template that the document uses. The special template is still the main template that Word uses, but Word always adds the features found in Normal.dot. Consequently, you should only make changes to Normal.dot that you want to see in every file that you create when using Word.

After you understand how the templates interact with your document, you can change template functionality in a way that makes creating the document easier. In general, you'll use template programs to make changes to the document as a whole and to all documents affected by that template. Listing 13-2 shows an example of the Templates collection in use. (You can find the source code for this example on the Dummies.com site at http://www. dummies.com/go/mueller.)

Listing 13-2   Listing Word Template Properties

```
Public Sub MyTemplates()
    ' Holds the current template.
    Dim CurrTemp As Template

    ' Holds the built-in properties.
    Dim CurrProp As DocumentProperty

    ' Holds the property name length.
    Dim PropLen As Integer

    ' Holds the output.
```

(continued)

Listing 13-2   *(continued)*

```
Dim Output As String

    ' Look at each template in the Templates collection.
    For Each CurrTemp In Application.Templates

        ' Get information about the current template.
        With CurrTemp
            Output = Output + _
                "Name:" + vbTab + vbTab + .Name + vbCrLf + _
                "Full Name:" + vbTab + .FullName + vbCrLf

            ' Check property values for the template.
            For Each CurrProp In _
                    .BuiltInDocumentProperties

                ' Some entries will fail.
                On Error Resume Next

                ' Determine the property name length.
                PropLen = Len(CurrProp.Name)

                ' Get the information.
                Output = Output + "Property: " + _
                    CurrProp.Name + _
                    IIf(PropLen < 40, vbTab, "") + _
                    IIf(PropLen < 32, vbTab, "") + _
                    IIf(PropLen < 24, vbTab, "") + _
                    IIf(PropLen < 14, vbTab, "") + _
                    IIf(PropLen < 6, vbTab, "") + _
                    CStr(CurrProp.Type) + vbTab + _
                    CStr(CurrProp.Value) + vbCrLf
            Next

            ' Add space at the end of the entry.
            Output = Output + vbCrLf + vbCrLf
        End With
    Next

    ' Output the result.
    MsgBox Output, _
            vbInformation Or vbOKOnly, _
            "Templates Currently in Use"
End Sub
```

The code begins by creating `Template` and `DocumentProperty` objects. These two objects hold the information that the program examines during execution. The `PropLen` variable contains the length of the current property name. The `Output` variable contains the output string for this example.

This example uses a double `For Each...Next` statement. The first `For Each...Next` statement controls selection of a template from the list in the `Application.Templates` collection. The second `For Each...Next` statement controls the selection of properties within the template by using the `.BuiltInDocumentProperties` collection.

Don't assume that Word templates contain only one set of properties. If you want to get a complete list of document properties, you also need to look at the `CustomDocumentProperties` collection. Theoretically, a template could contain custom property collections as well, so you need to check for other additions.

Notice that the code includes both the `.Name` and `.FullName` property values in `Output`. The `.Name` property value only includes the document template name, but the `.FullName` property includes the path information as well. If you want just the path information, use the `Path` property. The seeming replication of information in some Word classes helps you create programs with less work. In this case, you only need to know which property to use instead of parsing the information from a complex property.

The second loop begins with an `On Error Resume Next` statement. Always include this statement whenever you work with properties. The code calculates the length of the `CurrProp.Name` property next. You could include this calculation every place that it's needed in the code, but using this technique is more efficient and saves time writing code.

The `Output` variable receives the name of the property, the property type, and the property value next. Notice the use of the `IIf` function to determine how many tabs to add to the string. Avoid using spaces in this situation. Although the output is the same as using the `Space` function, the memory used by eight spaces (8 bytes) for each tab (1 byte) is much greater, and you could run out of string space to hold all the data. Figure 13-2 shows the output of this program.

The text in Figure 13-2 looks different from the text in Figure 13-1. The example in Figure 13-2 relies on the Courier New font that is supplied with Windows. Using a *monospaced font,* one in which every character takes precisely the same amount of space, makes aligning the text easier. The only problem with this approach is that the Courier New font is more difficult to read. You also have to use a custom dialog box, in most cases, to ensure that the output is in the desired font.

Using the Windows collection

The `Windows` collection contains one `Window` object entry for each window that you have open. You use the `Window` object to manage the overall view of a document. For example, you use this object to add or remove scrollbars or the ruler.

Templates Currently in Use			
Name:	Normal.dot		
Full Name:	D:\Program Files\Microsoft Office\Templates\Normal.dot		
Property:	Title	4	Normal Formatting
Property:	Subject	4	Template
Property:	Author	4	John Mueller
Property:	Keywords	4	Normal Template
Property:	Comments	4	Standard documents.
Property:	Template	4	Normal.dot
Property:	Last author	4	John Mueller
Property:	Revision number	4	59
Property:	Application name	4	Microsoft Word 11.0
Property:	Creation date	3	6/8/1994 12:22:00 PM
Property:	Last save time	3	3/25/2003 6:04:00 PM
Property:	Total editing time	1	22
Property:	Number of pages	1	1
Property:	Number of words	1	0
Property:	Number of characters	1	0
Property:	Security	1	0
Property:	Category	4	
Property:	Format	4	
Property:	Manager	4	
Property:	Company	4	DataCon Services
Property:	Number of bytes	1	62976
Property:	Number of lines	1	0
Property:	Number of paragraphs	1	0
Property:	Hyperlink base	4	
Property:	Number of characters (with spaces)	1	0

OK

Figure 13-2:
Rely on the properties found in both documents and templates for identification information.

Don't confuse a `Window` object with a `Pane` object. A `Window` object can contain up to two panes. (Older versions of Word let you create multiple panes — newer versions limit you to two.) The `Window` object is a container for the `Pane` object. You use the `Pane` object to view, add, delete, and otherwise manipulate the current content of a document. A disk file contains the data as of the last save — this object contains the data as it appears in memory.

The panes operate independently of each other. You can select an area of text in one pane and not have it affect the selection in the other pane. However, data changes in one pane do appear in the other pane. Listing 13-3 shows an example of the `Windows` collection. (You can find the source code for this example on the Dummies.com site at `http://www.dummies.com/go/mueller`.)

Listing 13-3   Determining Window Properties

```
Public Sub MyWindows()
    ' Holds a Window object.
    Dim MyWin As Window

    ' Holds the output.
    Dim Output As String

    ' Used for loop counting.
```

```
    Dim Counter As Integer

    ' Look at each Window in the Windows collection.
    For Each MyWin In Application.Windows

        ' Get the current window information.
        With MyWin
        Output = Output + "Caption: " + .Caption + _
            vbCrLf + "Panes: " + _
            CStr(.Panes.Count) + vbCrLf

        ' Check each of the panes for selected data.
        For Counter = 1 To .Panes.Count
            Output = Output + "Pane " + CStr(Counter) + _
                " Selection: " + _
                CStr(.Panes(Counter).Selection) + _
                vbCrLf
        Next

        ' Add a new pane if possible.
        If .Panes.Count = 1 Then
            .Panes.Add
        End If

        ' Add space to the output.
        Output = Output + vbCrLf

        End With
    Next

    ' Output the result.
    MsgBox Output, _
        vbInformation Or vbOKOnly, _
        "Windows Currently in Use"
End Sub
```

The example shown in Listing 13-3 begins like the other collection examples in this section (see Listings 13-1 and 13-2) by creating an individual object and some associated variables. The Application.Windows contains all the existing windows that are processed one at a time in the code.

Every Window object has a Caption property. This Caption appears as part of the Word title bar text. A Window doesn't have a Name property like many other objects because you never manipulate it by name.

After the code determines the Window caption, it looks at the number of panes associated with that window. In Office 2003, Office XP, and Office 2000, the value is always 1 or 2. The code processes each window in turn. In this case, it retrieves the selected text.

The code shows how you can add another pane to the code. If the user isn't using both panes, you can open a second pane, perform any work that you need to do to the data in that pane, and then close the pane when you finish. This technique lets you work on the data quickly and yet return the view to the user's original view. Figure 13-3 shows typical output for this example.

Figure 13-3:
Windows and panes work together to provide access to your data.

```
Windows Currently in Use                          [x]

  (i)     Caption: Temp.txt
          Panes: 1
          Pane 1 Selection: temporary

          Caption: WordML Example (XSLT).xml
          Panes: 1
          Pane 1 Selection: A WordML Document Example

          Caption: WordObjects.doc
          Panes: 2
          Pane 1 Selection: document
          Pane 2 Selection: T

                    [    OK    ]
```

When you run this program a second time, each of the open windows will have two panes open even if they only had one pane open to begin with. None of the windows will ever have more than two panes open. If you try to open more than two, VBA generates an error. (The precise error message can vary — sometimes the VBA error messages aren't very clear, and you need to look carefully for the cause.)

Accessing the Word Document

Accessing the Word document means accessing specific text elements so that you know what they contain. For example, you might want to process the text one paragraph or one sentence at a time. It's possible to select individual letters in Word along with individual objects, such as pictures. However, sentences are a good place to start because working with sentences exercises many of the calls that you'll need for other forms of access. Listing 13-4 shows an example that accesses sentences one at a time in the test document. (You can find the source code for this example on the Dummies.com site at http://www.dummies.com/go/mueller.)

Listing 13-4   Retrieving a Specific Sentence from a Document

```
Public Sub AccessTheText()
    ' Holds the current pane.
```

```
        Dim CurrPane As Pane

        ' Holds a specific paragraph on the page.
        Dim CurrPara As Paragraph

        ' Holds a single sentence.
        Dim CurrSent As String

        ' Holds the output.
        Dim Output As String

        ' Acts as a loop counter.
        Dim Counter As Integer

        ' Make sure you can access the pane properly.
        Application.Windows("WordObjects.doc").View _
            = wdNormalView

        ' Access the test document pane.
        Set CurrPane = _
            Application.Windows("WordObjects.doc").ActivePane

        ' Access the second paragraph in that pane.
        Set CurrPara = CurrPane.Document.Paragraphs(2)

        ' Access the second sentence in that paragraph.
        For Counter = 1 To CurrPara.Range.Sentences.Count

            ' Get the current sentence content.
            CurrSent = CurrPara.Range.Sentences(Counter)

            ' Add the content to the Output string.
            Output = Output + "Sentence " + CStr(Counter) + _
                ": " + CurrSent + vbCrLf
        Next

        ' Display the sentence.
        MsgBox Output
    End Sub
```

The code begins by creating the individual objects needed to hold various document elements. The kind of objects that you create depends on the tasks that you need to perform and the view option in some cases. For example, if you want to work with the Pages collection, the document must appear in the Print Layout view.

To ensure that you can access the document by using the method that you need, you must set the pane or the window to a specific view. The code sets the window to the Normal view by setting the View property to wdNormalView. Also notice that you must use the name and extension of a document to select its Window — using just the name isn't enough because you could load multiple documents with the same name and different extensions. Make sure that you add a Window number when necessary.

You must use the Pane object to access data within the document. It's usually a good idea to create an actual Pane object instead of going through the long object hierarchy to access it each time. This program actually takes a microscopic performance hit when using this technique, but the time that you save typing will be well worth it. Notice that the code uses the ActivePane property in this case. You can also use the Panes collection if desired.

One of the tricky parts about working in Normal view is that you need to access the document by using paragraphs. If the document has just a few paragraphs, debugging the code isn't difficult. However, life can become interesting for long documents because finding a particular paragraph can become difficult. You can use search techniques to make finding a paragraph easier in many cases.

Collections include a Count property that you can use to access individual members by using a For...Next loop instead of a For Each...Next loop. This example makes use of that feature to create a counter setup that displays the sentence number and the content of that sentence. When you run this program, VBA displays each sentence in the second paragraph of the document in turn. It won't display any other sentences.

The document hierarchy continues to words and individual characters. By using Listing 13-4, when you want to select individual words, select the CurrPara.Range.Sentences(Counter).Words collection. Use the CurrPara.Range.Sentences(Counter).Characters collection to select individual characters in the sentence.

Using the Registry with VBA

Microsoft assumes that you always want to access the Registry to store settings for your program. So it created special functions that let you store settings under one specific key, \HKEY_CURRENT_USER\Software\VBA. If you want to store program settings, simply use the SaveSetting function. Likewise, the GetSetting and GetAllSettings functions retrieve information from the Registry.

Unfortunately, these functions don't provide access to the rest of the Registry. The example in the upcoming "Selecting Objects in a Word Document" section shows why this is a problem. You need access to the entire Registry to write functional programs. Consequently, you have to augment the functionality VBA provides by accessing the Windows 32-bit Application Programming Interface (Win32 API) directly. The *Win32 API* is the entire set of functions that Windows supports. Listing 13-5 shows the code required to perform the task reading other parts of the Registry. (You can find the source code for this example on the Dummies.com site at http://www.dummies.com/go/mueller.)

Listing 13-5   Accessing the Registry with VBA

```
' This Windows API function opens a Registry key.
Public Declare Function RegOpenKey _
    Lib "advapi32.dll" _
    Alias "RegOpenKeyA" (ByVal HKey As Long, _
                         ByVal lpSubKey As String, _
                         phkResult As Long) As Boolean

' Use this enumeration for the top-level keys.
Public Enum ROOT_KEYS
    HKEY_CLASSES_ROOT = &H80000000
    HKEY_CURRENT_USER = &H80000001
    HKEY_LOCAL_MACHINE = &H80000002
    HKEY_USERS = &H80000003
    HKEY_PERFORMANCE_DATA = &H80000004
    HKEY_CURRENT_CONFIG = &H80000005
    HKEY_DYN_DATA = &H80000006
End Enum

' This Windows API function reads a value from a key.
Declare Function RegQueryValue _
    Lib "advapi32.dll" _
    Alias "RegQueryValueA" (ByVal HKey As Long, _
                            ByVal lpSubKey As String, _
                            ByVal lpValue As String, _
                            lpcbValue As Long) As Boolean

' This Windows API function closes a Registry key.
Public Declare Function RegCloseKey _
    Lib "advapi32.dll" (ByVal HKey As Long) As Boolean
```

VBA lets you access specific Win32 API functions by using the `Declare` keyword shown in these three examples. You must give your function a name, as usual. Use the same name as the Win32 API function whenever possible so that you remember the purpose of this function. VBA also requires that you provide the name of the Dynamic Link Library (DLL) file that contains the function by adding the `Lib` keyword. All Registry functions appear in `advapi32.dll` located in the `\Windows\System32` folder.

Two of these functions use the `Alias` keyword. A Win32 API function might have a common name, such as `RegOpenKey`. However, the DLL might actually hold two or more versions of the function. The `RegOpenKeyA` alias tells VBA to use the ASCII version of the function. You could also use the Unicode (or W) version of the function.

After you provide all the information required to locate the function, you supply a list of arguments. Again, it's a good idea to use the same names that the Microsoft documentation uses so that you remember the purpose of each argument.

Selecting Objects in a Word Document

You can link or embed objects into your Word document. Object Linking and Embedding (OLE) is a feature found in most high-end applications. Linking places a pointer to the information within the Word document. Every time that Word wants to display that object, it invokes the required OLE server (the application that usually manages the data) and tells it where to find the file on disk. The advantage to this method is that the OLE server updates the data every time that you view the object. Linking also keeps the Word document small because the pointer consumes very little space.

Embedding actually places the data from the file into the Word document. Every time that you view the object, Word passes the data to the OLE server for display and manipulation. The advantage of this method is that the data remains with the document, so you have to send only one file to someone if you want to share the information. Although the individual Word file is larger and doesn't receive updated information, an information package is usually smaller, especially if you compress it using something like WinZip.

No matter which form of object technology you use, Word considers it an `InlineShape`. The `InlineShapes` collection contains all the objects linked or embedded in the Word document. Because you can use OLE with so many applications, Microsoft had to devise an object handling strategy that will work with all Word-compatible objects. The example document supplied with the source code, `WordObjects`, has two embedded objects in it. The first is a picture, and the second is a sound. Listing 13-6 contains some code demonstrating techniques for working with those two objects. (You can find the source code for this example on the Dummies.com site at `http://www.dummies.com/go/mueller`.)

Listing 13-6   Using the Registry to Work with Objects

```
Public Sub AccessAnObject()
    ' Holds an indeterminate object.
    Dim AObj As InlineShape

    ' Holds the BMP file class.
    Dim BMPClass As String

    ' Holds picture statistical data.
    Dim Output As String

    ' Holds the Registry key reference.
    Dim RegKeyRef As Long

    ' Holds the length of the Registry data.
```

```
Dim RegLength As Long

' Get the BMP file class.
' Open the Registry key.
RegOpenKey ROOT_KEYS.HKEY_CLASSES_ROOT, _
          ".bmp", RegKeyRef

' Determine whether the key exists.
If RegKeyRef = 0 Then

   ' Display an error.
   MsgBox "Couldn't open BMP file Registry setting.", _
       vbOKOnly Or vbExclamation, _
       "Registry Error"

   ' Exit the sub.
   Exit Sub
End If

' Determine whether the required information exists. If
' so, get the data length.
RegQueryValue RegKeyRef, "", BMPClass, RegLength

' Fill the string with the required spaces.
BMPClass = VBA.String(RegLength, " ")

' Retrieve the value.
RegQueryValue RegKeyRef, "", BMPClass, RegLength
BMPClass = Left(BMPClass, Len(BMPClass) - 1)

' Close the Registry.
RegCloseKey (RegKeyRef)

' Check each inline shape.
For Each AObj In ThisDocument.InlineShapes

   ' Select the object and show that it is selected.
   AObj.Select
   MsgBox "Object Number " + _
      CStr(AObj.Field.Index) + " is Selected", _
      vbInformation Or vbOKOnly, "Object Select"

   ' If this is a sound object, play it.
   If AObj.OLEFormat.ClassType = "SoundRec" Then
      AObj.OLEFormat.DoVerb wdOLEVerbPrimary
   End If

   ' If this is a picture object, display some
   ' statistics.
   If AObj.OLEFormat.ClassType = BMPClass Then

      ' Get the height and width and then display it.
```

(continued)

Listing 13-6 *(continued)*

```
          Output = "Height: " + CStr(AObj.Height) + _
            vbCrLf + _
            CStr(Application.PointsToInches(AObj.Height)) _
            + " Inches" + vbCrLf + _
            "Width: " + CStr(AObj.Width) + vbCrLf + _
            CStr(Application.PointsToInches(AObj.Width)) _
            + " Inches"
          MsgBox Output, vbInformation Or vbOKOnly, _
            "Picture Statistics"
      End If
    Next
End Sub
```

The code begins by creating variables to hold the information used in the example. Note the inclusion of an `InlineShape` object to hold each of the objects in the document.

The next section uses the special Registry functions described in the earlier "Using the Registry with VBA" section of this chapter. This section requires a little more explanation than simply saying what the code does.

Whenever you double-click an icon in Windows Explorer, Windows goes to the Registry and asks what application to use to open that file. Windows stores this information by file extension in the `HKEY_CLASSES_ROOT` hive of the Registry. (The term *HKEY* stands for *hive key*.) Figure 13-4 shows the entry for the `.bmp` file extension.

Figure 13-4:
Use the Registry Editor to discover more about how OLE works.

The (`Default`) value tells Windows which application type to use to open the file. (Other Registry entries contain precise instructions for using this program.) Any file with a `.bmp` extension on my machine uses Paint Shop Pro as a default, but your machine setup could be different from mine. Because another application creates the objects linked or embedded in a document, Word needs the same kind of information as Windows does to open the OLE server. This information appears in the `ClassType` property of the `InlineShape.OLEFormat` object.

When you want to work with an object created by another application in Word, you can't necessarily assume that the program that you use to work with that file is the same program used on the machine executing the program. This is the purpose for the Registry code in this example. It shows how you can retrieve the program type information for a particular file extension such as .bmp.

The code begins by using RegOpenKey to open the Registry and get a reference (also called a *handle*) to a specific Registry key. This function requires the hive key, a *subkey* (the file extension), and a variable to hold the Registry key reference as arguments. You must include code that checks the key for a 0 return value. This value tells you that the key doesn't exist on the target machine. If the key doesn't exist, you can't open that object on that target machine because it lacks the required support.

After the code gets a Registry key reference, it uses it to ask for the program type information by using the RegQueryValue function. To request the information in the (Default) value, you send an empty string as the second argument. Otherwise, you can include a string that has a specific value name in it, such as the PerceivedType value shows in Figure 13-4. The third argument is a string that will hold the name of the program class when the function returns. The RegLength argument tells you how long the BMPClass value is.

The first call to the RegQueryValue function only determines the length of BMPClass. The code uses the VBA.String function to fill BMPClass with spaces. The Win32 API won't do this task for you like the VBA functions do, so it's something that you have to do manually. A second call to the RegQueryValue function fills BMPClass with the program type name.

However, there's still a problem with this string. If you look carefully in the Debugger, you'll notice that BMPClass has a funny character at the end. This is the 0 termination required by languages such as C. VBA doesn't need a 0 terminator, so the code gets rid of it by using the Left function. The final Registry step is to close the Registry by using the RegCloseKey function.

The code finally begins looking at the individual objects. It begins by selecting the object onscreen and displaying a message box. This code lets you see how the Select method works. It also shows which object the code is working with now.

The example file contains two objects. The WAV file relies on the SoundRec program type, in most cases, so I simply used that value for the example. You can certainly use the Registry technique to look up the program type in your programs. If the object is a sound file, the code plays it by using the DoVerb method with the wdOLEVerbPrimary argument. OLE supports a number of other *verbs* (action words). To see which verbs work with a particular object, right-click the object and see which Object menu entries appear on the context menu. For example, you can play (wdOLEVerbPrimary), edit (wdOLEVerbShow), or open (wdOLEVerbOpen) a sound file.

Notice how the code treats the picture object. In this case, the code compares the picture object with the program type received from the Registry. If the two match, the code displays the height and width of the picture. Notice how this code uses the `Application.PointsToInches` function to convert the point values that Word normally uses to inches. VBA includes a number of these handy conversion functions that you can use to present data in a format that the viewer will understand.

Manipulating Text

The task that you perform most often in Word is manipulating text. The section "Accessing the Word Document," earlier in this chapter, shows how to access the text in your document. You can access every text element, including individual letters, as needed. Selecting text is as easy as using the `Select` method. (See the section "Selecting Objects in a Word Document," also earlier in this chapter, for an example of how the `Select` method works.)

After you select the text, you can use simple properties to change its appearance or manipulate it in other ways. For example, you could change the text by making the selection equal to another value. The `Font` property contains a number of interesting features, including the ability to add special effects such as strikethrough and underlining. You can also use the `Font` property to change the font face or size.

The example in Listing 13-7 shows another type of text manipulation. You might need the ability to look for a particular word in a document and just highlight it. It's not necessary to change every occurrence of the word, so a standard search and replace won't work. All you want to do is find all the occurrences of the target word without a lot of extra work. (You can find the source code for this example on the Dummies.com site at `http://www.dummies.com/go/mueller`.)

Listing 13-7   Highlighting Text in Word

```
Public Sub HighlightText()
    ' Holds the current pane.
    Dim CurrPane As Pane

    ' Make sure you can access the pane properly.
    Application.Windows("WordObjects.doc").View _
        = wdNormalView

    ' Access the test document pane.
    Set CurrPane = _
        Application.Windows("WordObjects.doc").ActivePane

    ' Get the word to highlight.
```

```
Dim Highlight As String
Highlight = InputBox("Highlight which word?", _
                     "Highlight Word", _
                     "document")

' Go to the beginning of the document.
CurrPane.Selection.GoTo wdGoToLine, wdGoToFirst

' Creates a search for the word.
Dim DoSearch As Find
Set DoSearch = CurrPane.Selection.Find

' Perform the search.
With DoSearch

    ' Clear any existing formatting information.
    .ClearFormatting
    .MatchCase = False

    ' Continue until there is nothing else to search.
    While DoSearch.Execute(FindText:=Highlight)

        ' Highlight any found text in the right color.
        With CurrPane.Selection.FormattedText
            .HighlightColorIndex = wdTurquoise
        End With
    Wend
End With

' Go to the beginning of the document.
CurrPane.Selection.GoTo wdGoToLine, wdGoToFirst
End Sub
```

The code begins by accessing the current pane. It then uses the InputBox function to ask what word to search for in the document. Highlight contains the work on return from the call.

Before you begin a search of any kind, you should consider placing the selection point at a known location. The code does this with the .Selection. GoTo method. The arguments for this call literally tell the code to place the selection point on the first line.

Search and replace works with the current pane. The code uses the Find property to create DoSearch object. At this point, the code begins setting the search. You must always use the .ClearFormatting function to clear any existing formatting from the search, or the search is likely to fail. It's also possible to define replacement parameters. The code uses the DoSearch. Execute method to perform the search.

The highlight occurs with the CurrPane.Selection.FormattedText object. This object determines the appearance of the text as a whole, including special features such as highlighting. The code sets the .HighlightColorIndex property to `wdTurquoise`, which highlights any selected text onscreen. The text is highlighted automatically as part of the search process.

Unless you want to remove all those highlights by hand, you need a program to remove them for you. The program in Listing 13-8 removes only turquoise highlights. If you have highlights of other colors in the document, the program won't remove them.

Listing 13-8   Removing Specific Highlights from a Word Document

```
Public Sub RemoveHighlight()
    ' Holds the current pane.
    Dim CurrPane As Pane

    ' Make sure you can access the pane properly.
    Application.Windows("WordObjects.doc").View _
        = wdNormalView

    ' Access the test document pane.
    Set CurrPane = _
        Application.Windows("WordObjects.doc").ActivePane

    ' Go to the beginning of the document.
    CurrPane.Selection.GoTo wdGoToLine, wdGoToFirst

    ' Creates a search for the word.
    Dim DoSearch As Find
    Set DoSearch = CurrPane.Selection.Find

    ' Perform the search.
    With DoSearch

        ' Clear any existing formatting information.
        .ClearFormatting
        .Highlight = True
        .MatchCase = False

        ' Continue until there is nothing else to search.
        While DoSearch.Execute()

            ' Remove the highlight as needed.
            With CurrPane.Selection.FormattedText
                If .HighlightColorIndex = wdTurquoise Then
                    .HighlightColorIndex = wdNoHighlight
                End If
            End With
        Wend
    End With

    ' Go to the beginning of the document.
    CurrPane.Selection.GoTo wdGoToLine, wdGoToFirst
End Sub
```

The code for this program works similarly to the text search. However, notice that it searches for a highlight instead by setting the `.Highlight` to `True`. Unfortunately, `DoSearch` can't look for a specific highlight color, so the code sets up an `If...Then` statement that ensures that only turquoise highlights are removed.

One final point to consider: You can usually perform most tasks more than one way when working with VBA. In this case, you can substitute the statement `CurrPane.Selection.HomeKey Unit:=wdStory` for `CurrPane.Selection.GoTo wdGoToLine, wdGoToFirst` if you want because both statements perform the same task. I used the code shown in Listing 13-8 because I think it's easier to understand. However, there isn't any performance or other advantage when using either statement — both forms of the statement are equally correct.

Chapter 14

VBA Programming in Excel

. . . .

In This Chapter

▶ Working with the Excel-related objects

▶ Accessing and using Excel objects

▶ Changing the contents of individual cells

▶ Creating your own functions to use in Excel

▶ Adding pizzazz to your Excel worksheet

▶ Defining your own special purpose worksheets

. . . .

Microsoft Excel provides a wealth of opportunities for custom VBA programs. You can do everything from creating special equations to designing eye-grabbing presentations. With some effort, you can create detailed graphs and charts on the fly. It's also possible to design self-checking worksheets where a press of a button will verify the data that you entered.

Of all the Office products, the third-party, add-in product market for Excel is the largest and includes a vast array of product types, including add-ins that you can use with your VBA programs. Although you probably wouldn't want to write *War and Peace* with Excel, products are available that you can use to turn it into a simple word processor. Many products provide advanced math modeling and other calculation tasks. You'll also find an assortment of graphics products designed to make charting easier.

You should always check for an existing solution before you write a program that you have to debug and maintain. However, you still need to write programs for Excel because the potential of this program is far from exhausted. In this chapter, I provide the tools that you need to write exceptional Excel programs so that you can complete your work quickly and easily. In this chapter, I focus on the worksheet instead of charts because you'll likely spend more time in that area.

Understanding the Excel-Related Objects

Excel relies on some essential objects to provide access to the various data elements. Because of the nature of worksheets, you'll find that each of these objects can actually perform multiple duties. For example, you don't have to access a worksheet through a Workbook object unless you don't know the name of the worksheet. Most objects also include links to objects above and below the current position in the hierarchy so that you can use the object of convenience to access a data element.

You also have to consider the way that objects appear in the document. For example, a chart can appear as a separate item, or it can appear within a worksheet. When the chart appears as a separate item, you see it listed in Project Explorer and you can work with the object directly. Always access charts included within a worksheet by using the Sheet object.

This section focuses on Excel object issues. The demonstrations show how the various objects interact and what you need to consider while you design and build your Excel program. For example, you need to consider where to add charts and graphs while you build them so that they're most convenient in displaying the data.

Using the Workbooks collection

The Workbooks collection contains a list of all the workbooks open at any given time. From this list, you can select a single Workbook object to use in your program. The Workbook object contains general information about the file such as its name and location. You can also use the Workbook object to access any other major object in the document, which includes all Worksheet objects and standalone Chart objects. Listing 14-1 shows an example of the Workbooks collection in use. (You can find the source code for this example on the Dummies.com site at http://www.dummies.com/go/mueller.)

Listing 14-1   Using the Workbooks Collection

```
Public Sub WorkbookDemo()
    ' Holds the output data.
    Dim Output As String

    ' Get the test workbook.
    Dim CurrBook As Workbook
    Set CurrBook = Application.Workbooks("ExcelObjects.xls")

    ' Get the workbook name and location.
    Output = "Name: " + CurrBook.Name + vbCrLf + _
```

```
            "Full Name: " + CurrBook.FullName + vbCrLf + _
            "Path: " + CurrBook.Path + vbCrLf + vbCrLf

    ' Holds the current sheet.
    Dim CurrSheet As Worksheet

    ' Look for every sheet.
    Output = "Worksheet List:" + vbCrLf
    For Each CurrSheet In CurrBook.Worksheets
        Output = Output + CurrSheet.Name + vbCrLf
    Next

    ' Holds the current chart.
    Dim CurrChart As Chart

    ' Look for every chart.
    Output = Output + vbCrLf + "Chart List:" + vbCrLf
    For Each CurrChart In CurrBook.Charts
        Output = Output + CurrChart.Name + vbCrLf
    Next

    ' Display the output.
    MsgBox Output, vbInformation Or vbOKOnly, "Object List"
End Sub
```

The code begins by using the Application.Workbooks collection to retrieve a single Workbook object. Notice that you must use the full name of the Excel file, including the file extension, as an index into the collection. The resulting Workbook object contains the name and path information for the document. It also contains settings such as the summary information. You can use this object to control windows and also add new main elements such as a worksheet.

After the code has access to the workbook, it uses the CurrBook object to access the list of worksheets. As usual, the code relies on a For Each...Next statement. You can also use an index to access individual worksheets in your code. The Worksheet, CurrSheet, contains properties and methods for manipulating any data that the Worksheet contains, including embedded objects such as charts or even pictures. Every worksheet appears in the CurrBook object list by its object name (not the friendly name that you give it), so you can access them without using the Worksheets collection.

Unlike worksheets, only independent charts appear as part of CurrBook. You use the same technique to access a Chart object as a Worksheet object. The only difference is that you must use the Charts collection. Note that chart names appear in the list of objects presented by CurrBook, so you can also access the chart directly as an object without using the Charts collection. Figure 14-1 shows typical output from this program.

Figure 14-1:
Retrieving
a list of
worksheets
and charts.

Although you must use the object name to access a worksheet or chart directly in CurrBook, the name property used for a collection is actually the friendly name. It's easy to become confused. The Project window always lists both the friendly and the object name, so always look to it for guidance when the name that you should use is unclear.

Using the Sheets collection

The Sheets collection is the easiest method for accessing worksheets in many situations. You don't have to drill down through the Excel object hierarchy to find the worksheet that you want. However, accessing the worksheets at the top of the hierarchy means that you don't have the objects that exist at lower levels available either, so this technique is a tradeoff.

Designing a basic example

You can use the Sheets collection to access all kinds of sheets, not just worksheets. Any standalone Chart objects also appear in this collection. Look at the example in the earlier "Using the Workbooks collection" section, and you see that it treats charts and worksheets as separate objects. Listing 14-2 shows an example of the Sheets collection in use. (You can find the source code for this example on the Dummies.com site at http://www.dummies.com/go/mueller.)

Listing 14-2   Using the Sheets Collection

```
Public Sub ListSheets()
    ' An individual entry.
    Dim ThisEntry As Variant

    ' Holds the output data.
    Dim Output As String

    ' Get the current number of worksheets.
    Output = "Sheet Count: " + _
```

```
        CStr(Application.Sheets.Count)

    ' List each worksheet in turn.
    For Each ThisEntry In Application.Sheets

        ' Verify there is a sheet to work with.
        If ThisEntry.Type = XlSheetType.xlWorksheet Then
            Output = Output + vbCrLf + ThisEntry.Name
        End If
    Next

    ' Display the result.
    MsgBox Output, _
           vbInformation or vbOKOnly, _
           "Worksheet List"
End Sub
```

The code for this example begins by creating a Variant to hold the various sheet types. If you use a Worksheet or a Chart object, the code will fail because the Sheets enumeration can return any valid type — not just one valid type. The problem with using a Variant is that VBA can't provide balloon help or automatic completion. You must be sure that you type the correct method and property names without the usual help.

After the code creates the required variables, it gets the number of sheets in the workbook. This number includes all the worksheets and charts and not just the worksheets.

A For Each...Next loop retrieves each sheet in turn. Notice how the code uses an If...Then statement to compare the Variant type with the XlSheetType.xlWorksheet constant. Using this technique lets you separate the worksheets from other Sheets collection types as needed. Figure 14-2 shows the output from this example.

Figure 14-2:
Retrieving a list of worksheets.

Note that the number of sheets doesn't match the number of names in the list. The ExcelObjects.xls example file supplied with the source code contains three worksheets and three charts. I embedded one of the charts on a worksheet, so the total number of Sheets collection members is five.

Extending test code for practical use

You might look at some of the example programs that you create to discover something new and then wonder how you can use these examples in an application. Example code (also called *test code*) is often more practical than you think; you simply have to look at it from another perspective. For example, the code in the "Designing a basic example" section, earlier in this chapter, shows how to list a particular type of member from the Sheets collection, but it might not look that useful. Listing 14-3 contains an example of how you can extend that example to do something more practical.

Listing 14-3   Determining the Name of the Last Sheet

```
Public Function GetLastSheet() As String
    ' An individual entry.
    Dim ThisEntry As Variant

    ' Holds the output data.
    Dim Output As String

    ' List each worksheet in turn.
    For Each ThisEntry In Application.Sheets

        ' Verify there is a sheet to work with.
        If ThisEntry.Type = XlSheetType.xlWorksheet Then
            Output = ThisEntry.Name
        End If
    Next

    ' Display the result.
    GetLastSheet = Output
End Function
```

The GetLastSheet function performs essentially the same task as the listing example, but now it tells you the name of the last worksheet in a Sheets collection. The examples in the upcoming "Adding and formatting a worksheet" and "Deleting a worksheet" sections rely on this function — you can't perform the task with any other technique.

Normally, when you want to add another sheet to the end of the collection, you use the Application.Sheets.Add After:=Worksheets(Worksheets. Count) statement. This command adds the new worksheet to the very end of the collection, which might not be convenient in many cases. You might prefer to store charts at the end of the list and worksheets at the beginning of the list.

The example code in the upcoming "Adding and formatting a worksheet" section performs the Add method in a special way. It places the new worksheet at the end of the worksheets and not at the end of the entire list objects. This code uses the function to add a worksheet by using this statement: Application. Sheets.Add After:=Worksheets(GetLastSheet), Type:=XlSheetType. xlWorksheet. See the next section for additional details.

Adding and formatting a worksheet

You might need to use code to add a worksheet to a workbook for a number of reasons. For example, the information that you need might be a calculated value that Excel doesn't include, or you might need to get the information from an outside source. Listing 14-4 shows some techniques that you can use to add a worksheet to a workbook.

Listing 14-4 Adding a Worksheet to a Workbook

```
Public Sub AddSheetToEnd()
    ' Create a new sheet.
    Dim NewWorksheet As Worksheet
    Set NewWorksheet = _
        Application.Sheets.Add( _
            After:=Worksheets(GetLastSheet), _
            Type:=XlSheetType.xlWorksheet)

    ' Rename the worksheet.
    NewWorksheet.Name = "Added Worksheet"

    ' Place a title in the worksheet.
    NewWorksheet.Cells(1, 1) = "Sample Data"

    ' Add some headings.
    NewWorksheet.Cells(3, 1) = "Label"
    NewWorksheet.Cells(3, 2) = "Data"
    NewWorksheet.Cells(3, 3) = "Sum"

    ' Format the title and headings.
    With NewWorksheet.Range("A1", "B1")
        .Font.Bold = True
        .Font.Size = 12
        .Borders.LineStyle = XlLineStyle.xlContinuous
        .Borders.Weight = XlBorderWeight.xlThick
        .Interior.Pattern = XlPattern.xlPatternSolid
        .Interior.Color = RGB(255, 255, 0)
    End With
    NewWorksheet.Range("A3", "C3").Font.Bold = True

    ' Create some data entries.
    Dim Counter As Integer
    For Counter = 1 To 6

        ' Add some data labels.
        NewWorksheet.Cells(Counter + 3, 1) = _
            "Element " + CStr(Counter)

        ' Add a random integer value between 1 and 10.
        NewWorksheet.Cells(Counter + 3, 2) = _
```

(continued)

Listing 14-4 *(continued)*

```
            CInt(Rnd() * 10)
        ' Add an equation to the third column.
        If Counter = 1 Then
            NewWorksheet.Cells(Counter + 3, 3) = _
                "= B" + CStr(Counter + 3)
        Else
            NewWorksheet.Cells(Counter + 3, 3) = _
                "= C" + CStr(Counter + 2) + _
                " + B" + CStr(Counter + 3)
        End If
    Next
End Sub
```

The code begins by adding a new worksheet to the Sheets collection (and therefore the workbook) by using the Add method. Make sure that you make a variable that is equal to the output of the Add method when you want to add data or format the worksheet after creating it. Notice the Type argument for the Add method. This argument defines the kind of object to add. This feature lets you use the same call to add any legal object to the Sheets collection by changing this one argument.

After the code adds the new worksheet, it uses the NewWorksheet object to perform formatting and add data. The NewWorksheet.Name property affects the name that you see on the tab at the bottom of the page. Note that the example doesn't include code to prevent you from adding this worksheet twice. Make sure that you call the function only one time, or it will fail at the point where VBA attempts to rename the worksheet.

The code adds a title and some headings. These entries appear in the default font and style unless you change them.

You use the Range collection to make formatting changes. The code begins by modifying the heading area. It changes the font to bold, makes the font a different size, adds a thick line around the affected boxes, and finally makes the inside of the box yellow. Notice the use of various enumerations to make it easier to provide values that VBA understands. Also, notice the use of the RGB function to create a color value. The headings appear in bold type but are the same as the other text in all other ways.

The example code shows how to add three kinds of data to an Excel worksheet. The first entry is a simple string that labels the data values. The second entry is an integer value. Notice the use of the Rnd function to create a random value between 1 and 10. The code uses the CInt function to convert the value from a Single to an Integer. The third entry is a *function*, which is a special kind of string that begins with an equals sign. Figure 14-3 shows the output from this program.

Figure 14-3:
Defining all
worksheet
elements by
using code.

Figure 14-3 demonstrates that the code met all its objectives. The Added Worksheet appears at the end of the worksheet list but before Last Chart. Look at the Formula bar and notice that Excel converted the formula string into an actual formula. The text characteristics of the title and heading are all correct. (Although you can't see the title block cell color in the book, running the example code shows that it appears yellow.) The data elements include a label, a random number, and a sum as expected.

Deleting a worksheet

You won't need to use code to delete a worksheet very often. In fact, you should avoid deleting a worksheet using this technique because your code might not always detect important information that the worksheet contains. However, if you create a temporary worksheet for some quick calculations or you want to perform an automated cleanup of old data, using code can be quite helpful.

Removing a worksheet from a Sheets collection is relatively simple. Here's an example of how you can perform this task.

```
Public Sub RemoveLastSheet()
    ' Remove the last worksheet.
    Application.Sheets(GetLastSheet).Delete
End Sub
```

Notice this code removes the last sheet in the example workbook. This example is generic enough that you can use it to remove the last worksheet in any workbook. However, to see how this example works, you can remove the worksheet added in the section "Adding and formatting a worksheet," earlier in this chapter.

Using the Charts collection

One of the most useful purposes of the Charts collection is building a custom chart whenever you need one. The advantage of creating uncommon charts by using code is that they take up less space. In addition, you can create variations on a theme without a lot of work. Listing 14-5 shows an example of the Charts collection in action. (You can find the source code for this example on the Dummies.com site at http://www.dummies.com/go/mueller.)

Listing 14-5   Creating an Excel Chart

```
Public Sub BuildChart()
   ' Create a new chart.
   Dim NewChart As Chart
   Set NewChart = Charts.Add(After:=Charts(Charts.Count))

   ' Change the Name.
   NewChart.Name = "Added Chart"

   ' Create a series for the chart.
   Dim TheSeries As Series
   NewChart.SeriesCollection.Add _
      Source:=Worksheets("My Data Sheet").Range("B$3:B$8")
   Set TheSeries = NewChart.SeriesCollection(1)

   ' Change the chart type.
   TheSeries.ChartType = xl3DPie

   ' Change the series title.
   TheSeries.Name = "Data from My Data Sheet"

   ' Perform some data formatting.
   With TheSeries
      .XValues = _
         Worksheets("My Data Sheet").Range("A$3:A$8")
      .HasDataLabels = True
      .DataLabels.ShowValue = True
      .DataLabels.Font.Italic = True
      .DataLabels.Font.Size = 14
   End With

   ' Modify the chart's legend.
   With NewChart
      .HasLegend = True
      .Legend.Font.Size = 14
   End With

   ' Modify the 3-D view.
   With NewChart
      .Pie3DGroup.FirstSliceAngle = 90
      .Elevation = 45
```

```
    End With

    ' Format the chart title.
    With NewChart.ChartTitle
        .Font.Bold = True
        .Font.Size = 18
        .Border.LineStyle = XlLineStyle.xlContinuous
        .Border.Weight = XlBorderWeight.xlMedium
    End With

    ' Format the Plot area.
    With NewChart.PlotArea
        .Interior.Color = RGB(255, 255, 255)
        .Border.LineStyle = XlLineStyle.xlLineStyleNone
        .Height = 450
        .Width = 450
        .Top = 75
        .Left = 25
    End With
End Sub
```

The code begins by creating a new chart. This chart should appear as the last chart in the workbook but not necessarily as the last item in the workbook. Any worksheets that appear after the existing last chart also appear after the new chart. The NewChart.Name property changes the name that appears on the tab at the bottom of the chart — the property doesn't change the chart title.

The chart is blank at this point. To display any data, you must add at least one data series to the chart. A pie chart only uses one data series at a time, but other charts can support (or might even require) multiple data series. For example, a bubble chart requires multiple data series. Consequently, the next task that the code performs is creating a data series based on the My Data Sheet worksheet supplied with the example. Notice that the code can't set TheSeries equal to the output of the Add method in this case, so it uses an extra step to get the new series from the SeriesCollection collection.

It's important to change the ChartType property at the outset if you want to see the correct changes while you build and debug your program. Otherwise, the chart displays the default chart type, and you might not see the changes that you expect. For example, the Legend property works differently when you use a pie chart versus a bar chart.

The code formats the data series next. Performing this step now is helpful because it displays all the *raw* (unformatted) data onscreen. The XValues property determines the entries in the legend for a pie chart. On the other hand, these values appear at the bottom of the display for a bar chart. In both cases, you want to display the labels onscreen so that you can see their effect on the overall display area.

Notice the appearance of the HasDataLabels and the HasLegend properties in the code. If you don't include these properties, the code will display some rather odd error messages, none of which relate to the problem at hand. When you have problems resolving data-label or legend-formatting errors, always verify that you've added these two property settings to your code.

The 3D property settings appear in several places. Notice the Pie3DGroup object in the code. VBA supports other kinds of objects for other kinds of charts, so you must use the correct object for the type of chart that you want to create. Some global 3-D settings do appear as part of the chart. For example, the Elevation property, which affects the angle of presentation, is part of the global settings group. Don't assume that two settings that appear on the same page of a property sheet will also appear in the same object in VBA.

Changing the ChartTitle format is almost a requirement because VBA uses the default font for every entry that the code creates. The example code shows a few of the changes that you might want to make. However, VBA provides a relatively large number of formatting features that you can choose. For example, the larger font size normally used by the ChartTitle lets you use special effects like Shadow.

You might notice that some formatting options don't work in every place that you could use them. For example, VBA complains if you try to set the NewChart.ChartTitle.Border.LineStyle property to XlLineStyle. xlDouble. The only problem is that Microsoft doesn't document these limitations, so you need to exercise care when testing your programs. Make sure that all the options that you select work in every situation in which they're used.

The plot area is one of the last elements that you should work on because every other setting change that you make will affect it. The example shows some of the changes that you always want to make to the plot area. The plot area background begins as gray, which actually makes some types of chart difficult to read if you don't change it. It's also a good idea to get rid of the border around some charts. (You'll want to keep it for bar charts in many cases.) Finally, you generally want to optimize the position and size of the chart to make it as large as possible. Figure 14-4 shows the output from this example.

Using the Windows collection

Excel records one Window object in the Windows collection for every file that you open. Consequently, the Windows collection doesn't tell you much about the data except at a very high level. For example, you could use the Window object to determine the names of files that you have opened. The Window object can also determine the active Sheet object (see the section "Using the Sheets collection," earlier in this chapter, for details) and tell you about general settings, such as whether Excel displays grids on the worksheets. In general, you won't use the Windows collection for low-level data manipulation in Excel because there are easier methods of getting access to what you need. Listing 14-6 shows an example of the Windows collection at work. (You can find the source code for this example on the Dummies.com site at http://www.dummies.com/go/mueller.)

Listing 14-6 Listing Application Windows

```
Public Sub ListWindows()
    ' Holds a Window object.
    Dim MyWin As Window

    ' Holds the output.
    Dim Output As String

    ' Look at each Window in the Windows collection.
    For Each MyWin In Application.Windows

        ' Get the current window information.
        With MyWin
        Output = Output + "Caption: " + .Caption + vbCrLf + _
            "Display Tabs: " + _
            IIf(MyWin.DisplayWorkbookTabs, "Yes", "No") + _
            vbCrLf + "Zoom Factor: " + CStr(MyWin.Zoom) + _
            vbCrLf + "Panes: "

        ' Determine the number of panes.
        If .ActiveSheet.Type = -4167 Then

            ' Store the number of panes.
            Output = Output + CStr(.Panes.Count) + vbCrLf

            ' Add a new pane if possible.
            If .Panes.Count = 1 Then
                .SplitHorizontal = 200
                .SplitVertical = 200

            ' Remove extra panes if possible.
            ElseIf .Panes.Count = 4 Then
                .SplitHorizontal = 0
                .SplitVertical = 0
            End If
        Else
            Output = Output + "No Panes on a Chart" + vbCrLf
        End If

        ' Add space to the output.
        Output = Output + vbCrLf

    End With
```

(continued)

Listing 14-6 *(continued)*

```
    Next

    ' Output the result.
    MsgBox Output, _
           vbInformation Or vbOKOnly, _
           "Windows Currently in Use"
End Sub
```

The code begins by creating a `Window` object from the `Application.` `Windows` collection. It uses this object to determine some characteristics about the window such as

✔ The window name (not the tab name)

✔ Whether the workbook tabs are visible

✔ The current zoom factor

Excel will present a few problems when you use this approach. Notice that the code looks for a worksheet by using the constant number -4167. The number for charts is equally odd: -4102. These aren't the constants used for other code in this chapter, and this issue points out one reason why you want to avoid using the `Windows` collection when you can.

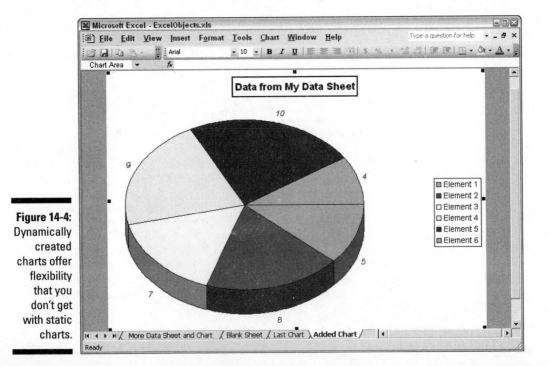

Figure 14-4:
Dynamically
created
charts offer
flexibility
that you
don't get
with static
charts.

Charts don't have panes. However, you can split a worksheet both horizontally and vertically for a total of four panes. The code shows how to perform both types of splits and also how to close them. Notice that you don't use the standard `Panes.Add` method that other applications such as Word use. When you want to split the view, you must tell VBA how many pixels to display on the left or the top of the split. Figure 14-5 shows the output from this example.

Windows Currently in Use

> Caption: ExcelObjects.xls
> Display Tabs: Yes
> Zoom Factor: 75
> Panes: No Panes on a Chart
>
> Caption: Apples.xls
> Display Tabs: Yes
> Zoom Factor: 100
> Panes: 4
>
> Caption: Main Orchard.xls
> Display Tabs: Yes
> Zoom Factor: 100
> Panes: 4
>
> OK

Figure 14-5:
Displaying
Excel
window
statistics.

Selecting Objects within Excel

You can place any object that you want in an Excel worksheet, including pictures and sounds. These kinds of objects work very much the same in Excel as they do in Word. (See the "Selecting Objects in a Word Document" section of Chapter 13.) The main difference is that you use the `OLEObjects` collection of the sheet that holds the object. However, Excel can also embed `Chart` objects in a worksheet. Because this is such a special feature, I show you in this section how to work with embedded `Chart` objects.

The same data can say different things depending on how you present it. A pie chart tells the viewer about parts of a whole, and a bar chart compares individual values. The problem with charts that you create in Excel is that they're static — they continue to say the same thing unless you redesign them. Fortunately, you can control the appearance of an embedded chart just as easily as a standalone chart. The code in Listing 14-7 demonstrates a rotating chart technique. (You can find the source code for this example on the Dummies.com site at `http://www.dummies.com/go/mueller`.)

Listing 14-7   Designing a Rotating Chart Presentation

```
Public Sub SelectObject()
    ' Select the worksheet.
    Sheet2.Select

    ' Select the object.
    Sheet2.ChartObjects(1).Select

    ' Create a chart object.
    Dim EmbeddedChart As Chart
    Set EmbeddedChart = Sheet2.ChartObjects(1).Chart

    ' Make sure the chart has a title.
    EmbeddedChart.HasTitle = True

    ' Look for the chart object.
    With EmbeddedChart

        ' Rotate between chart types. Change the title as
        ' needed to match the chart type.
        Select Case .ChartType
            Case XlChartType.xlPie
                .ChartType = xlArea
                .ChartTitle.Caption = "More Data (Area)"
            Case XlChartType.xlArea
                .ChartType = xlLine
                .ChartTitle.Caption = "More Data (Line)"
            Case XlChartType.xlLine
                .ChartType = xlColumnClustered
                .ChartTitle.Caption = "More Data (Column)"
            Case XlChartType.xlColumnClustered
                .ChartType = xlPie
                .ChartTitle.Caption = "More Data (Pie)"
        End Select
    End With
End Sub
```

The code begins by selecting the correct worksheet and the chart embedded on that worksheet. The ChartObjects collection contains one entry for each embedded chart on the worksheet. The Select method highlights the chart of interest on the worksheet.

Unlike many collections, the ChartObjects collection doesn't return the selected chart by default. You must specifically request the chart by using the Sheet2.ChartObjects(1).Chart property.

After the code gets hold of the chart, it checks the HasTitle property. It's possible that this property is set to False, so you must check it each time; otherwise, changing the ChartTitle object results in an error.

The `Select Case` statement relies on the current `ChartType` property value to choose the next chart. The code sets the `ChartType` property value to one of the standard constants. It then changes the chart's caption to match the chart type. Notice that you must use the `ChartTitle.Caption` property to change the title. The `ChartTitle` object is self contained and includes a number of other formatting properties. Figure 14-6 shows typical output from this program.

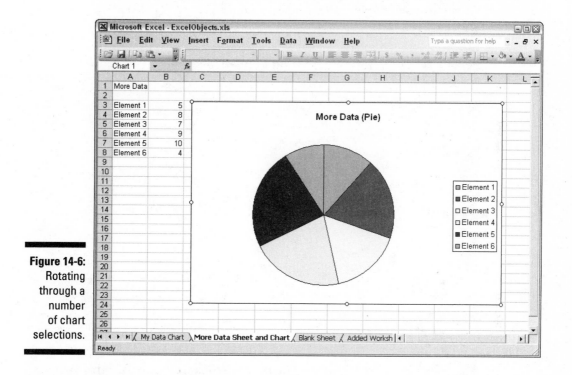

Figure 14-6:
Rotating
through a
number
of chart
selections.

Developing Custom Functions in Excel

Formulas are the lifeblood of Excel. You can't find too many worksheets that are devoid of formulas because you need formulas to figure out new values based on your existing data. Microsoft includes a wealth of standard formulas in Excel. In fact, it's possible that you'll never need anything more than the Microsoft formulas. However, formulas are extremely important, so it's handy to know how to create one of your own.

All formulas in Excel rely on functions. If you want to create a special formula for your worksheet, all you need is a function to perform the task. The functions that you create appear in the User Defined category of the Insert Function dialog box that you access by using the Insert⇨Function command.

Performing data conversion

One of the more interesting uses for specialized formulas is data conversion. A data conversion can convert one type of data to another, or it can manipulate the data in some way. Listing 14-8 shows an example of a function that reverses the order of letters in a string. (You can find the source code for this example on the Dummies.com site at `http://www.dummies.com/go/mueller`.)

Listing 14-8   Performing a String Conversion

```
Public Function ConvertString(Original As String) As String
   ' Used for loops.
   Dim Counter As Integer

   ' Contains the string length.
   Dim StrLen As Integer
   StrLen = Len(Original)

   ' Holds the output string.
   Dim Output As String
   Output = ""

   ' Reverse the string.
   For Counter = StrLen To 1 Step -1
      Output = Output + Mid(Original, Counter, 1)
   Next

   ' Return the result.
   ConvertString = Output
End Function
```

The code begins by getting the length of the input string. It uses this value as part of a `For...Next` loop. Notice how the function relies on the `Mid` function to retrieve one letter at a time from the end of the string to build `Output`. The function ends by returning the final `Output` value. To use this function, simply type =**ConvertString("Hello")** into the cell of a worksheet, where `"Hello"` is the string that you want to convert.

Defining math calculations

Another common type of formula is the math equation. The Pythagoras function shown in Listing 14-9 computes the length of the hypotenuse of a triangle, given the length of two sides. (You can find the source code for this example on the Dummies.com site at `http://www.dummies.com/go/mueller`.)

Listing 14-9   Calculating the Hypotenuse of a Triangle

```
Public Function Pythagoras(Side1 As Double, _
    Side2 As Double) As Double

    ' Perform the calculation.
    Pythagoras = Math.Sqr((Side1 * Side1) + (Side2 * Side2))

End Function
```

Math calculations are usually simple in that you don't have to create any special variables to use them. However, splitting complex calculations into pieces can help you debug them. To use this function, type **=Pythagoras(3,4)**.

Adding comments to your functions

When you open the Insert Function dialog box, Excel displays a message saying that there's no help for your function. You can use one of two techniques to add comments to your functions. Use the following procedure to add the comment with the first technique.

1. **Select the Tools⇨Macro⇨Macros command.**

   VBA displays the Macro dialog box.

2. **Type the name of your function in the Macro Name field.**

   Notice that VBA doesn't highlight the Create button because it knows that the function exists even though the function doesn't appear in the macro list.

3. **Click Options.**

   Excel displays the Macro Options dialog box.

4. **Type a description for the function in the Description field but don't change anything else.**

5. **Click OK.**

   The Macro dialog box appears.

6. **Click Cancel.**

   Excel closes the Macro dialog box.

7. **Save the file and close Excel.**

When you open the file again, the functions have a description. Closing and reopening Excel is necessary to reload the file.

The advantage of the second technique shown in Listing 14-10 is speed. You can use this technique to add descriptions to several functions quickly. Begin by exporting the file from the VBA Integrated Development Environment (IDE). (See the "Exporting a module from a program" section in Chapter 6.) Open the file by using a text editor such as Notepad. Immediately after the function declaration, type a VB_Description attribute such as this one.

Listing 14-10   Adding a Comment by Using an Attribute

```
Public Function Pythagoras(Side1 As Double, _
   Side2 As Double) As Double
Attribute Pythagoras.VB_Description = "Returns the value of the hypotenuse."

   ' Perform the calculation.
   Pythagoras = Math.Sqr((Side1 * Side1) + (Side2 * Side2))

End Function
```

Notice the way that the description appears in the file. You must type the keyword Attribute, followed by the name of the function and the keyword VB_Description. Type the text that you want to appear as a description for the function in the Insert Function dialog box.

Save the file. Remove the old copy of the file from the modules list and import the new copy. (See the "Importing a module in a program" section of Chapter 6.) You see the description in the Insert Function dialog box even though you can't see it in the VBA IDE.

Chapter 15

VBA Programming in Access

• •

In This Chapter

▶ Working with Access-related objects

▶ Developing programs with a database engine in mind

▶ Creating utility programs with the database objects

▶ Using Structured Query Language (SQL) statements in your code

▶ Designing form-based applications

▶ Designing automatic execution applications

• •

Microsoft Access is a database management system (DBMS) that provides a number of opportunities for developing programs with VBA. In fact, it's safe to say that some people make a good living performing this very task. The kinds of tasks that you can perform by using a database are also varied — everything from writing reports to creating new and better methods for data entry. You can also use Access as a data storage method for everything from scientific needs to your CD collection.

This chapter introduces you to database programming in Access. I'm assuming that you know how to use Access and that you have already used it to create elements such as tables, which are composed of *records* (an individual entry in the table) and *fields* (the individual entries in the record). Consider this chapter your doorway to a much larger world. I could easily write an entire book on the topic of database management and still not exhaust the topic. In fact, database management books consume a large part of my personal library. Consequently, this chapter discusses just the VBA portion of Microsoft Access. By using VBA, you can

✔ Make the task of managing your Access data easier by reducing data entry requirements or ensuring the data the user enters meets certain requirements

✔ Perform data manipulation, such as extracting just the records that you need

✔ Provide customized data output, such as reports

Because *database management* (the organized storage of data in one or more tables) is such a large topic, you need to consider just how you'll use database management to answer an immediate need. Small, easy projects are the best way to start with Microsoft Access. However, you should also choose a database project that makes a difference. My first project was a contact management database that I've improved over the years and still use today. This contact management system is a good way to use Access, and it's something I care about, so I understand Access better today — because *I* wrote the contact management system — than if I had chosen an inconsequential project.

This chapter also focuses on some key areas that you can use immediately to increase your personal productivity and to help others in a small group (office) setting. For example, I increased my personal productivity by using an Access database to maintain lists of interesting words that I learn. I also have one that maintains the inventory for my office. Folks can use either of these databases to discover new VBA programming techniques, improve their personal productivity, and help other people in a small office setting.

Microsoft Access is actually a very good database to use for a number of office tasks. It's small, you don't need a server to use it, and it doesn't require complex knowledge that only a computer expert could love. Although Access includes all the support required to work on a server, you can also create databases for personal use. You could create something as simple as a To Do list that will make you more productive, even though you wouldn't necessarily want to share it with anyone else.

Understanding the Access-Related Objects

Microsoft Access provides more objects than just about any other Office application that you'll use. You can create a database, populate it with information, and print it out without ever using the user interface. In addition, these objects are interesting because they perform so many tasks well. Access even has a special object (see the upcoming "Accessing special commands with the DoCmd object" section) that performs little utility tasks. You need to know about a variety of collections and objects in order to perform many tasks programmatically. (See the object hierarchy chart at `http://msdn.microsoft.com/library/en-us/vbaac10/html/acsumAccessObjHierarchy.asp` for a complete list of Access objects.)

Don't assume that you need to perform every task by using code. In fact, it's to your advantage to play around with the user interface for some time before you even consider using VBA with Access. The user interface includes a wealth of features for creating objects that you need by using the Access Designer rather than imagining them by using code.

The macro system provided with Access is also superior (and different) from other Office applications. Access macros reside separately from VBA, and you can use them to perform a number of tasks. In fact, you'll find that macros are a required addition to VBA to create some types of programs. Access presents some unique problems and opportunities for the VBA user.

Understanding Access and sub-procedure use

When you create a program for Word or Excel, you normally create it by adding sub-procedures (the Sub statement). However, when you work with Access, you normally use a Function statement instead. If you want to execute the function independently, you need to create a macro with the RunCode action. The Function Name field contains the name of the function and any arguments that it requires. Figure 15-1 shows an example of such a macro.

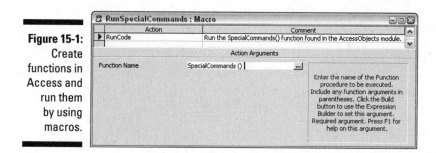

Figure 15-1: Create functions in Access and run them by using macros.

When you do decide to create sub-procedures, you must call the sub-procedure by using a function. Although a sub-procedure will execute within the VBA Integrated Development Environment (IDE), it won't do you much good outside that environment.

Using the Application object effectively

Access has a number of interesting and useful features in the Application object. When using other Office applications, the Application object tends to provide a means for access collections such as the Sheets collection in Excel. In Access, you can use the Application object to perform other tasks. Listing 15-1 shows an example of a few of the features that you should try. (You can find the source code for this example on the Dummies.com site at http://www.dummies.com/go/mueller.)

Listing 15-1   Using a Progress Meter in Access

```
Public Function UseApplication()
    ' Create an output string.
    Dim Output As String

    ' Fill it with text version of a numeric error.
    Output = Application.AccessError(14)

    ' Display the result.
    MsgBox "Error number 14 is " + Chr(&H22) + Output + _
        Chr(&H22), vbInformation, "Error Number Text"

    ' Add this database to the favorites list.
    Application.AddToFavorites

    ' Perform some system commands.
    ' Create a progress meter.
    Application.SysCmd acSysCmdInitMeter, "Progress Meter", 5
    Dim Counter As Integer

    ' Update the meter until finished.
    For Counter = 1 To 5
        Application.SysCmd acSysCmdUpdateMeter, Counter
        MsgBox "Click to proceed", vbInformation, "Progress"
    Next

    ' Remove the meter.
    Application.SysCmd acSysCmdRemoveMeter

    ' Say you're done by changing the status bar text.
    Application.SysCmd acSysCmdSetStatus, _
                    "Progress meter is done."
End Function
```

The example performs three unique tasks, but you have many others that you can use. The first task is to determine what an error code means. You often receive error numbers from VBA that you then have to look up somewhere (such as online, in a help file, or by asking someone online) in hopes of finding a meaning. The Application.AccessError method takes the guesswork out of finding a human readable explanation for a numeric error.

You might want to include the next method in an installation program or as part of the automatic execution sequence. The Application.AddToFavorites method places a pointer to the database in your Favorites folder. You can access the database by using the Start⇨Favorites menu or from within Internet Explorer.

When you write a program that performs a number of tasks, it could require some time to complete. In fact, you could begin thinking that the task is taking so long that the computer has failed. A progress meter can help in this situation by providing visual feedback that something is indeed going on with the computer.

The `Application.SysCmd` method can display a progress meter in the status bar when you call it with the `acSysCmdInitMeter` as the first argument. The second argument contains the text that you want to display in the status bar while the progress meter is visible. The third argument tells how many segments that the project meter requires. You should include one segment per each major task that the program performs. Figure 15-2 shows a typical example of the progress meter for this program.

Figure 15-2:
A progress
meter.

Notice how the example uses a `For...Next` loop to update the progress meter. You use the `Application.SysCmd acSysCmdUpdateMeter` method call to provide update information. The second argument should contain the amount of the update — a higher number increases the length of the progress meter indicator. You can use this feature to your advantage. Counting down instead of up can show negative progress, such as backing out of an unsuccessful database update.

When you finish using the progress meter, you remove it by calling the `Application.SysCmd acSysCmdRemoveMeter` method. Normally, this act displays the word `Ready` in the status bar. However, you can make the status bar say anything that you want by calling the `Application.SysCmdacSysCmdSetStatus` method. The second argument contains the text that you want to display in this case. The example uses this technique to tell you that the progress meter portion of the example is complete.

Defining your work area with the Workspaces collection

You can use the `Workspaces` collection for a number of tasks. Each `Workspace` object within the collection contains an environment in which you can perform database- or Access-related tasks. The `Workspaces` collection contains a single, default `Workspace` object when you first start Access, which is enough to perform most of the work that you need to do.

Most Access programming tasks never require that you open more than one database at a time, which is why the default `Workspace` is sufficient. You can use this default `Workspace` to perform a number of tasks, such as adding a new user or performing database maintenance. Listing 15-2 shows an example of a generic function for adding a user to a database. (You can find the source code for this example on the Dummies.com site at `http://www.dummies.com/go/mueller`.)

Listing 15-2   Adding a User to a Database

```
Public Function ConfigureUser()
    ' Get the default workspace.
    Dim CurWrk As Workspace
    Set CurWrk = DBEngine.Workspaces(0)

    ' Get the username and password.
    Dim Username As String
    Dim Password As String
    Username = InputBox("Type a user name.", "New User")
    Password = InputBox("Type a password.", "New User")

    ' Create a new user.
    Dim NewUser As User
    Set NewUser = CurWrk.CreateUser(Name:=Username, _
                               Password:=Password, _
                               PID:=Username)

    ' Add the user to the database.
    CurWrk.Users.Append NewUser

    ' Modify the user setup for a default user.
    Dim AddGroup As Group
    Set AddGroup = NewUser.CreateGroup("Users", "Users")
    NewUser.Groups.Append AddGroup
End Function
```

The code begins by accessing the default `Workspace` object in the `Workspaces` collection. Notice that the code uses the `DBEngine` object as the source of the `Workspaces` collection. Even though you shouldn't have to use this extra reference, the program fails intermittently if you don't. The default `Workspace` object doesn't actually exist until you call upon the `Workspaces` collection the first time. Access creates this object automatically during the first request. You can add additional workspaces to the `Workspaces` collection by calling the `CreateWorkspace` method.

The next step is to get a username and password by calling the `InputBox` function. You could also use a custom form or request the information as part of the calling syntax for the function. The point is to obtain the required user information. In some cases, you might even want to include multiple options to add to the flexibility of your program.

After the code gets the username and password, it creates the `NewUser` object. The `CurWrk.CreateUser` method fills the `NewUser` object with data. You must provide a name, password, and Personal Identifier (PID) as arguments. This example uses the `Username` value as the PID. You can use any string containing between 4 and 20 characters. The `Username` should be unique, so using it as the `PID` value tends to ensure this fact.

However, creating the `NewUser` object doesn't add the user to the database even though you used the `CurWrk.CreateUser` method to perform the task. The code uses the `CurWrk.Users.Append` method to add the user to the list of users in the database.

At this point, you have a new user without any rights. To add rights, you must assign the user to a group. This three-step task begins by creating a group entry in the `NewUser` object. When the group has the same name as an existing group, Access adds the user to the existing group instead of creating a new one. The user has the same rights as everyone else in that group. Consequently, the `NewUser.CreateGroup` method can result in a new group, or it can simply reference an existing group. The code adds the user to the existing group in the database by using the `NewUser.Groups.Append` method.

Working with the DBEngine object

The `DBEngine` object is useful for performing several tasks. You can use it to access the `Workspaces` collection, as shown in the earlier "Defining your work area with the Workspaces collection" section. In this section, I present the most useful features of the `DBEngine` object. See the help topic at `http://msdn.microsoft.com/library/en-us/office97/html/output/F1/D2/S5A291.asp` for a complete reference.

This object is also useful for some database maintenance tasks. It's important to perform tasks such as compacting the database from time to time (normally accomplished by executing the Tools⇨Database Utilities⇨Compact and Repair Database command). Using the `DBEngine.CompactDatabase` method helps you perform this task. You can even use this object to register an Open Database Connectivity (ODBC) source automatically by calling the `DBEngine.RegisterDatabase` method. (You manually register an ODBC source using the Data Sources [ODBC] applet in the Control Panel.)

You might not realize that Access can work in one of several database modes by using a number of different technologies. When you use the `DBEngine` approach, you can choose between the *Microsoft Jet Engine* (the set of DLLs that Access uses natively for communicating with the database) or *ODBCDirect* (a special set of DLLs that many programming environments, including Access, can use to communicate with the database) by using the `DBEngine.DefaultType` property. The Microsoft Jet Engine approach is best suited to situations where you know the location of the MDB file and want to work directly with it. The ODBCDirect approach is best suited for named sources created with the Data Sources (ODBC) applet of the Control Panel.

However, one of the most useful ways to use the DBEngine object is to perform some types of security tasks. For example, you can use the DBEngine object to modify workgroup setups and also change the default settings for the database as a whole. Listing 15-3 shows an example of how you can get the default settings. (You can find the source code for this example on the Dummies.com site at http://www.dummies.com/go/mueller.)

Listing 15-3   Getting the Default DBEngine Settings

```
Public Function GetDBEngineProperties()
    ' Create an output string.
    Dim Output As String

    ' Make a place for the property values.
    Dim CurProp As Property

    ' Some properties won't have a value.
    On Error Resume Next

    ' Get the current properties.
    For Each CurProp In DBEngine.Properties
        Output = Output + CurProp.Name + ": " + _
            CStr(CurProp.Value) + vbCrLf
    Next

    ' Display the results.
    MsgBox Output, vbInformation, "DBEngine Properties"
End Function
```

Many of the objects in Access have a Properties collection. Each Property is a separate object that controls some aspect of the database operation. The properties define a database characteristic or the location of configuration information, as shown in Figure 15-3. This is a standard list of properties for the DBEngine when you use it in Microsoft Jet Engine mode.

Figure 15-3:
Use the DBEngine properties to determine the database characteristics.

```
DBEngine Properties                                                    ☒

   (i)    Version: 3.6
          LoginTimeout: 20
          IniPath: Software\Microsoft\Office\11.0\Access\Jet\4.0
          DefaultType: 2
          SystemDB: D:\Documents and Settings\John\Application Data\Microsoft\Access\System.mdw

                         [        OK        ]
```

The essential information for Access appears in the Version property. This property tells you the version of Data Access Objects (DAO) installed on the host machine. When this value is less than 3.6, you encounter problems getting some DAO features listed in the help file to work. Consequently, when you run your program on another machine, and it fails — even though it worked on your machine — verify the DAO version number.

The IniPath property contains the location of the information for Access in the Registry. See the "Using the Registry with VBA" section of Chapter 13 for details on using the Registry. The contents of the Registry vary by machine and installation. However, you can usually find a list of database conversion entries in HKEY_LOCAL_MACHINE as well as the path to the security settings for this user under HKEY_CURRENT_USER.

Getting the security settings is a little more difficult. Listing 15-4 shows an example of how you can determine the settings for a particular object type such as a table or a report. These are general settings for the entire class of objects and not a specific object. (You can find the source code for this example on the Dummies.com site at http://www.dummies.com/go/mueller.)

Listing 15-4   Getting DBEngine Security Settings

```
Public Function GetDBEngineSecurity()
   ' Create an output string.
   Dim Output As String

   ' Set the system database value if necessary.
   If DBEngine.SystemDB = "" Then
      DBEngine.SystemDB = "System.mdw"
   End If

   ' Get the current database.
   Dim TheDB As Database
   Set TheDB = DBEngine.Workspaces(0).Databases(0)

   ' Create a container object to hold the security data.
   Dim AContainer As Container

   ' Check each container for data.
   For Each AContainer In TheDB.Containers

      With AContainer

      ' Store the name of the permission object.
      Output = Output + .Name + ":" + vbCrLf

      ' Check the flag values.
      If .AllPermissions And dbSecReadDef Then
         Output = Output + "Can Read Definition" + vbCrLf
```

(continued)

Listing 15-4 *(continued)*

```
        End If

        ... other permissions ...

        If .AllPermissions And dbSecDBOpen Then
            Output = Output + "Can Open" + vbCrLf
        End If
        End With

        ' Display the results.
        MsgBox Output, vbInformation, "DBEngine Security"

        ' Erase the data.
        Output = ""
    Next

End Function
```

The code begins by checking the DBEngine.SystemDB property value. When this property is blank, the DBEngine object can't retrieve security information. You must make this check before you do any other work with the DBEngine object. Generally, setting the property as shown will let you retrieve the security information.

Access places security information in the Containers collection. Each Container object has properties such as the permission object name. One of the more important features is the AllPermissions property. This property looks like any Long value that you might have seen in the past, but it really consists of a number of individual flag values. A *flag* is an individual bit within the Long value. Setting the flag to 1 turns that entry on, and setting it to 0 turns it off. Consequently, if you want to let someone read the definition for a particular property object, you set the dbSecReadDef flag on.

The If...Then statements perform a logical And on the AllPermissions property. Each flag entry, such as dbSecDBOpen, has one bit set. If this bit is also set in the AllPermissions property, the If...Then statement expression is true. Figure 15-4 shows typical output from this example when you use the default configuration or log in as the admin account.

Setting the flag value in the AllPermissions property requires a little different technique. The idea is to perform a Boolean operation that will result in the right bit result in the AllPermissions property. Here's typical code for setting a flag on or off within the AllPermissions property.

```
' Set the flag on.
.AllPermissions = .AllPermissions Or dbSecDBOpen

' Set the flag off.
.AllPermissions =.AllPermissions And Not dbSecDBOpen
```

DBEngine Security

DataAccessPages:
Can Read Definition
Can Write Definition
Can Retrieve Data
Can Insert Data
Can Replace Data
Can Delete Data
Can Administrate
Can Create New
Can Open Exclusively
Can Open

OK

Figure 15-4:
Every object
type has a
separate
security
container
that you can
validate.

You can use the Windows Calculator to make this more understandable. When you place the calculator in Bin mode, it displays the individual bits of the number that you type. Combine this utility with the Intermediate or the Locals window to work out the effect of the flag changes. The Not, And, Or, and Xor buttons on the Calculator work just like the commands in VBA, so you can check for the results that you want before you commit them to code. (See the "Defining hex and octal values" section of Chapter 4 for details on using the Windows Calculator.)

Using the CurrentDB and related objects

The latest version of Access has new and interesting ways to perform a task. The CurrentDB object originally appeared in Office 2000 as an updated version of the DBEngine.Workspaces(0).Databases(0) object. You should use the CurrentDB object, whenever possible, to perform actual database work because this object includes a few new features that makes it a better fit for multi-user environments. However, when you want to use multiple workspaces, you still need to use the DBEngine.Workspaces collection.

You use the CurrentDB object to gain full control over the information contained in the current MDB file. This is a complete database object and not a single table. Listing 15-5 shows an example of how you can use the CurrentDB and its related objects. See the upcoming "Understanding the Database objects" section for details on elements such as the Recordsets and Fields collections. (You can find the source code for this example on the Dummies.com site at http://www.dummies.com/go/mueller.)

Listing 15-5   Getting Database Configuration Information

```
Public Function CheckCurrentDB()
   ' Create an individual table definition.
   Dim CurTblDef As TableDef

   ' Create an individual recordset.
   Dim CurRec As Recordset

   ' Create an individual field.
   Dim CurField As Field

   ' Create an output string.
   Dim Output As String

   ' Check each recordset in the database.
   For Each CurTblDef In CurrentDb.TableDefs

      ' Open a recordset for each table definition.
      Set CurRec = CurrentDb.OpenRecordset(CurTblDef.Name)

      ' Get the recordset name.
      Output = Output + CurRec.Name + vbCrLf

      ' Check for records.
      If CurRec.RecordCount = 0 Then

         ' Tell the user and exit.
         Output = Output + "No Records Available"
         GoTo SkipFields

      End If

      ' Check each field definition in the recordset.
      For Each CurField In CurRec.Fields

         ' Get the field name, type, and current value.
         Output = Output + "Name: " + CurField.Name + _
            vbCrLf + vbTab + "Type: " + _
            CvtType(CurField.Type) + vbCrLf + vbTab + _
            "Value: "

         ' Some values are null.
         If IsNull(CurField.Value) Then
            Output = Output + "Null" + vbCrLf
         Else
            Output = Output + CStr(CurField.Value) + vbCrLf
         End If
      Next

SkipFields:
   ' Display the results.
```

```
        MsgBox Output, vbInformation, "CurrentDB Information"

        ' Erase the data.
        Output = ""

        ' Close each recordset in turn.
        CurRec.Close
    Next
End Function
```

The code begins by creating objects that represent various database elements that you've used in the past. For example, a `TableDef` object is a representation of the table design that you create by using the Access Designer. The `CurrentDB` object contains a `TableDefs` collection with every table that the MDB file contains. It might surprise you to learn that Access has seven or more internal tables that it maintains in addition to the tables that you create. When you run this program on the sample database, you see eight table definitions because there really are eight tables in the database. These internal tables can provide useful information, but you generally don't want to use them.

Although the example code doesn't show them, the `CurrentDB` object also contains a `QueryDefs` collection for queries and a `Containers` collection for security objects. You use these objects in the same way that you use the objects for the `Workspaces` collection. See the earlier "Working with the DBEngine object" section for details.

To work with a particular table or query, you must create a `Recordset` object. The code performs this task by using the `OpenRecordset` method. The first argument for this method contains the name of the table that you want to open or the query that you want to create. The example shows one technique for opening an individual table when you don't know the table name when you write the code.

The presence of a table doesn't necessary indicate that it contains any data. You can check for this condition by using the `RecordCount` property. If this property is `0`, the table lacks records, and you shouldn't attempt to do anything but add records or determine configuration information. The example code shows one situation where you really do need to use a `GoTo` statement. In this case, you must skip the record-specific code if there are no records to process.

The record processing code works with individual fields, much as you will when writing code to change the information in the database. The code gets the field name, type, and its current value. A field can contain a `Null` (or nothing) value. It's important to remember that VBA uses `Null` for values and `Nothing` for objects. The `IsNull` function returns `True` when a field is `Null`. You must use this technique instead of the `Is Nothing` method that is used with objects.

The Type field also requires special processing in this case. When you convert an enumerated value to a string and that value resides in a variable, VBA returns a number and not the string value of the enumeration. If you want to see a string value, you need to write an enumeration conversion function such as the `CvtType` function shown in Listing 15-6. (You can find the source code for this example on the Dummies.com site at `http://www.dummies.com/go/mueller`.)

Listing 15-6   Converting a Numeric Type Value into a String

```
Public Function CvtType(DataType As Long) As String
   ' Use a case statement to choose a data type.
   Select Case DataType
      Case DataTypeEnum.dbBigInt
         CvtType = "dbBigInt"
      ... Other Cases ...
      Case DataTypeEnum.dbVarBinary
         CvtType = "dbVarBinary"
      Case Else
         CvtType = "Type Unknown"
   End Select
End Function
```

This function ends up as a giant `Select Case` statement. Always include a `Case Else` clause in case the function receives a nonstandard value. Otherwise, your code could fail. Figure 15-5 shows typical output from this example.

Figure 15-5:
Use
`TableDef`,
`Record`,
and `Field`
objects to
work with
tables.

Figure 15-5 shows one of the hidden Access tables that you encounter when working with the `CurrentDB` object. Notice that the example provides the data types and values for each field, along with the appropriate field name. Although it's fun to poke around a bit, exercise care when working with the `CurrentDB` object because you could damage one of these hidden system tables.

Understanding the Database objects

Access provides a number of `Database` objects that you commonly use to create programs. Here's a list of the common objects and collections that you use for database programs:

- ✔ `Connections` collection: You must create at least one connection for each Access database. The connection determines how the program communicates with the database. However, you can create more than one connection when using ADO. By way of contrast, when using DAO, the `Connection` object and the `Database` object are the same. The `Connections` collection contains one `Connection` object for each database connection.

- ✔ `Databases` collection: A `Database` object is the representation of the physical storage for all the tables, queries, reports, and other database elements. The `Database` object is the container — not the content. The `Databases` collection contains one `Database` object for each database that the program has opened.

- ✔ `Recordsets` collection: A `Recordset` object is the representation of one data set. A data set could reference a single table, or it could reference multiple tables by using a query. A *query* is an SQL statement that defines the data that you want to retrieve and what technique to use to combine data from multiple tables. (See the upcoming "Understanding SQL: A Quick Overview" section for details.) The `Recordsets` collection contains one `Recordset` object for each query made against a `Database` object. You can create multiple `Recordset` objects for each database.

- ✔ `Command` object: This is the representation of an SQL statement in object form. The `Command` object also contains any arguments required by the SQL statement. You execute a command against a `Connection` object to open the query and retrieve a `Recordset` object for use in your program.

- ✔ `Fields` collection: A `Recordset` object contains one or more `Field` objects that define each record. The `Fields` collection contains the list of `Field` objects for a given `Recordset`.

- ✔ `TableDefs` collection: Every time that you create a new table by using the Access Table Designer, Access adds a `TableDef` object to the `TableDefs` collection of the database. The `TableDef` object defines every element of the table, including field names and data types.

- ✔ QueryDefs collection: A *query* defines how you want to get data from the database. Access provides the means to create static Query objects by using the Query Designer and stores each QueryDef (query definition) object in the QueryDefs collection.

- ✔ Relations collection: A *table* represents a single set of related data. A *data set* can contain one or more tables that contain data in a particular relationship. For example, a customer record can reference multiple invoice records. The customer record and the invoice records reside in different tables. A Relation object defines the references between two tables. Access stores each of these Relation objects in the Relations collection.

Accessing special commands with the DoCmd object

The DoCmd object provides you with a number of interesting methods that look similar to the list of macros that you find in the Macro dialog box (refer to Figure 15-1). You can't perform every macro task by calling on DoCmd object services, but this object is exceptionally useful if you want to perform some tasks in code instead of writing a macro to do them. Think of the DoCmd object as a means of bypassing the Access macro requirements, in some situations, so that you can make your VBA code easier to read as shown in Listing 15-7. (You can find the source code for this example on the Dummies.com site at http://www.dummies.com/go/mueller.)

Listing 15-7 Using the DoCmd Object for Special Tasks

```
Public Function SpecialCommands()
   ' Sound a beep.
   MsgBox "Sounding a beep!", vbInformation, "DoCmd Event"
   DoCmd.Beep

   ' Turn echo off and then back on.
   DoCmd.Echo False, "Echo is off!"
   MsgBox "Echo is off!", vbInformation, "DoCmd Event"
   DoCmd.Echo True, "Echo is on!"
   MsgBox "Echo is on!", vbInformation, "DoCmd Event"

   ' Open and close a query.
   DoCmd.OpenQuery "GetWordList", acViewNormal, acReadOnly
   MsgBox "Query is open!", vbInformation, "DoCmd Event"
   DoCmd.Close acQuery, "GetWordList"
   MsgBox "Query is closed!", vbInformation, "DoCmd Event"

   ' Run a macro.
```

```
    DoCmd.RunMacro "RunSayHello"
End Function

Public Function SayHello()
    ' Say hello to the user.
    MsgBox "Hello!", vbExclamation, "Say Hello Message"
End Function
```

This code performs a number of interesting tasks. First, it tells the system to beep. In most cases, you want to avoid using the Beep method because it only tells the user that there's an error and doesn't say what error the user made or how to fix it. In some cases, such as when a user reaches the end of the database records, using the Beep method works fine because the meaning of the beep is clear to most users.

Access normally echoes every change to the environment onscreen. An *echo* is the display of a command and its consequences. Having the commands flash onscreen while your program performs its task is distracting and could cause some users problems. Consequently, you might want to turn the echo off by using the DoCmd.Echo method. The first argument is True or False depending on whether you want to turn echo on or off. The second argument is a string that VBA displays on the status bar. It's important to display this information so the user knows that Access is working in the background.

You can also use the DoCmd object to open and close various kinds of Access objects such as tables, reports, and queries. For example, you can use it to open and close a query by calling the OpenQuery and general Close methods.

Notice that you can define the query that you want to open, the view that you want to use, and the kind of access to provide. The example opens the GetWordList query in the Normal view for read-only access. You could just as easily open a query in the Design view for read/write access.

The Close method works for a variety of objects. If you use Close by itself, VBA closes the currently selected object. However, you can also provide the kind of object that you want closed, along with the object name. This second method is safer because you won't close by mistake an object that you really want open. Closing an object means it's no longer available for any use, so closing an object by mistake could mean that your program experiences an error even if the code is normally correct.

You can also use DoCmd to run a macro by using the RunMacro method. This macro indirectly runs the SayHello function. You could also call the SayHello function directly, but macros often contain a series of instructions that you wouldn't want to include in your code.

A few of the DoCmd object functions seem to have odd results or might not work at all. For example, the AddMenu function doesn't appear to work, and Microsoft has documented this issue on its Web site. Make sure that you test the program using the same platform that the user will use when you use the DoCmd object in your code. (If you don't know what platform the user will have, you'd better research the user to find out.)

Understanding SQL: A Quick Overview

SQL (pronounced *see*-quel) is a specialized language used by many Database Management Systems (DBMSes) to manipulate data. You normally don't need to use SQL in Access programs because you can create a query by using the Access Query Designer. The Query Designer is one of the first tools that you learn to use because you need it to link tables together and create complex datasets. None of the techniques that you use for designing a database changes when you write VBA programs — you can still create queries and use them just as you always have.

Creating a SQL query the easy way

The only time that you need to consider using SQL directly is if you want to get data from an external source such as SQL Server or you need a temporary query that you don't want cluttering up the Access environment. I won't show you in this book how to gain access to external data sources because using external data sources could fill an entire book. However, the following procedure gives you a very fast and easy method for creating temporary queries.

1. **Create a query as you normally do.**

   Figure 15-6 shows a somewhat complex query for the example database. It includes all the fields from the Word List table. The query has two criteria. Notice that the first criterion uses the VBA Left function.

Figure 15-6:
Create a temporary SQL query with the same technique you usually use.

2. **Right-click the upper pane and then choose SQL View from the context menu that appears.**

   Access displays the SQL for the query that you just created graphically. Figure 15-7 shows the SQL for the test query shown in Figure 15-6.

Figure 15-7:
View the
SQL query
with the SQL
View option.

```
Test Query : Select Query
SELECT [Word List].*
FROM [Word List]
WHERE (((Left([Acronym],1))="C") AND (([Word List].IsAcronym)=True));
```

3. **Highlight the SQL query (all the text shown in Figure 15-7) and then click the Copy button on the toolbar.**

   Access places the query on the Clipboard.

4. **Open the VBA IDE, position the cursor, and then click the Paste button on the toolbar.**

   VBA pastes the query text for you.

5. **Close the SQL query without saving it.**

TIP

Note that you can always test your query before you use it in code by using the Datasheet View option. Using this technique ensures that you only write the code once to get the precise results that you want.

Using the SQL query

After you create a SQL query, you can use it in a program to get information from the database. Listing 15-8 shows a short example that uses the test query to get a list of words with acronyms that begin with the letter C. (You can find the source code for this example on the Dummies.com site at http://www.dummies.com/go/mueller.)

Listing 15-8   Performing a Database Query in VBA

```
Public Function QueryCAcronyms()
    ' Create a recordset.
    Dim Rec As Recordset
    Set Rec = _
        CurrentDb.OpenRecordset( _
            "SELECT [Word List].* " + _
            "FROM [Word List] " + _
```

(continued)

Listing 15-8 *(continued)*

```
            "WHERE (((Left([Acronym],1))='C') " + _
            "AND (([Word List].IsAcronym)=True))", _
        Type:=dbOpenDynaset)

    ' Create an output string.
    Dim Output As String

    ' Check each record in the recordset.
    While Not Rec.EOF

        ' Get the information.
        Output = Output + Rec.Fields("Acronym") + vbTab + _
                 Rec.Fields("Word") + vbCrLf

        ' Move to the next record.
        Rec.MoveNext
    Wend

    ' Display the result.
    MsgBox Output, vbInformation, "Words and Acronyms"

    ' Close the recordset.
    Rec.Close
End Function
```

Notice that you still use the `CurrentDb.OpenRecordset` method to get the `Recordset` object. The query is simple text, so you can substitute variables as input. For example, you might add a `Letter` argument to the program that lets you define which letter to use for the search.

A `Recordset` provides the `EOF` property that tells when you reach the end of the file (or recordset). Notice that the code addresses the content of the recordset by using indexed `Fields` collection entries. In this case, the recordset doesn't contain the whole table, just those records that match the criteria.

The `Rec.MoveNext` method is the most important piece of code in this loop. You must provide some means of moving from record to record, or the code will never reach the end of the recordset. The result of leaving out this piece of code is an endless loop. Whenever you run into this problem, press Ctrl+C to interrupt program execution.

The code uses the `Rec.Close` method to close the recordset. Always close the recordset when you finish using it. Otherwise, you might experience problems using the database later without a machine reboot. For example, when you lock a table for exclusive use and you don't close it when you're done, Access keeps the table locked, and no one else (not even you) can use it until you reboot the machine.

Discovering more about SQL

SQL isn't something that you can understand in a few short lessons. You don't need to spend a lot of time learning SQL to create simple commands, such as retrieving information from a single table, but the commands get more complicated when you ask SQL to do more for you. (The more advanced commands are also product specific in some cases, so you need to exercise caution.) The best way to build your knowledge of SQL is a little at a time, such as through a newsletter. One such newsletter is SQL Server Professional eXTRA. You can subscribe to it at `http://www.freeenewsletters.com/`.

A number of online sites also make SQL easy and interesting to learn. A Gentle Introduction to SQL (`http://sqlzoo.net/`) provides a number of tutorials and some great how-to links. The advantage of this Web site is that the author provides links for multiple flavors of SQL, which means that you can see how other products use SQL. You get a step-by-step tutorial on standard SQL at `http://www.w3schools.com/sql/default.asp`. The site at `http://www.sqlcourse.com` provides an interactive course where an interpreter tells you how well you do typing basic commands. Finally, the SQL Tutorial site at `http://www.1keydata.com/sql/sql.html` provides clear demonstrations of individual commands.

When you simply need information about SQL, you should try a few other Web sites. A complete set of reserved words (SQL commands) appears on the Microsoft Web site at `http://msdn.microsoft.com/library/en-us/tsqlref/ts_ra-rz_9oj7.asp`. You can find an outstanding list of SQL resources on the Ocelot Web site at `http://www.ocelot.ca/`. The links and book reviews are especially helpful.

Adding Form-Related Applications

The example database, queries, data, and associated form in this chapter all come from 1 of about 15 databases that I use personally. This word list is handy because it contains all the words that I've ever had to define in a book. A personal word list is one of the handier database programs that you can maintain because finding the meaning of words (especially jargon related to a specific industry) can prove difficult.

In other examples in this chapter, I show you bits and pieces of the tables and queries that the database contains. In this section, I discuss the form used to query, add, and retrieve words. The form includes a number of helpful buttons and the word information shown in Figure 15-8.

You often need to hide and show fields as needed on a form to reduce clutter and potential confusion. The Is This an Acronym field performs this task by hiding the Acronym field when it isn't needed. Right-click this field and then select Properties from the context menu that appears. Select the Event tab, and you'll see a list of events for the check box. Whenever someone marks the check box, the form executes the AcronymCheck macro. This macro runs the `SetAcronymLabel` function shown in Listing 15-9. (You can find the source code for this example on the Dummies.com site at `http://www.dummies.com/go/mueller`.)

Figure 15-8:
Design forms with the idea that you can perform specialized tasks with macros and programs.

Listing 15-9   Hiding or Showing a Form Field as Needed

```
     Public Function SetAcronymLabel()
  ' Check the status of the Acronym check box.
  If Forms![DataCon Word List]![IsAcronym] = True Then
      Forms![DataCon Word List]![Acronym Label].Visible = True
      Forms![DataCon Word List]![Acronym].Visible = True
  Else
      Forms![DataCon Word List]![Acronym Label].Visible = False
      Forms![DataCon Word List]![Acronym].Visible = False
  End If
End Function
```

This macro selects the `DataCon Word List` form from the `Forms` collection and locates the IsAcronym field on that form. If this field is `True`, which means the database entry has an acronym, the macro makes the Acronym field and its associated label visible. Otherwise, it hides both items.

I set this program up to accept three kinds of entries. An entry can contain a word and definition, an acronym and definition, or all three. I often need to send a definition of a word to someone else, so I created a special button that copies the information from the database to the Clipboard so that I can paste it in an e-mail message. Of course, I don't want to send someone an old definition — one that I haven't updated for a while — so this function has to check the date when I last updated the definition. In addition, it's handy to know when I used an entry last so that I can get rid of old words that I no longer need. Consequently, the Copy to Clipboard button shown in Figure 15-8 has a lot of work to do as shown here. Listing 15-10 contains code that you can use to copy a record to the Clipboard.

Listing 15-10   Copying a Record to the Clipboard

```
    Public Function Create_Record_Copy()
' Create some variables.
Dim strWord As String
Dim strAcronym As String
Dim strDefinition As String
Dim strDate As String
Dim RecordDate As Date

' Some records will start out with a null date that indicates it
' hasn't been checked since the check was implemented.
Forms![DataCon Word List]![Last_Updated].SetFocus
If Forms![DataCon Word List]![Last_Updated].Text = "" Then
    MsgBox "This definition hasn't been checked before, so ask " _
           "John to check it!", vbOKOnly, "Must Check Definition"
    Forms![DataCon Word List]![Copy_Text] = " "
    Exit Function
End If

' Get the last updated date from the record.
strDate = Forms![DataCon Word List]![Last_Updated]
RecordDate = DateValue(Forms![DataCon Word List]![Last_Updated])

' If there is a date, add 366 to it to represent one year.
RecordDate = RecordDate + 366

' The date on some records will be too old, which means it's time
' for another check.
If RecordDate < Now() Then
    MsgBox "The definition dated " + strDate + " is too old, add " _
           "word to the list!", vbOKOnly, "Time to Redefine"
    Forms![DataCon Word List]![Copy_Text] = " "
    Exit Function
End If

' Set the last used field to today.
Forms![DataCon Word List]![Last_Used] = Now()

' Get the values of the word and definition since they'll always be present.
strWord = Forms![DataCon Word List]![Word]
```

(continued)

Listing 15-10 *(continued)*

```
    strDefinition = Forms![DataCon Word List]![Definition]

    ' Place the data we want to copy on the form.
    Forms![DataCon Word List]![Copy_Text] = strWord + " -- " + strDefinition

    ' Check to see if we need to store the acronym value as well.
    If Forms![DataCon Word List]![IsAcronym] = True Then

        ' If we do need to store the acronym, then place it in a variable.
        strAcronym = Forms![DataCon Word List]![Acronym]

        ' Check to see if there is a definition for this acronym.
        If UCase(strDefinition) = "N/A" Then

            ' If not, then simply place the word and its meaning on the
            ' Clipboard.
            Forms![DataCon Word List]![Copy_Text] = _
                strAcronym + " -- " + strWord
        Else

            ' Otherwise, place the acronym and associated definition on the
            ' Clipboard.
            Forms![DataCon Word List]![Copy_Text] = _
                strAcronym + " -- See " + strWord + Chr(13) + Chr(10) + _
                strWord + " (" + strAcronym + ") -- " + strDefinition
        End If
    End If
End Function
```

The code begins by checking the last date of update. Notice that it sets the focus to the Last_Updated control. When this field is blank, the program displays a message to me saying that I need to update the definition. If the form does contain a Last_Updated value, the code retrieves this value and adds 366 to it. I require that I update my definitions every year, so if it's been more than a year since the last update, the code displays an error message and exits.

After the code knows that the definition isn't too old, it sets the Last_Used field to today's date. This entry lets me know when I last used the definition so I can remove old entries later.

The code begins the process of creating the text that it will place on the Clipboard at this point. The simplest case is a word and definition without an acronym, so the code performs that copying process first. The code checks for an acronym next and exits when there isn't one.

When there's an acronym, the code tests to see whether there's a definition. The second case is when there's an acronym and associated series of words but no definition. A definition of N/A signifies this condition, and the code copies just the acronym and associated words to the Clipboard.

The third condition is one when there's a word, an acronym, and a definition. In this case, the code copies all three entries to the Clipboard.

Creating Automatic Applications

The focus of automatic execution in Access is the Autoexec macro. When you want a database to perform a task automatically upon opening, create a macro named Autoexec. Any actions that you add to this macro will execute when you open the database file. This feature works like any other macro, so you can easily add one or more `RunCode` actions to execute programs associated with the file.

Chapter 16

Applications that Work Together

*Y*ou might never have an interest in using any program other than Word or Excel by themselves. It's possible to create some interesting and useful documents with either program. As a database administrator (DBA), you might never need to wander outside the world provided by Access. However, as you move on in your career, you find that you wear more hats and need to manage your data more effectively. Often, this means combining several tools because one tool can't perform a portion of a task effectively. Yes, you can always force Word to create spreadsheets and use Excel as a word processor, but this really isn't efficient.

This chapter shows you how to write programs where a main application such as Word, Excel, or Access calls upon a subordinate application to perform some work. I chose to concentrate on Office products in this chapter because that's what I discuss in most of the book. However, don't limit yourself to the examples in this chapter. Any application that supports VBA can act as a main or subordinate program. For example, you can just as easily ask CorelDRAW to perform services for Word as ask Excel.

Understanding Why You Should Work with More than One Application

Feature bloat (where the vendor adds useless or unnecessary features) is an incredible problem in applications today. Part of the problem is that users ask vendors to keep adding features to programs so that they don't have to leave the comfortable confines of the single program that they know instead of learning how to use other programs. Another part of the problem is that vendors want to provide you with a good reason to upgrade to the next version of a product. They hope that adding new features will grab your attention as something that you must have. Whether the feature is a request or a marketing idea is beside the point; the problems of feature bloat are numerous.

With feature bloat, a single program consumes more resources such as memory and disk space. In addition, the added complexity makes the program less stable (it tends to cause errors more often) and increases the program's learning curve. The features are often poorly defined and don't work as well as the same feature offered by another program that is dedicated to that purpose. For example, the drawing features in Word can't compare to the drawing features in a program such as CorelDRAW.

The problems with feature bloat addressed by this chapter are functionality and efficiency. Dedicated applications usually provide better functionality than an add-in for an application dedicated to some other purpose. In addition, the dedicated application can usually perform the task faster and with fewer data compatibility problems. Using the dedicated program costs more when you first set a system up, but it pays the investment back by making the system more flexible.

Your main application might not include a feature that you desperately need. For example, when you want to send an e-mail, you need to use a project such as Outlook to do it. Don't assume that *e-mail* means *content*. A program might need to send an e-mail to report an application or a system error to the network administrator. It could also track usage statistics and send them to a central collection point for analysis. You might even want a user to fill out a survey after he uses a new program that you create for a specific length of time.

It would be easy to limit your multi-application programs to simple data exchange or data manipulation. However, you can also use the multiple application technique in a workgroup environment for collaboration. When you complete a task on a project, a program can send your completed data to the next person in line for their additions. The other person might find out about the new file through an e-mail message or an addition to her task list. Your program can interact with the next application in line and also send notifications.

Processing Outlook E-Mail Messages with Word

Outlook is a capable e-mail program. You can use it to get your personal mail or to view newsgroups online. However, you might run into situations when the formatting features that Outlook provides are less than useful. That's the purpose of the example in this case. Word requests the messages that you mark in Outlook and formats them in preparation for printing or just viewing. I use this program to create quick reference resources from my e-mail.

The marking feature of this program is especially helpful because you can mark just some of the messages in a thread instead of outputting them all. This program uses a red flag, but you could modify it to use any flag. In addition, the program automatically marks the message as completed after processing it. This means that you don't have to clear the flags individually.

Unfortunately, the program shown in Listing 16-1 works only with Outlook and not Outlook Express. You can't work with Outlook Express messages directly with VBA unless you're willing to create your own library or use a third-party COM object such as DBX2XML (http://www.bizon.org/ilya/dbx2xml.htm). After you translate an Outlook Express DBX (e-mail) file into XML, you can easily import it by using the XML features provided with Office. Here's the code for this example. (You can find the source code for this example on the Dummies.com site at http://www.dummies.com/go/mueller.)

Listing 16-1   Working with Flagged Outlook Messages

```
Public Sub GetFlagged()
   ' Create the Outlook application reference.
   Dim OutlookApp As Outlook.Application
   Set OutlookApp = CreateObject("Outlook.Application")

   ' Create the MAPI namespace reference.
   Dim MAPI_NS As Outlook.NameSpace
   Set MAPI_NS = OutlookApp.GetNamespace("MAPI")

   ' Create a reference to the Inbox.
   Dim Inbox As Outlook.MAPIFolder
   Set Inbox = MAPI_NS.GetDefaultFolder(olFolderInbox)

   ' Holds the current message.
   Dim CurMsg As Outlook.MailItem

   ' Look at all of the messages.
   For Each CurMsg In Inbox.Items

      ' Determine whether this message requires processing.
```

(continued)

Listing 16-1 *(continued)*

```
          If CurMsg.FlagStatus = olFlagMarked And _
          CurMsg.FlagIcon = olRedFlagIcon Then

              ' Place the information in the Word document.
              With ActiveWindow.ActivePane.Selection

                  ' Create a From header and content.
                  .BoldRun
                  .TypeText "From: "
                  .BoldRun
                  .TypeText CurMsg.SenderName + " <" + _
                      CurMsg.SenderEmailAddress + ">"

                  ' Go to the next line.
                  .InsertParagraph
                  .GoTo What:=wdGoToLine, Which:=wdGoToLast

                  ' Create a Subject header and content.
                  .BoldRun
                  .TypeText "Subject: "
                  .BoldRun
                  .TypeText CurMsg.Subject
                  .InsertParagraph
                  .GoTo What:=wdGoToLine, Which:=wdGoToLast

                  ' Create a Content header and content.
                  .BoldRun
                  .TypeText "Content: "
                  .BoldRun
                  .TypeText CurMsg.Body

                  ' Create a page separator.
                  .InsertParagraph
                  .InsertBreak wdPageBreak
                  .GoTo What:=wdGoToLine, Which:=wdGoToLast
              End With

              ' Show this action is complete.
              CurMsg.FlagStatus = olFlagComplete

          End If
      Next
  End Sub
```

The code begins by creating some Outlook objects, including the application, namespace, folder, and an individual message. You might wonder how you gain access to these objects. Add a reference to the Microsoft Outlook Object Library to your program by using the Tools⇨References command.

You can use several techniques to create OutlookApp. For example, the code could use Set OutlookApp = new Outlook.Application. This technique works fine as long as Outlook is already running. However, using this statement can cause an error when Outlook isn't running, so whenever possible, you should use the `CreateObject` method shown in the example to ensure reliable program operation.

Outlook might eventually have the ability to use more than one communication technique. For now, Outlooks uses Messaging Application Programming Interface (MAPI). You must create a reference to the communication technique or namespace in the program. The code uses the namespace to get a message folder (or other data, such as a contact) by using the `GetDefaultFolder` method.

After the code creates the objects that it needs, it uses a `For Each...Next` loop to check each message in the folder. This program uses the Inbox, but you can use the same technique on any folder. If the message is marked with a red flag, the program processes it. Notice that you must make two checks to see whether the message requires processing. First, you must ensure that the message is marked by using the `FlagStatus` property. Second, you check the color of the flag by using the `FlagIcon` property (which seems a tad counterintuitive, even for Microsoft).

The program spends most of its time writing to the document, so the code uses a `With ActiveWindow.ActivePane.Selection` statement. The formatting in this example is simple. All the headings appear in bold; everything else appears in normal text.

The message format is very predictable, so it performs a minimum of text processing commands. It uses the `TypeText` method to send text to the current document. Notice the use of the `InsertParagraph` method. Inserting the paragraph mark doesn't move the selection point. If you don't also use the `GoTo` method to change the selection point, the program will happily continue inserting text at the beginning of the first time. Each message loop ends by inserting a page break after the message by using the `InsertBreak wdPageBreak` method. I like each message to start on a new page, but you can certainly change this behavior.

The final step in this program is to change the message flag status. Use the `CurMsg.FlagStatus = olFlagComplete` statement to perform this task. The reason why you want to use a completed flag is that it signifies that you've completed working with this message. If you cleared the flag, you might go back later and mark the message for printing again.

Sending E-Mail Messages with Outlook

Creating e-mails with Outlook is straightforward. If you don't like the formatting capabilities of Outlook, you can always create the message in Word and use the Word document as content for the e-mail. However, these two methods of message creation assume that a list of people will receive precisely the same message. When you want to create every message with the same general content and some messages with special content, you need a program.

I often need to send customized announcements by using e-mail, so I created the program shown in Listing 16-2. This example is a simplified version of my program, but it presents all the code that you need to create your own custom version. The program relies on a specially formatted Word document that includes tags for particular kinds of information. Figure 16-1 shows the document for this example.

The Word document used for this example (download from the Web site at `http://www.dummies.com/go/mueller`) has three sections. Using section breaks makes each document area obvious and has advantages when the code processes the document. (See Listing 16-2 and the accompanying code description for details on the advantages of using this technique.) The first section of the example document in Figure 16-1 contains the e-mail subject. Just like any e-mail, the subject must appear on a single line.

The second section of the example document in Figure 16-1 contains the general text — the information that you want everyone to see. This section can contain as many or as few lines as you want. The example won't process any formatting information, and it doesn't recognize objects such as pictures.

Figure 16-1:
Using a
specially
formatted
document to
create
e-mails.

The third section of the example document in Figure 16-1 contains the person's name, e-mail address, and any special text. The identification could include just the name or just the address, but the example uses both. Notice that you must include the e-mail address in angle brackets, as shown in the figure. Any special text must appear in a single paragraph. You must mark the paragraph with the Special tag as shown in Figure 16-1. Listing 16-2 shows the code to process this Word document as e-mail messages. Here's the code for this example. (You can find the source code for this example on the Dummies.com site at http://www.dummies.com/go/mueller.)

Listing 16-2   Processing a Word Document into an Outlook Message

```
Public Sub CreateMessage()

   With ActiveWindow.Selection

      ' Go to the beginning of the document.
      .GoTo What:=wdGoToLine, Which:=wdGoToFirst

      ' Holds the subject and general text.
      Dim Subject As String
      Dim General As String

      ' Get the subject.
      ' Start by selecting the first word.
      .End = .Start + 8
      ' Make sure it's a subject.
      If .Text = "Subject:" Then
         'Go to the next line and select the subject.
         .GoTo What:=wdGoToLine, Which:=wdGoToNext
         .EndOf Unit:=wdParagraph, Extend:=wdExtend
         .End = .End - 1
         Subject = .Text
      Else
         ' Display an error message.
         MsgBox "You must include a subject line!", _
            vbCritical, "File Formatting Error"
         Exit Sub
      End If


      ' Get the general text.
      ' Start by selecting the keyword.
      .GoTo What:=wdGoToLine, Which:=wdGoToNext
      .Start = .Start + 1
      .End = .Start + 8
      ' Make sure it's the general text.
      If .Text = "General:" Then
         'Go to the next line and select the general text.
         .GoTo What:=wdGoToLine, Which:=wdGoToNext
         .EndOf Unit:=wdSection, Extend:=wdExtend
         .End = .End - 1
```

(continued)

Listing 16-2 *(continued)*

```
        General = .Text
    End If
End With

' Tracks the end of the text.
Dim EndOfText As Boolean
EndOfText = False

' Holds the user name.
Dim UserName As String

' Holds any special greeting.
Dim Special As String

' Create the Outlook application reference.
Dim OutlookApp As Outlook.Application
Set OutlookApp = CreateObject("Outlook.Application")

' Create the MAPI namespace reference.
Dim MAPI_NS As Outlook.NameSpace
Set MAPI_NS = OutlookApp.GetNamespace("MAPI")

' Create a reference to the Inbox.
Dim Outbox As Outlook.MAPIFolder
Set Outbox = MAPI_NS.GetDefaultFolder(olFolderOutbox)

' Holds the current message.
Dim CurMsg As Outlook.MailItem

' Holds the existing and new start range.
Dim OldStart As Long
Dim MyRange As Range

' Process the next section.
ActiveWindow.Selection.GoTo What:=wdGoToSection, _
    Which:=wdGoToNext

' Keep processing until there is no more text.
While Not EndOfText

    ' Get the user name and e-mail address.
    With ActiveWindow.Selection
        .EndOf Unit:=wdParagraph, Extend:=wdExtend
        UserName = .Text

        ' Determine if the next line is a special greeting.
        OldStart = .Start
        Set MyRange = .GoTo(What:=wdGoToLine, _
```

```
                Which:=wdGoToNext)
            If MyRange.Start = OldStart Then
                EndOfText = True
            End If
        .End = .Start + 8
        ' Make sure it's a subject.
        If .Text = "Special:" Then
            ' Select the Special text.
            .Start = .End + 1
            .EndOf Unit:=wdParagraph, Extend:=wdExtend
            .End = .End - 1
            Special = .Text
            .HomeKey
        Else
            ' Reset the Special text.
            Special = ""

            ' Go back to the previous text.
            .GoTo What:=wdGoToLine, Which:=wdGoToPrevious
        End If

        ' Select the next name in the list. If this is the
        ' end of the text section, set the indicator.
        OldStart = .Start
        Set MyRange = .GoTo(What:=wdGoToLine, _
            Which:=wdGoToNext)
        If MyRange.Start = OldStart Then
            EndOfText = True
        End If
    End With

    Set CurMsg = Outbox.Items.Add()

    ' Add some content.
    CurMsg.Recipients.Add UserName
    CurMsg.Subject = Subject
    CurMsg.Body = General + vbCrLf + vbCrLf + Special

    ' Send the message.
    CurMsg.Send

Wend

' Display the number of messages sent.
MsgBox CStr(Outbox.Items.Count) + " message sent.", _
    vbInformation, "Messages Sent"
End Sub
```

The code begins by processing the subject and general message. One of the most important considerations is that you have to keep the selection pointer and range in the correct places throughout the processing, or the messages won't appear correctly.

The reason for the peculiar document format shown in Figure 16-1 becomes a little more obvious when you read the code for this example. The document takes maximum advantage of the text selection features that Word provides. Notice that after the code determines that the Subject tag appears on the first line, it moves to the second line and selects the entire line by calling the EndOf method. Unfortunately, this method also selects the paragraph mark, and you don't want to see that in the message title. (The paragraph mark appears as a square because Outlook can't make it visible.) Consequently, the program uses selection range math to change the selection. The .End = .End - 1 statement simply changes the selection so that it doesn't include the paragraph mark.

Selecting text correctly is a big issue when working with Word. The subject and general text use similar selection techniques. However, the code uses the Unit:=wdSection argument of the EndOf method in the second case to select the rest of the section. Using this technique lets you select an indeterminate number of paragraphs, which makes the program more flexible.

This example uses the same Outlook objects as those used in the earlier "Processing Outlook E-Mail Messages with Word" section. See this section for a description of the Application, NameSpace, MAPIFolder, and MailItem objects. The only difference is that this example writes to these objects instead of reading from them.

Processing the names and special text requires a little extra work because you don't know whether every name will have special text associated with it. In addition, the document could contain any number of names, so the code needs to know when it has reached the end of the document (or it will continue adding names forever). A special variable, EndOfText, tracks the end of the document condition.

The code begins by selecting the user name. It doesn't matter whether you provide a name, an e-mail address, or both because Outlook knows how to handle all three conditions.

Checking for a special greeting comes next. The code doesn't know whether the text exists, so it must make an assumption, validate the results, and take the appropriate action. This example assumes that the special text exists. It selects the text in the next line to see whether it begins with the Special keyword. If this word is present, the example selects the text that follows the keyword and places it in the Special string. Otherwise, the code clears the Special string and places the cursor on the previous line so that processing continues as if nothing happened.

The code has to track the last line. There are two possibilities. The entry could include a special line of text, or it might simply contain a recipient identity. The first range check that appears as part of the special greeting code checks for a condition where the last line is a recipient identity. The second range check code looks for a condition where the last line is a special greeting. You need both checks to ensure that the code works properly because in the second case, the code won't actually be at the last line until it processes the special message. Leaving out this second check lets the code post an extra e-mail message. However, if you leave out the first check, the code that returns the selection pointer to the previous line will prevent the loop from ending.

The loop ends with the code required to send the message that the code creates. The message includes a recipient, the subject, and the text (including a special message). The Send method places the message in the Outlook Outbox.

Sending Notes from Word to Excel

You might find the need to create a utility simply because a task becomes unwieldy in the host program. For example, many of my worksheets contain extensive notes. Editing those notes in Excel can become a real problem after the note gets to a certain size. However, Word provides a great editor, and I can make the notes as long as needed. The example shown in Listing 16-3 includes part of a program that I created for moving notes between Word and Excel so that they're easier to edit. (You can find the source code for this example on the Dummies.com site at http://www.dummies.com/go/mueller.)

Listing 16-3   Moving Notes from Word to Excel

```
Public Sheet As Integer
Public Row As String
Public Column As String

Public Sub SendNote()
   ' The text used as a note.
   Dim NoteText As String

   With ActiveWindow.Selection

      ' Go to the beginning of the document.
      .GoTo What:=wdGoToLine, Which:=wdGoToFirst

      ' Select the document text.
      .EndOf Unit:=wdSection, Extend:=wdExtend

      ' Get the text.
      NoteText = .Text
```

(continued)

Listing 16-3 *(continued)*

```
      End With

      ' Create a file dialog.
      Dim GetFile As FileDialog
      Set GetFile = Application.FileDialog(msoFileDialogOpen)
      GetFile.AllowMultiSelect = False
      GetFile.Filters.Clear
      GetFile.Filters.Add "Excel Files", "*.XL*"

      ' Get the Excel file.
      GetFile.Show

      ' Get the selected file.
      Dim Filename As String
      Filename = GetFile.SelectedItems(1)

      ' Open the Excel workbook.
      Dim TheBook As Excel.Workbook
      Set TheBook = Excel.Workbooks.Open(Filename)

      ' Request the sheet and cell number for the note.
      NoteSelect.Show

      ' Get the worksheet.
      Dim TheSheet As Excel.Worksheet
      Set TheSheet = TheBook.Sheets(1)

      ' Add the comment.
      TheSheet.Range(Column + Row).AddComment NoteText

      ' Close the workbook.
      TheBook.Close True
End Sub
```

The code begins by getting the note text from the Word document. This means placing the cursor at the beginning of the document, selecting a range of text, and copying that text to a local variable.

The next step is to figure out which Excel file to modify. The GetFile object is a file dialog box. Unfortunately, the file dialog box filters for Word point to Word documents, so the code has to change the filter by using the Filters.Clear and Filters.Add methods. It's also important to set GetFile so that it won't allow multiple selections — this program only works with one file at a time.

After the code displays the dialog box and you select a file, GetFile contains the name of the selection. This is the full path to the file, so you can select a file anywhere, and the code still works.

It's time to open the Excel file. You won't actually see Excel open — everything takes place in the background. The code uses the value in `Filename` as input to the `Excel.Workbooks.Open` method.

Notice that everything to do with Excel begins with the word Excel. Word and Excel often use objects with the same name. Adding the word *Excel* avoids confusion.

This program also requires a custom form. Figure 16-2 shows what this form looks like. The `NoteSelect` form appears onscreen long enough for you to select a sheet, column, and row for the note.

Figure 16-2:
Design
forms as
needed to
get program
input.

After the code knows what you want to write and where to place the information, it can open the Excel worksheet by using the `Sheets` collection. Notice how the code combines the `Column` and `Row` values to create a range for the comment. The `AddComment` method accepts the note text. Always make sure that you close the `Workbook` object when you're finished, or you'll end up with multiple background copies of Excel.

The `NoteSelect` form has a few interesting features. The code shown in Listing 16-4 makes the OK button shown in Figure 16-2 functional.

Listing 16-4   Getting the Sheet, Row, and Column Values

```
Private Sub btnOK_Click()
    ' Add error handling.
    On Error GoTo EntryError

    ' Check the Sheet range.
    If Not CInt(txtSheet.Value) > 0 Then
        MsgBox "Please type a number greater than 0.", _
            vbOKOnly Or vbCritical, "Data Entry Error"
        Exit Sub
```

(continued)

Listing 16-4 *(continued)*

```
    End If

    ' Check the Row range.
    If Not CInt(txtRow.Value) > 0 Then
        MsgBox "Please type a row number greater than 0.", _
            vbOKOnly Or vbCritical, "Data Entry Error"
        Exit Sub
    End If

    ' Check the Column range.
    If Not Asc(txtColumn.Value) > 64 Then
        MsgBox "Please type a letter greater than A.", _
            vbOKOnly Or vbCritical, "Data Entry Error"
        Exit Sub
    End If

    ' Save the data values.
    SendExcelNotes.Sheet = CInt(txtSheet.Value)
    SendExcelNotes.Row = txtRow.Value
    SendExcelNotes.Column = txtColumn.Value

    ' Close the dialog box.
    Me.Hide

    ' Exit the Sub.
    Exit Sub

EntryError:
    ' Tell the user what went wrong.
    MsgBox "You must enter a number for the Sheet and " + _
        "Row fields, and a letter for the Column field.", _
        vbOKOnly Or vbCritical, "Data Entry Error"

    ' Return the fields to appropriate values.
    txtSheet.Value = "1"
    txtRow.Value = "1"
    txtColumn.Value = "A"
End Sub
```

Whenever you need external input from the user, including yourself, it pays to add error trapping. Even I type the wrong text sometimes and find the error trapping helpful in preventing data damage. This form uses two levels of error trapping. First, it checks the data type. When the data type is wrong (such as typing a letter when you really meant to type a number), the program normally goes to the EntryError label for standard error handling.

Notice that the code after the EntryError label performs two tasks. First, it displays an error message that tells you what went wrong. Second, it returns the three values to default settings. This technique ensures that you can see the correct input, and it reduces the chances of additional errors. Of course, if you have a long form to fill out, this might not be the best solution. You might want to simply say that the data is incorrect and try to point out the problem field (a task that can prove hard to tackle).

The second level of error trapping is *range checking* (making sure that the entry value falls within a specific range of numbers). You can't completely prevent errors, but you can reduce the risk of fatal errors. In this case, the code checks to ensure that the sheet and row numbers are greater than 1 and that you typed a letter A or greater (remember that letters have a numeric value to the computer as described in Listings 4-2 and 4-3 in Chapter 4) as the column value. Unfortunately, that's about all the range checking that you can do.

After the code checks the input, it places the information in three global variables found in the `SendExcelNotes` module. These global variables supply the placement information that you can see earlier in this section.

The code ends by hiding the form. Unless you specifically hide the form, it will stay visible, and clicking the OK button doesn't appear to have any effect.

Part V
The Part of Tens

The 5th Wave   By Rich Tennant

"This isn't a quantitative or a qualitative estimate of the job. This is a wish-upon-a-star estimate of the project."

In this part . . .

Chapter 17 contains ten cool things that you can do with VBA. Don't assume that this is the end of the road. VBA has no limitations, and neither do you. I listed only ten new things that you can do, but there are perhaps thousands of things that you could do. All the examples in this part of the book come from my personal library. I wanted to share some of my experiences with you — a fellow VBA programmer.

Use Chapter 18 to discover new resources that you can use to build your own VBA library. This chapter contains ten types of resources that you can use to make your VBA programming experience better, easier, faster, or more fun. VBA is a language that lets you decide what you want your host application to do. The VBA resources in this chapter give you ideas of what's possible.

Chapter 17

Ten Really Cool Things You Can Do with VBA

You can write an impressive number of programs with VBA and not even begin to use all the features that it provides. That's the thing that I find most interesting about working with VBA. When you need to perform a task, there's usually at least one way to accomplish it and generally more than one way.

If you've already read most of the chapters in this book, you're well on your way to becoming a hotshot VBA programmer. You have all the skills required to write any program that your mind can think to create and many programs that you can't even imagine at the moment. That's the goal of this chapter: After you master the programming techniques, it's time to start considering what you can do with them.

The coolest thing that you can ever do with VBA is to make it your personal tool for accomplishing tasks that you want to do. It doesn't matter how you use the program — personal programs are just as worthwhile as those that you create for your business or fellow workers. The fact that you did something for your personal satisfaction and to meet your personal needs is the best feeling that there is. You now have the power to write any program that you need. Make sure that you take time to play.

Using Files with the Open Command

Many of the Microsoft and third-party online VBA references mention the Open function, which is an older method of working with files that you won't use for opening standard application files. However, you might need to open an INI (initialization settings) file or a file containing data produced in another application that Office doesn't support directly. This function requires a number of arguments, including the name of the file and the kind of access that you require. Listing 17-1 is a simple example of how you can use the Open function to open a text file on the local drive. This text file contains data that could have resided on a mainframe or in another PC program. The example translates this data and places it in Excel. (You can find the source code for this example on the Dummies.com site at http://www.dummies.com/go/mueller.)

Listing 17-1   Opening and Translating a Text File into an Excel Worksheet

```
Public Sub OldOpen()
   ' Create the input strings.
   Dim DataLine As String
   Dim ThisCell As String

   ' Used for looping.
   Dim Counter As Integer
   Counter = 1
   Dim CellCounter As Integer

   ' Open the file.
   Open ThisWorkbook.Path + "\Temp.txt" For Input As #1

   ' Read the data one line at a time.
   While Not EOF(1)
      Line Input #1, DataLine

      ' Verify whether there is a tab in the text. If so,
      ' place each text element in a separate column.
      If InStr(1, DataLine, vbTab) Then

         ' Set the cell counter.
         CellCounter = 1

         ' Keep processing the line of text until finished.
```

```
        While (Len(DataLine) > 0)

            ' Verify that the text still has tabs in it.
            If InStr(1, DataLine, vbTab) Then

                ' Get the text to the left of the tab and place it in the cell.
                ThisCell = Left(DataLine, InStr(1, DataLine, vbTab) - 1)
                Sheet1.Cells(Counter, CellCounter) = ThisCell

                ' Make the current text the remaining tabbed text element.
                DataLine = Mid(DataLine, InStr(1, DataLine, vbTab) + 1)

                ' Go to the next cell.
                CellCounter = CellCounter + 1
            Else
                ' The text is free of tabs. Make the cell equal to this last
                ' line and then clear the data line.
                Sheet1.Cells(Counter, CellCounter) = DataLine
                DataLine = ""
            End If
        Wend
    Else

        ' Place the data in the worksheet.
        Sheet1.Cells(Counter, 1) = DataLine
    End If

    ' Update the counter.
    Counter = Counter + 1
    Wend

    ' Close the file.
    Close #1
End Sub
```

This code reads a text file into a worksheet. Each line of text appears in a separate worksheet row. When the text file contains tabs, it places each tabbed element in a separate cell. The effect is precisely the same as this code:

```
Public Sub UseOpen()
    ' Open a text file as a workbook.
    Dim TempBook As Workbook
    Set TempBook = Workbooks.Open(ThisWorkbook.Path + "\Temp.txt")
End Sub
```

When working with native application files, such as the .doc extension for Word, the FileSystemObject method of working with files that I demonstrate in Chapter 10 is normally superior because it provides better access to the drive system and works more consistently than the Open function. In addition, you only need to think about one or two objects and not a host of individual functions.

You still need the Open function to perform certain tasks. The most important is the use of *binary* (non-text) files. If you decide to work with binary files outside of the objects that the host application provides, you must use the Open function. The Erlandsen Data Consulting Web site at http://www.erlandsendata.no/english/vba/fileaccess/binary.htm provides a good example of using binary data records. You can find an interesting alternative to using the Open function for binary data at the DeveloperFusion.com Web site at http://www.developerfusion.com/show/2542/. This method relies on using the ADODB object.

Record-based access also requires the Open function. You can create a file with fixed length records. You can use these text-based files to exchange information between databases. The Erlandsen Data Consulting Web site at http://www.erlandsendata.no/english/vba/fileaccess/random.htm provides a good example of how to use the Open function for random file access.

The most important consideration for using the Open function is that it provides better control than some of the newer methods that VBA provides. The first example in this section uses a lot of code precisely because you have to do everything, but that means that you get to decide how things will work. Using a newer function requires less code, but it also means that you have to do things the Microsoft way, which means a loss of flexibility and in some cases, functionality.

Defining Database Connections

When you develop complex programs, you might find that you want to use data directly from a database, such as Access. In Chapter 15, I show you how to use Data Access Objects (DAO) to accomplish this task. DAO works fine for many tasks, but you gain additional flexibility by using ActiveX Data Objects (ADO) to access databases, including Access, from other programs. This example relies on the Microsoft ActiveX Data Objects 2.7 Library. You can add this library by using the Tools⇨References command. The code in Listing 17-2 places the contents of the Word List table of the AccessObjects database into an Excel worksheet. (You can find the source code for this example on the Dummies.com site at http://www.dummies.com/go/mueller.)

Listing 17-2   Exporting an Access Table to an Excel Worksheet

```
Public Sub GetData()
    ' Create the database connection.
    Dim DBConn As ADODB.Connection
    Set DBConn = New ADODB.Connection
    DBConn.ConnectionString = _
        "Driver={Microsoft Access Driver (*.mdb)};" + _
        "Dbq=" + ThisWorkbook.Path + "\AccessObjects.MDB;" + _
        "Uid=admin;Pwd="

    ' Open the database.
    DBConn.Open

    ' Create a recordset.
    Dim DBRec As ADODB.Recordset
    Set DBRec = New ADODB.Recordset

    ' Set the recordset parameters.
    DBRec.ActiveConnection = DBConn
    DBRec.Source = _
        "Select * From [Word List] Where IsAcronym=True"

    ' Open the recordset.
    DBRec.Open

    ' Display the fields as headers.
    Dim CurrentCell As Integer
    CurrentCell = 1
    Dim AField As ADODB.Field
    For Each AField In DBRec.Fields
        Sheet2.Cells(1, CurrentCell) = AField.Name
        CurrentCell = CurrentCell + 1
    Next

    ' Display the data.
    Dim RowCount As Integer
    RowCount = 3
    While Not DBRec.EOF
        CurrentCell = 1
        For Each AField In DBRec.Fields
            Sheet2.Cells(RowCount, CurrentCell) = AField.Value
            CurrentCell = CurrentCell + 1
        Next
        DBRec.MoveNext
        RowCount = RowCount + 1
    Wend

    ' Close the dabase.
    DBConn.Close
End Sub
```

This program resides in Excel, yet it uses Access data. You can use a combination of sorting, filtering, and different source statements to create the dataset that you need for a particular program. For that matter, you pick the fields that you want or manipulate the data in various ways. The point is that you can perform various kinds of data merges within your programs. Make sure that you close the database connection to ensure that you don't lose data or corrupt the database file in some way.

Automating PowerPoint Presentations

PowerPoint, more than any other application, can benefit from the cross-application benefits that I demonstrate in Chapter 16. A single VBA program could rely on Word for the text in a PowerPoint presentation, Access for the presentation data, and Excel for presentation graphs and statistics. The important idea is to use each of the applications for their intended purpose. PowerPoint is a consolidation tool: It's best used to consolidate the data that you create in other applications into a presentation. Think of this program as a container for the other kinds of data that you create, and the requirements for creating programs for it become a little easier to understand.

Creating Data Connections with OLE

Most of the examples in this book concentrate on creating new data, moving data from one application to another, or manipulating data in some way. An application might contain data in precisely the format that you need, so all you really need is a reference to it. That's where Object Linking and Embedding (OLE) comes into play. You can use this technology to simply place a copy of the data in another document. This technique is equivalent to using the Edit⇨ Paste Special or the Insert⇨Object command. Listing 17-3 shows an example of adding a data connection by using OLE. (You can find the source code for this example on the Dummies.com site at http://www.dummies.com/go/mueller.)

Listing 17-3   Using OLE with VBA

```
Public Sub AddOLE()
    ' Create a reference to the current objects.
    Dim Objs As OLEObjects
    Set Objs = Sheet3.OLEObjects

    ' Add a new object.
    Objs.Add Filename:=ThisWorkbook.Path + "\Cuckoo.wav", _
        Link:=False, Top:=20, Left:=40, _
        IconLabel:="The Cuckoo Sound"
End Sub
```

The biggest reason to use this technique is to automate data additions to a document. For example, you might want to construct a letter template that automatically adds graphics based on the customer or the type of account. In other cases, you could use this technique to automate the object-insertion process for less-skilled users.

Adding Functionality with Controls

In Chapter 7, I provide a wealth of tips and hints about using standard VBA controls. I also show you how to add new controls to your VBA palette in the that chapter's "Adding controls to the Toolbox" section. However, that chapter doesn't really convey the power that controls can have over your development efforts. A *control* is code that someone else has already debugged and tested for you. It includes some type of graphic element (unlike components, which include only code). In short, controls represent the fastest and easiest method of adding functionality to your program.

You get controls from a variety of sources. For example, if you want to add the ability to display PDFs to Word, just add an Acrobat Reader control to your palette. Adobe installs this control whenever you install Acrobat Reader (http://www.adobe.com/products/acrobat/readermain.html), so you don't even have to do anything special to receive the functionality.

Other programmers make their controls available for use. You have to exercise care in downloading controls from the Internet, but some sites are quite reliable. Here's a list of some sites where you can look for controls:

- ✔ **c/net Download.com:** http://download.com.com/
- ✔ **Tucows:** http://www.tucows.com/
- ✔ **SofoTex.com:** http://www.sofotex.com/download/Programming/ActiveX/
- ✔ **Download Safari:** http://www.downloadsafari.com/
- ✔ **SHAREWAREORDER:** http://www.sharewareorder.com/

After you download a control, you have to install it on your system. I set aside a special folder for controls that I download so that I can find and remove them later. To add a control to your system, type **RegSvr32 *<Name of Control>*** at the command line and then press Enter. Windows displays a success message when the control is registered for use. Now you can add it to your VBA project.

When you find that you no longer need a control, you have to unregister it first so that the Windows Registry remains clean. To remove a control, open a command prompt with the Start⇨Programs⇨Accessories⇨ Command Prompt command, type **RegSvr32 –u** *<Name of Control>*, and then press Enter. Windows will display a success message. At this point, you can erase the file.

Getting and Using Components

You have no idea how many useful components reside on your machine. I know that I've delved into the components on my machine for years and have yet to try them all. The undiscovered country of code that you can use to enhance your programs extends to many areas. You can use .NET in your programs because many features of the .NET Framework appear as standard components. The same concept extends to Java applets, utilities that Windows provides, or just about any other piece of code that you can imagine.

The magic word to access any component on your machine is `CreateObject`. This function appears in many examples in this book. However, before you can use a component, you need to know that it exists.

The *OLE/COM Object Viewer utility* is a special program that displays all the components on your machine. This tool comes as part of Visual Studio and a few other Microsoft products, but you can also download it from the Microsoft Web site at `http://www.microsoft.com/com/resources/ oleview.asp`. The purpose of this program is to show all the components and controls on your machine. Simply double-click the file that you download to install the utility on your machine.

When you open the OLE/COM Object Viewer, you'll see categories of objects that you can use. For example, all the controls on your machine appear in the Controls folder. These categories help VBA know which items to display in the dialog boxes that let you add new controls to the Toolbox or new component references.

Using the OLE/COM Object Viewer can provide you with names of new components to try. It can also tell you about the component. For example, look at the InprocServer32 entry on the Registry tab, and you'll see the location of the file that supports the component. In many cases, this location information tells you who created the control and also provides clues on how you can use the component to improve your code.

Using Microsoft's Online Documentation

In the Registry example in Chapter 13, I show you that you can use Windows 32-bit Application Programming Interface (Win32 API) calls directly in VBA. You can also access the .NET Framework by using new features in Office 2003. Microsoft also provides a vast array of components and controls that you can use. All this free code sounds great until you realize that you don't have any documentation for it.

Fortunately, Microsoft does provide a wealth of online documentation to go with the free code that it provides. The Microsoft Developer Network (MSDN) Library at `http://msdn.microsoft.com/library/` lets you search for just about any current Microsoft product. The table of contents on the left side of the site helps you refine your search after you locate something interesting. In addition to the MSDN Library, you also want to check the Microsoft Knowledge Base at `http://support.microsoft.com/default.aspx` for updates, programming tips, and additional information.

Creating Your Own Jigs and Templates

You might think that I create every module, form, or code module by hand. In some respects, this is true. I do write any custom code by hand. However, there's no reason for me to write my name and create basic functions or sub-procedures that I know I'm going to use every time. I don't feel any obligation to write the code to create basic structures. VBA is your ally; use it to make your workload just a little less. Listing 17-4 shows an example of a template that automatically creates a module and fills it with standard data. Note that you must add a reference to the Microsoft Visual Basic for Applications Extensibility component for this example. (You can find the source code for this example on the Dummies.com site at `http://www.dummies.com/go/mueller`.)

Listing 17-4   Automating the Module Creation Process

```
Public Sub ModuleStart()
   ' Create the new module.
   Dim NewMod As Module
   Set NewMod = Modules.Add

   ' Get the module name.
   Dim ModName As String
   ModName = InputBox("Type the Module Name", "Name")
   NewMod.Name = ModName

   ' Get the new projects
```

(continued)

Listing 17-4 *(continued)*

```
Dim MyProj As CodeModule
Set MyProj = Application.VBE.VBProjects(1).VBComponents(ModName).CodeModule

' Open the file.
MyProj.CodePane.Show

' Add the required option statement, module header, and opening Sub.
MyProj.InsertLines 1, "Option Explicit" + vbCrLf + vbCrLf + _
    "' Module Name: " + ModName + vbCrLf + "' Author: " + _
    Application.UserName + vbCrLf + "' Date: " + CStr(DateTime.Now) + _
    vbCrLf + vbCrLf + "Public Sub Main()" + vbCrLf + vbCrLf + "End Sub"
End Sub
```

Developing Reusable Libraries

When you build new programs with VBA, keep reusability in mind. Many examples in this book appear as a single, large piece of code to make them easier to explain. My own code contains smaller modules that accept one or more arguments as input. Each module performs one task exceptionally well. Using this technique means that code that I write today can also perform work tomorrow.

All my tested code goes into a utility module (named Utility.bas). When I begin a new project, I import Utility.bas and instantly have a lot of the code that I need written. The functions and sub-procedures in the main module for my program calls each of these utility modules and asks them to perform their special task. Some programmers call this the *Lego approach* to writing code because of the similarity to the toy's modularity of interchangeable pieces. Reusable libraries can save you a great deal of time and make mundane programming tasks a lot easier and fun.

Chapter 18

Ten Kinds of VBA Resources

*Y*ou aren't alone in your quest for the perfect VBA program. Many other companies and individuals produce resources that you can view on or download from the Internet. The resources come in a variety of forms — everything from informational Web sites to newsgroups where you can talk with other people who use VBA to free tools and code. In this chapter, I don't present every VBA resource, but I do present some interesting ideas. The first three sites that you should visit to answer your VBA question are

✔ **Microsoft Visual Basic for Applications home page:**
   `http://msdn.microsoft.com/vba/`

✔ **Microsoft Visual Basic home page:**
   `http://msdn.microsoft.com/vbasic/`

✔ **Microsoft Office home page:** `http://msdn.microsoft.com/office/`

Using Magazines and Periodicals

Articles come in all shapes, sizes, complexity levels, and forms. Some magazines specialize in a particular reader group, and others tackle a specific product. You can find high-quality articles in both free and paid form. The length of the articles varies according to the magazine and its goals. In short, you can find one or more magazines that meet particular needs.

Traditional paper magazines and periodicals

Traditional paper magazines and periodicals offer a permanent form of documentation that you can keep on your bookshelf for reference and read just about anywhere. This list is by no means complete but has the advantage of providing a Web reference:

- **Microsoft Certified Professional Magazine Online:** http://www.mcpmag.com/

- **Visual Studio Magazine:** http://www.fawcette.com/vsm/

- **Access-SQL-VB Advisor Magazine:** http://accessvbsqladvisor.com/

- **VBUG Magazine:** http://www.vbug.co.uk/magazine/

Free electronic newsletters

Free newsletters often contain short articles, tips, links, and the occasional coding example. (You might see them listed as *e-newsletters* or *eNewsletters*.) They're a good source of continuous information for building your VBA knowledge base. Here are a few of the better examples:

- **Woody's Office Watch:** http://woodyswatch.com/

- **Element K Journals:** http://www.elementkjournals.com/tips.asp

- **The Office Experts:** http://www.theofficeexperts.com/newsletter.htm

- **Microsoft Office Tips:** http://www.worldstart.com/msofficetips.htm

- **DevX.com:** http://www.windx.com/

- **OzGrid Excel Newsletter:** http://www.microsoftexceltraining.com/News/ExcelSubtotalsEfficientVBA.htm

- ✔ **informIT:** http://www.informit.com/articles/
- ✔ **Wanita's Office Newsletter:** http://www.topica.com/lists/wanitasoffice/?cid=2743
- ✔ **AbleOwl:** http://www.sheet.com/live/entry/index.php

Many of these sites also provide free downloads. For example, you can find downloads on The Office Experts site at http://www.theofficeexperts.com/downloads.htm. A few of the sites, such as OzGrid Excel Newsletter (http://www.microsoftexceltraining.com/Links/2home.htm), provide lists of interesting links. Some sites, such as AbleOwl, provide news about seminars as well as training and support. The reason why I listed these sites here is that they focus on a newsletter — the other features add to an already great site.

Newsletters that you pay for

Newsletter subscriptions that you pay for provide more information and longer articles than free electronic newsletters. However, newsletters don't quite provide the same amount of information as a magazine. Some newsletters that you pay for are quite advanced, and you get detailed programming examples that many magazines won't cover. Most newsletters that you pay for also come in printed form instead of the e-mail form of free electronic newsletters. Here are a few sites that offer newsletters that you pay for:

- ✔ **Pinnacle Publishing:** http://www.pinnaclepublishing.com/
- ✔ **Microsoft Developer Network:** http://msdn.microsoft.com/subscriptions/
- ✔ **Smart Solutions:** http://www.msofficemag.net/default.asp

Finding Interesting Newsgroups and List Servers

Most methods of information gathering are *unidirectional:* A vendor or advanced computer user chooses to share code, techniques, or general information through a Web site or newsletter. Although this method of sending information works great for most needs, it's still nice to have two-way communication when you have a question. Newsgroups can really help in this case. All you need to do is point your news reader to the correct group to learn more.

You can also access a newsgroup by typing the news server and newsgroup name in your browser or other Internet address bar like this: `news://news.microsoft.com/microsoft.public.word.vba.addins`. This second technique works well when your ISP doesn't support a particular newsgroup, but you know the name of the news server that hosts the newsgroup.

List servers work like newsgroups except that you use your e-mail or a Web site to correspond with other people. You normally have to sign up for a list server, and they're usually moderated to keep conversations on track. You might find that these tightly focused and controlled sources of information help you get what you need quickly or they might be too confining for words.

This chapter doesn't list the Microsoft or third-party Visual Basic newsgroups; however, because VBA is a true subset of Visual Basic, you can usually find good information in these newsgroups as well. It's better to go to a VBA specific newsgroup when you can but look to Visual Basic newsgroups when you can't find what you need.

Microsoft-specific newsgroups

Microsoft provides a number of VBA newsgroups. In fact, you can probably find everything that you need to talk with other VBA users in this one place. Most ISPs carry the Microsoft newsgroups. However, you can also access Microsoft's newsgroups directly by using its server at `news.microsoft.com`. (If you want to use your browser, you'd type `news://news.microsoft.com/microsoft.public.access.modulesdaovba` as example; however, it's usually easier to find the newsgroup in your newsgroup reader.) Here are some of the VBA newsgroups that you can visit for additional information. (***Note:*** Most of these sites are product specific, so you need to go to the VBA site for your particular product, such as Access or Excel.)

- ✔ `microsoft.public.access.modulesdaovba`
- ✔ `microsoft.public.access.modulesdaovba.ado`
- ✔ `microsoft.public.frontpage.programming.vba`
- ✔ `microsoft.public.office.developer.outlook.vba`
- ✔ `microsoft.public.office.developer.vba`
- ✔ `microsoft.public.outlook.program_vba`
- ✔ `microsoft.public.project.vba`
- ✔ `microsoft.public.visio.developer.vba`
- ✔ `microsoft.public.word.vba.addins`
- ✔ `microsoft.public.word.vba.beginners`

✔ microsoft.public.word.vba.customization

✔ microsoft.public.word.vba.general

✔ microsoft.public.word.vba.userforms

✔ microsoft.public.word.word97.vba

Third-party newsgroups

Newsgroups are either news-reader-based or Web-based. The number of third-party, news-reader-based newsgroups that you find depends on your ISP and could depend on the vendor. In some cases, you find that the vendor runs a special news server that you can access by using the same technique as for the Microsoft newsgroups. Web-based newsgroups rely on a special Web site interface that you access with your browser. Here are a few of the third-party newsgroups that you can find without too many problems.

✔ autodesk.autocad.customization.vba

✔ ingr.cserve.msbbeta.vba-prog

✔ **Expresso Code Cafe:** http://www.vbdesign.net/expresso/

✔ **VBWire VB Forums:** http://www.vbforums.com

✔ **Experts Exchange:** http://www.expertsexchange.com/Applications/MS_Office/

Don't forget to try third-party, general newsgroups, too. For example, you can find various Corel products newsgroups where you can ask about the CorelDRAW or WordPerfect form of VBA at corel.developers (and the associated sub-newsgroups). You can also ask general support questions at corel.support, which includes a number of sub-newsgroups.

List servers that you access through e-mail and Web sites

List servers have several advantages over newsgroups. For one thing, the *noise level* (unwanted postings) is much lower. These groups are very focused, which means that you normally get good information. A moderator keeps discussions on track, so there's less chance of seeing a discussion entitled "Great New VBA Trick" that's actually about Uncle Al's birthday party. In many cases, you subscribe by sending the list owner or another special e-mail address an e-mail with the word Subscribe as the subject. Here are some list servers that you can try:

- ✔ **AccessRabbit:** `mailto:AccessRabbit-subscribe@topica.com`
- ✔ **Office 2000 Tips:** `mailto:canicas-subscribe@topica.com`
- ✔ **Microsoft Office Freelist Group:** `http://www.freelists.org/cgi-bin/webpage?webpage_id=mso`

Locating Just the Right Code

A number of Web sites cater to the VBA user by proving example code that you can use anywhere in your own code. Most of these sites copyright their code so that you can't use it for profit or as part of a magazine article. The developer provides the code as is, so you might need to debug it a little or modify it to meet your needs. The point is that the code helps you understand a programming concept better, which makes writing your own version of the example much faster. Use these links as your gateway to some great coding examples:

- ✔ **VB2theMax:** `http://www.vb2themax.com/`
- ✔ **MVPs.org:** `http://www.mvps.org/`
- ✔ **Walker Software:** `http://www.papwalker.com/links.html`
- ✔ **Contract CADD Group:** `http://www.contractcaddgroup.com/download/`
- ✔ **FreeVBCode:** `http://www.freevbcode.com`
- ✔ **VBCode.com:** `http://www.vbcode.com`
- ✔ **Word-VBA Code Samples:** `http://www.jojo-zawawi.com/code-samples-pages/code-samples.htm`

Some of these sites include more than just code. For example, the VB2theMax site includes newsletters, articles, tips, and other resources in addition to code downloads. Make sure that you take time to explore these sites fully.

Getting Tools to Make Programming Easier

When you build more programs, you'll begin to notice that VBA doesn't always provide all the features that you need. In some cases, you might find that the VBA IDE lacks functionality. You might think that Microsoft hasn't really addressed every need and that some tasks require too many steps to complete. Instead of reinventing the wheel and writing the addition yourself, consider using one of these third-party products.

✔ **MZ-Tools** (`http://www.mztools.com/`): An interesting addition to the VBA Integrated Development Environment (IDE) that provides missing functionality. The menu-driven product contains a wealth of features to make your next coding session faster and less error prone.

✔ **EducationOnlineforComputers.com** (`http://www.educationonlineforcomputers.com/`): A list of interesting links for discovering new facts about VBA in general and Microsoft office products in specific.

✔ **Add-ins.com** (`http://www.add-ins.com/`): A listing of various add-ins that you can use to enhance your Office experience. Many of these add-ins are also programmable. All these products are shrink wrapped, which means that you must buy before you try.

✔ **The Spreadsheet Page** (`http://www.j-walk.com/ss/`): A collection of tips, hint, code, and useful downloads. Everything is either *freeware* (no payment required) or *shareware* (try before you buy).

✔ **ZDNet Downloads** (`http://downloads-zdnet.com.com/`): You need to search this site carefully for development tools. However, the search is worthwhile because this site contains a wealth of development tools and utilities.

✔ **PRIME Freeware Products** (`http://www.primeconsulting.com/freeware/`): The products at this site are all free. You can find everything from a list of VBA annoyances for Office 97 users to a bookmark pop-up utility that makes using this feature easier. The site includes a number of other free resource links.

Downloading ActiveX Controls and Third-Party Components

A developer can never have too many controls and components. You don't necessarily have to use them all every time that you write a program. A well-stocked toolbox of controls and components simply makes it easier to find just the tool that you need. Use the following sites as a starting point to building your own control and component toolbox:

✔ **VBA Store at ComponentSource:** `http://www2.componentsource.com/Marketplace/`

✔ **ActiveX.COM:** `http://www.active-x.com/`

✔ **c/net Download.com:** `http://download.com.com/`

✔ **TopShareware:** `http://www.topshareware.com/`

Using Me as a Resource

The last resource in this chapter is me. That's right, you can call on me at any time to help you with any question that you might have with this book. No, I won't write your next college paper for you, but I can answer your questions on how collections work.

I also want to hear your thoughts about this book. What do you think I can do to improve it? What would you like to see in the next edition? If you think that I can provide more information in a certain area, feel free to let me know. Any errors or problems that you find are also issues that I want to know about.

You can contact me at JMueller@mwt.net. Unless I'm on vacation (rare), I'll usually answer you in around two days. Even if I don't have an answer immediately, I'll let you know that I received your e-mail. While I collect information that I think other people want to know, I'll put it in a book link on my Web site at http://www.mwt.net/~jmueller/. Make sure that you check my Web page for updates. Of course, you'll also find the source code and a few extras on the Dummies.com site at http://www.dummies.com/go/mueller.

Index